1991

INSIDE
TELEVISION
PRODUCING

Richard D. Lindheim • Richard A. Blum

Focal Press
Boston London

To Lambert and his family and
to Jennifer, Jason, and Eve Blum

Focal Press is an imprint of Butterworth–Heinemann.

Recognizing the importance of preserving what has been written, it is the policy of Butterworth–Heinemann to have the books it publishes printed on acid-free paper, and we exert our best efforts to that end.

Library of Congress Cataloging-in-Publication Data

Lindheim, Richard D.
  Inside television producing / Richard D. Lindheim, Richard A. Blum.
    p. cm.
  Includes bibliographical references and index.
  ISBN 0–240–80019–2
    1. Television—Production and direction.   I. Blum, Richard A.
  II. Title.
PN1992.75.L56 1991
791.45′0232—dc20   90–48114
                                                                   CIP

British Library Cataloguing in Publication Data

Lindheim, Richard D.
  Inside television producing.
  1. Television programmes. Production
  I. Title II. Blum, Richard A.
  791.450232

  ISBN 0–240–80019–2

Butterworth–Heinemann
80 Montvale Avenue
Stoneham, MA 02180

10 9 8 7 6 5 4 3 2 1

Printed in the United States of America

Contents

Acknowledgments

We would like to thank the many professionals who shared their ideas, comments, and insights with us. In particular, Barry Kemp and Dick Wolf extended a great deal of time and thought to ensure that our readers were presented with an accurate look at the dynamics and complexities of producing. They allowed us to follow their progress in the pilot productions of two then-new shows—a comedy series *(Coach)*, and a dramatic action series *(Law and Order)*. Throughout the difficult process of creating, producing, and supervising these new pilots, they made special efforts to remain accessible at every turn and were interested and pleased to share their knowledge and experiences. As a result, the readers of this book have a unique chronology to examine the process of development and production of new television programs.

Similarly, John Stephens provided extensive insights into the process of line producing. His technical and creative expertise helped clarify the role of the line producer and the working responsibilities of individual crew members.

During the early stages of this book, our researcher, Cindy Fabian, coordinated activities, compiled a daily log, and supervised the transcription of the interviews. She diligently followed the progress of each show, and we are grateful for her dedication and follow-through.

At Universal Television, we appreciate the assistance from Kerry McCluggage, Ed Masket, Joan Sittenfield, and other executives who permitted our observation, offered suggestions, and graciously granted releases for material appearing in this book. And a special thanks to Olga DeSales, whose decision to retire was probably abetted by her transcriptions for this book.

On the family front, our thanks to the Lindheim family and friends for enduring the numerous hours of modeming, which kept the telephone off limits. And our thanks to the Blum family—Jason, Jennifer, Eve, and Stephen—for enduring yet another book.

Friends have also had their impact. Special thanks to Norman Tamarkin for his remarkable talent and reliable insights, Frank Tavares for his valuable advice and long friendship, Michele Orwin for sharing her thoughts on the art of writing, Janice Smith for her camaraderie, and David Gioviannoni for responding to the alarm when computer problems arose.

Introduction

Throughout the world, billions of people regularly view television programs on satellite, cable TV, networks, and local stations. The fact that so many programs reach so many people almost belies the reality that one key individual is responsible for developing and supervising every aspect of each show. That person is the executive producer. From the simplest situation comedy to the most sophisticated drama, the program's executive producer, aided by his or her staff, has faced and accomplished a Herculean task.

Viewers easily recall the names of their favorite stars and would have little difficulty explaining the roles of actors, directors, or writers. The names of the executive producers, however, are infrequently recognized. Exceptions include "superstar" executive producers like Stephen Bochco, Stephen Cannell, Michael Mann, and Aaron Spelling. Still, their work activities are seldom fully understood.

A producer is supposed to be in charge of all production, but there are so many different facets of producing, that the functions can be truly confusing. Even within the television industry itself, the role of the producer is often cloaked in ambiguity. The title is often misused and is frequently awarded to writers of stature, who do not know the work of a producer and who never perform producing functions. Moreover, since there is no strong guild to protect the use of the title, anyone can print a business card and declare himself or herself a producer.

To complicate matters, most shows have executive producers, supervising producers, co-producers, line producers, and associate producers. Without the aid of a job description, it is difficult to know who is really responsible for what. Compounding the problem is the fact that producers in motion pictures and television have the same title but different responsibilities. In cinema, producers secure financing, while the director is in charge of the creative elements. In television, the producers reign supreme.

Television executive producers are the visionaries who create, manage, and supervise every aspect of a program. They are intricately involved in every decision, from the show's concept to its final edited form. They work against enormous odds to develop a show and orchestrate its production—a coordination of talent, ideas, and exacting challenges. Problems spring up at every turn, sometimes with apparently contradictory solutions. For example, producers fight for the highest-quality production, while simultaneously battling to keep costs within the predetermined budget.

Television producing involves an extraordinary ability to juggle the demands of creativity and practicality. Like puppet masters, producers must pull many strings and coordinate a multiplicity of skills and people to provide eventually a coherent vision to their audience. Given the different needs of management, technicians, actors, and crew, it is a wonder that producers can achieve any of their initial goals.

This book is designed to break through the mystique of producing. It offers a blueprint of what it means to be a working television producer. Whether you are interested in producing for television or in analyzing the role of the producer in the industry, this book will help you sift through the unique demands of the craft.

These are some of the topics explored in depth:

- What is a producer, and what does he or she do?
- How does a producer create new television shows for the major networks?
- Who are the key players needed for production?
- What is the difference between producing for film and videotape?
- What is the difference between producing drama and comedy?
- What are the daily activities of a television producer?
- What are the tricks a producer uses to keep costs down and quality up?
- How are critical production decisions reached?

The experiences reported, discussed, and analyzed here are consistent with the responsibilities faced by virtually any working television producer. The diverse views, choices, and producing functions explored are readily extrapolated for any television arena, including networks, cable, pay TV, syndication, and independent production venues.

THE APPROACH OF THIS BOOK

The book is divided into four major sections. Part I provides a detailed overview of the key functions of a producer. Chapter 2 explores how the producer can be defined according to title, workplace, and job function. It clarifies the different titles and roles in the hierarchy of television producing, from executive producer to subordinate producers. It also differentiates between producing for television and motion pictures. Within the workplace, a producer may function independently or work within a studio environment. The financial implications of those choices are considered. Also examined is job function: a producer is classified as the creative producer or the line producer. A ***creative producer*** supervises all aspects of artistic concerns. Responsibilities are clarified, including story and script concerns, challenges faced in the first year of a new show, and ongoing challenges to keep a series interesting for audiences. A ***line producer*** is responsible for all technical aspects of the production. Each of those areas is scrutinized.

Chapter 3 examines specific assignments faced by all producers. Development activities are discussed, including creation of new series concepts, stories, character development, and pilot scripts. Scripts are the basis for budget and production analysis. This chapter explains budget responsibilities, including the common practice of a studio producer working on a *pattern budget* (a budget assigned by the studio and considered highly classified). Budget-cutting strategies are analyzed in depth. The complexities of production scheduling are also detailed.

Preproduction involves an enormous range of activities and choices. Each major challenge is thoroughly documented. The casting process is clarified, from casting lead actors and secondary parts to studio readings and network casting sessions.

Before production, the producer must decide whether to shoot on the sound stage or on location. Another critical decision is whether to shoot on film or tape. The different technical options are explored, including the advantages and disadvantages of single-camera film, multi-camera tape, multi-camera film, and block and tape. Production meetings and rehearsal techniques are also discussed.

Postproduction activities are fully explained, including the intricacies of editing on film and tape, dubbing, ADR work (automatic dialogue replacement), music, and main titles.

Producing, like many other aspects of the television business, is interdisciplinary. The executive producer acts as captain of the production ship—responsible for people under his or her command, yet answerable to a supervising admiral of the fleet. Those critical relationships are thoroughly analyzed in Chapter 4. The executive producer functions with many individuals who help put the show together: the line producer, director, lead actors, writers, casting director, and production personnel. Producers also rely heavily on key crew members to accomplish the technical tasks of production. Among the crew positions clarified are unit production manager, cameraman or director of photography, assistant directors, script supervisor, art director, set director, wardrobe and makeup personnel, transportation coordinators, studio location manager, and stunt coordinator.

As for line of authority, the executive producer reports to senior-level management at studios, networks, and production companies. The complex nature of those relationships are unraveled. Given the intricate, multi-faceted nature of producing for television, the challenges of the field are highly unusual. Some of the keys to successful producing that are illuminated are setting priorities, dealing with compromises, and maintaining integrity of artistic vision.

In short, Part I defines the essential tools, techniques, and resources available for any television producer. It serves as a basic guide for the intricacies of the craft.

In Part II and Part III, those techniques are put into practice. Complete case histories are highlighted for two new television series as they evolved—*Coach*, a half-hour comedy, and *Law and Order*, a one-hour action drama. Their producers, Barry Kemp and Dick Wolf, respectively, permitted us to chronicle their daily activities during the creation and production of these new television pilots.

Both producers are highly esteemed for work in their respective genres. Barry Kemp, creator and producer of *Coach*, was a key executive on the comedy series, *Taxi*, and was creator and executive producer of the *Newhart* comedy series. Dick Wolf, producer of *Law and Order*, was a major writer on *Hill Street Blues* and was executive producer of *Miami Vice*.

Their perceptions offer an unparalleled opportunity to understand the function of television producers, their daily routine, and the methods by which they respond to the crucial challenges that arise along the way. They provide intimate portraits of how successful producers deal with unexpected problems—as they occur.

These sections are organized around the central concerns of the producer at each stage of the production process.

"The Development Process" looks at the conception and development of the new series. The producers of *Coach* and *Law and Order* explain how their shows were conceived and evolved from idea to pre-production planning. The chapters on the two shows illuminate the producers' thoughts and ideas about the new concepts, encompassing problems of story and script development, casting the lead characters, and selecting the appropriate production format.

"The Production Process" follows daily problems encountered throughout the productions of the pilots. It incorporates a daily log of activities, including casting, set design, and production implementation. Barry Kemp selected a three-camera, in-studio, live-audience format. Dick Wolf selected a cinema verité film format for on-location shooting. Both decisions had significant ramifications on the look of each show. The postproduction requirements for *Coach* and *Law and Order* differed considerably, with the film drama taking much more time and presenting significant technical dilemmas.

"Evaluation of the Production" offers an opportunity for the producers to assess their respective program's strengths and weaknesses. They were interviewed immediately after production was completed. From that perspective, they candidly evaluated their own effectiveness as producers and speculated on what they would do differently if starting again. The network reactions to the shows are also profiled, offering an intriguing backdrop for understanding they way producers deal with matters like scheduling and network management.

Barry Kemp gives us an evaluation of his work. What strengths and weaknesses did he find? What problems might have been overcome another way? The network's response to the *Coach* pilot from researchers and program executives is also revealed. It explains the rationale behind the unusual airing of the pilot show the day following the premiere of the series. It also traces the tenuous nature of the show's scheduling.

Dick Wolf wanted a specific tone for his show. He deliberately set out to break aesthetic expectations for the viewing audience. His experiments and choices are thoroughly documented, from preproduction planning, to casting lead characters, to dealing with unusual complexities of postproduction. In the evaluation section, Dick Wolf candidly analyzes the problems, choices, and production quality of the *Law and Order* pilot. He offers a vivid and insightful assessment of the producer's role in television. The network's reactions to the show are also fully documented, as is the uncanny story of the show's disposition.

In Part IV, the critical and social responsibilities of the producer are analyzed. The producer is busy working day to day on immediate problems of production. Yet the final product will be seen by millions of people. The issue of "responsible" producing is complicated by the fact that different views prevail on artistic freedom, censorship, and the nature and impact of sex and violence in television shows.

To provide a comprehensive inquiry, critical considerations are examined from three different perspectives—television management, social scientists, and independent producers. In our view, the divergent points of view can be consolidated through the producer's critical perspectives.

The Bibliography is selected and annotated to provide an extensive resource on all aspects of television producing.

The Appendix provides the actual shooting scripts for the pilots of *Coach* and *Law and Order*. These are the working documents around which all decisions evolved and around which everything else functioned—including casting, budgeting, and production scheduling.

An Overview
of Producing

2

What Is a Producer?

HOW THE TITLE DEFINES A PRODUCER

Defining a Producer

The title *producer* generates considerable confusion. It is difficult to offer a concise definition, because the title is amorphous and can be ascribed to a wide variety of functions. Adding to the confusion is the fact that individuals may perform the same job function but have different producing titles.

In truth, the title *producer* is self-designated. While working producers may not like to admit this, there is no specific training, knowledge, or background needed to proclaim oneself a producer, nor is there any prerequisite in education or experience. Unlike other craftspeople who are governed by industry unions, there is no guild protection or minimum requirements.

Many abuses of the producer title are the result. Some successful actors demand that their companion-friend-lover-associate get "executive producer" credit. Others want their business managers to get "associate producer" credit. Joanna Lee, who has written and produced a number of after-school TV specials, recalls a situation she faced: "I let the director get a producer's credit," Lee says, "But I said no when he wanted to make his editor the supervising producer. I don't even know what that means."[1]

There is a Producer's Guild of America, but it lacks clout. In 1983 the National Labor Relations Board ruled that producers cannot form

---

[1] *American Film* (March 1990): 12.

a union, because their jobs are essentially managerial. The only significant producer's organization is The Producer's Caucus, a self-appointed,
informal coalition of producers, dedicated to watchdog activities relating
to networks' demands and to creative matters.

Therefore, a producer can be anyone who calls himself or herself
such. Print a business card, order letterhead stationery, call yourself a
producer, and you too can be a producer—at least in title.

Clarifying Producing Titles

Perhaps the most frequently asked question of established producers is
the distinction between various producing titles in television. What is the
difference between executive producer, co-executive producer, supervising producer, producer, co-producer, and associate producer?

Confusion reigns because titles are used both as a job classification
and as a measure of prominence. The more esteemed titles are negotiated in contracts, much like actors negotiate star billing. With the exception of associate producer, all of the titles can apply to either a line
producer (overseeing the technical aspects of the show) or a creative
producer (overseeing the script and creative areas of the show). The
difference between line producers and creative producers will be discussed in detail shortly.

For the moment, let's look at the hierarchy of producing titles in
television:

Executive producer

Co-executive producer

Supervising producer

Producer

Co-producer

Associate producer

A sole credit as **executive producer** is the most prestigious title for
a producer in television. It designates the "star" producer. All other
producers function in subordinate roles to this individual. If two producers are granted executive producer status, they usually require separate *cards,* that is, separate listings in the credits. In the title sequence,
positioning is also important. An executive-producer credit at the end
of the program is more flattering than a listing in the beginning. Equal
executive producers share the same card at the conclusion of the program.

Co-executive producers are slightly less eminent than executive producers, although their work responsibilities are the same.

Supervising producers are frequently the workhorses of the producing team. In many instances the executive producer is involved in overseeing a number of projects, and it is the supervising producer who is the top-ranked individual on the project. It is also common for the supervising producer to be a fast-rising, younger person, learning the profession from older, more experienced executive producers.

The sole title *producer* is further down in the ranking, and *co-producers* represent the lowest position. Producers managing technical aspects of the show are usually younger people who hope to move up the production ladder. Those who manage creative matters are probably functioning as staff writers or story editors.

The title *associate producer* is the only one that actually describes a specific job function. This individual reports to a senior line producer, and his or her responsibilities center primarily on the postproduction process. One task is to supervise actors on the ADR (automatic dialogue replacement) stage (the *looping* stage). In that setting, dialogue can be replaced or re-recorded if the original dialogue was muffled or lost.

The associate also films inserts which can be used in the editing process. *Inserts* are close-ups of objects that are needed to make the visual sequences cohesive. Typical inserts include close-ups of notes, letters, newspaper headlines, or bullet holes in the wall.

In addition, the associate producer works with music and sound-effects editors, coordinates activities of the *dubbing* stage (where sound and music are mixed with the dialogue tracks), and checks the final product for any technical problems.

John Stephens is one of the most experienced line producers in television, having produced television movies, miniseries, and film series such as *Gunsmoke, Buck Rogers, How the West Was Won,* and *Simon and Simon.* He underscored the importance of a technically proficient associate producer:

> I rely completely upon my associate producer for postproduction chores. . . . [When we produced *Simon and Simon*] I always let him know what I wanted. There is so much going on, he has to know everything [to stay on top of our production requirements]. He's in on the "spotting" sessions for music and effects. Then, I leave the dubbing entirely to him. . . . I trust my associate producer totally.[2]

---

[2]Quotes in this chapter attributed to John Stephens are from personal communication in 1988.

The Role of the Producer in Television and Motion Pictures

The confusion over the roles of a producer are compounded further by the difference between producing for television and for motion pictures. In the realm of motion pictures, a producer is the "money man," the individual who obtains and manages the financing. That person may have a say in the selection of writer, star, or director, but he or she does not become intricately involved in the creative process of making the film. Instead, it is the director who has creative control over the production. If there is a major star involved in the movie, he or she may also have influence on the project. The motion picture producer usually limits his or her involvement to issues involving costs and scheduling.

In television, the situation is quite different. Since the networks finance much of the production costs, with the difference supplied by the studio or production organization, there is less need for a financial wizard.

Television has awarded the title *producer* to those who creatively guide the production from concept to postproduction. Usually these are writers who can provide artistic continuity and essential creative visions to a project.

There is a logical explanation for the rise of the producer in television and the subsidiary role played by the director. It may be best understood by examining the demanding production requirements for a television series. If a network commits to a new series, it expects 22 episodes delivered each season. Those episodes are shot on a continuous schedule. No one director can possibly handle all the programs. A show must utilize at least three directors: one for shooting the current episode, another for preparing the subsequent show, and another for supervising editing of the episode completed.

Typically, a show will have even more directors, and those directors move from series to series. For that reason, directors are not intricately in touch with the day-to-day operations and problems of a particular series.

The same situation applies to television series writers. Given the time constraints and production requirements, no writer can conceive all the episodes of a series. The producer needs minimally a staff of two or three writers (story editors or story consultants). This small staff is augmented by a body of freelance writers who solicit assignments and work on a number of different series. Generally, the scripts that arrive from freelance writers vary substantially in quality and acceptability. Freelance writers are rarely familiar with the intricacies of the series, and it is axiomatic that all scripts will need some degree of rewriting.

Given the context of television, it is easy to understand why the skills of a creative producer are crucial. Directors are hired by the producer, the writing staff is chosen by the producer, the freelance writers are approved by the producer, and the script revisions are prescribed by the producer.

HOW JOB FUNCTION DEFINES THE ROLE OF THE PRODUCER

While it is difficult to determine roles by titles, it is possible to categorize two types of producers: the *creative producer,* who is often a writer, and the *line producer,* who supervises daily operations of the production. Let us look at the responsibilities of the creative producer first.

The Creative Producer

Many years ago, the head producer of a television series was rarely a writer. He or she turned to the show's head writer (the story editor) to perform script revisions. As television shows became more elaborate, a producer who could also write had an advantage over the conventional producer. He or she could do script revisions without assistance.

Eventually, most key producers of television series became writers, including Stephen Cannell *(Hunter, The A-Team, 21 Jump Street)*, Peter Fischer *(Murder, She Wrote)*, Stephen Bochco *(L.A. Law)*, Gary David Goldberg *(Cheers)*, and Glenn Caron *(Moonlighting)*.

While the elevation of writers to television producers solved one problem, it created others. The writer/creator of a successful show is unquestionably the best writer for that series. However, as a producer, he or she rarely has time to write original material. In addition to production tasks, producers are constantly rewriting the work of others. Consequently, the most gifted writers in television are quickly elevated to positions in which they no longer write.

Since the disciplines of writing and producing are different, excelling in one field does not guarantee success in the other. There are many instances where talented writers have become terrible producers. The telltale signs are series that run way over budget, have little advance script material ready prior to production, have a high staff turnover, and have constant difficulty in meeting network airdate schedules.

In those situations where the writer-producer is too new at the job or not strong enough in production skills, it is common practice for studios to assign a nonwriting producer to the executive staff. Even when the writer-producer is exceptionally talented, it has become common practice for the hyphenate producer to join with a nonwriting producer in helming the production of the series. For example, Peter Fischer, writer/creator of *Murder, She Wrote* works hand-in-hand with line producer Robert O'Neill. Steve Cannell and Jo Swerling, Jr., have a similar long-standing relationship. Glen Larson has Harker Wade, and Aaron Spelling has had a long collaboration with E. Duke Vincent.

With a strong alliance to complement their skills, creative producers are free to concentrate on the stylistic problems of a show, including stories, scripts, casting, and visual style.

Supervising Stories and Scripts

It is the responsibility of the creative producer to oversee all the scripts for a season of television shows. Most often, the producer has written the pilot and will write the initial episode for a new series. These can serve as a blueprint for other writers.

As the Writer's Guild of America repeatedly and correctly declares, the script is the inception of any television project. In addition to telling a story, a pilot script conveys the style of a show, delves into the characters and their motivations, and sets the tone for a whole series. The producer must peg the show's dramatic values, which run on a continuum from stark realism to slapstick comedy. Episodic scripts attempt to emulate the pilot on a weekly basis.

In some ways creative producing for a television series can be compared to writing a 22-chapter novel every season. An individual episode is just a moment of time and conflict for characters in that world. For that reason, a series should be examined on the basis of the full run of season's episodes. Changes that occur over the course of a season affect the show's longevity.

The producer's goal, of course, is to keep the series fresh and interesting—for the production team, as well as the viewing audience. That task varies considerably between the first year of a series and subsequent seasons.

Surviving the First Year of a New Series

During the first year of any new television series, the principal creative struggle is simply to survive. Good scripts are scarce, and daily rewrites are the rule. The entire creative team, from producers and writers to actors and directors, is finding its way. These trial-and-error efforts are usually evident to the discerning viewer.

In that first year, many series spin out of control, losing their audience as they struggle to find a direction, and as they search for storytelling stability. Other shows, through luck or expertise, find a successful path and muster their creative forces in the right direction. But it never comes easily. The first year is usually filled with horror stories, culminating in the exhilaration of success or the despair of Nielsen ratings oblivion.

While there have been extensive discussions and planning sessions about the direction of the series between creative producers, writers, and network and studio executives, actual production frequently renders these plans obsolete. The program itself assumes its own form and direction. A creative producer must be attuned to the natural rhythms of a series, adapting to the emerging identity of the new show, like a butterfly, changing the script and story direction as necessary.

Some classic examples might be helpful. In concept and early episodes, *Happy Days* centered about the life and activities of Richie Cunningham, as played by Ron Howard. There was, however, an incidental character named *Fonzie*, played by Henry Winkler. Shortly after the series premiered to mediocre ratings, the audience desire to see more of "The Fonz" became evident. The series was subsequently shifted to feature Fonzie, and the show became an enormous long-running hit.

Garry Marshall, producer of *Happy Days*, recalls his battle with the network to preserve the character of the Fonz as he saw that character emerging:

> ABC had a theory that *Happy Days* must have a gang of hoodlums from the other side of the tracks. I said, "Well, we'll see," and then gave them Fonzie, alone. They said, "Where's the gang?" and I said, "You don't need a gang. This man is good enough, he's symbolic." They watched and (finally) agreed.[3]

Similarly, *Family Ties* was initially conceived as a family generation-gap comedy about liberal parents, products of the 1960s, having to deal with their Reagan-like conservative son, a product of the 1980s. As audiences gravitated to Michael J. Fox, however, the initial concept was downplayed and the son, rather than the parents, became the show's centerpiece.

In the pilot and early episodes of *CHIPS*, the Ponch character, played by Eric Estrada, was a bumbler, who unsuccessfully chased after women and was a thorn in the side of his superior. The initial ratings were poor. Research indicated that audiences wanted to like Ponch, but were displeased by this characterization. The character was modified. Ponch became good at his job. Women chased him, rather than vice versa, and the series became a popular hit.

Sometimes, changes occur right after the pilot is produced. In *The A-Team*, a female character was initially part of the team, but she quickly

---

[3]Horace Newcomb and Robert S. Alley, *The Producer's Medium* (New York: Oxford University Press, 1983), pp. 245–246.

disappeared. In the pilot for *Simon and Simon,* A.J. Simon was virtually engaged to a young lady whose father owned a rival detective agency. Both the woman and her father quickly vanished from the series.

Even if there are no drastic concept changes, the discovery process holds surprises at every turn. It is common for actors and directors to stumble through the early episodes of a series, with revised script pages delivered to their homes the night before shooting. In an early episode of *Miami Vice,* which took place in the Everglades, producer Michael Mann was on the set, swatting away mosquitoes and rewriting the script in longhand as it was being shot.

It is a wonder that any television series survives the experimentation of the first year. It is a hardship on the producers as well as the actors and directors. But if the series survives and is renewed for a subsequent year, production life becomes easier and the challenges change.

Fighting Predictability in Ongoing Series

After the first year, production of a television series usually settles down to a dull roar. The crew becomes acclimated to one another and efficient working relationships evolve. The actors become comfortable in their roles and often have better insight into their characters than do the writers who created them. The actors "live" the character every day for the nine-month shooting schedule of a typical series.

In an ongoing series, the producing team has also secured a core of writers whose sensibilities are consistent with the tone of the series. Staff members and freelancers with multiple writing assignments form the foundation for the episodes.

Similarly, through the trial-and-error wanderings of the first year, a cache of directors emerge, whose sensibilities fit the requirements of the series. Often a series will rely on two or three directors for an entire year, using outside directors only occasionally as relief from the grueling production schedule.

What then are the problems for a creative producer in this coordinated, ongoing work situation? Principally, fighting boredom and burnout. The creative producer must ensure that the process does not become automatic and formulaic. If one episode blends into another, following the same blueprint in cookie-cutter fashion, the actors become bored. Ultimately, so does the viewing audience.

The creative producer must constantly strive to surprise, shock, and delight. There are a few techniques that can be employed. If there is more than one leading character in the series, the producers can shift the focus from week to week. In *Miami Vice,* one week the story featured Crockett; the next week it would focus on his partner, Tubbs. Occasionally, subsidiary characters like Castillo were central to the story. In

L.A. Law, the focus shifts easily from one law partner to another. In *thirtysomething,* each episode centers around different characters and conflicts in personal relationships.

Producers also look for new revelations and insights about their continuing characters. What can they reveal about a character's past life to the audience? How do these revelations reflect on the character today?

Finally, producers work to balance the episodes over the course of the season. The best series have an element of unpredictability about them. Even the most dramatic series will occasionally have a humorous episode, and vice versa. *Quantum Leap* will shift in two weeks from a light-hearted episode, where the central character, Sam Beckett, is trapped in the body of a teenage nerd, to an episode that deals forcibly and dramatically with prejudice.

A situation comedy will stretch into dramatic themes and conflicts. One of the highest-rated episodes of *Family Ties* dealt with teen suicide. It is exemplary if the viewer is surprised to find the show dramatic one week, mysterious the next, humorous the next. Producers who practice the art of balance are better able to keep a series popular than are those who settle for week-to-week conformity.

After the third year, even greater changes usually are needed. Actors and writers can unintentionally fall into routines. The series starts going stale. A good creative producer realizes that review, rethinking, and overhaul must be attempted.

Commonly, the third year is the point in a series' life cycle when new regular characters are introduced and some older characters disappear. Perhaps the home locations and sets are also changed for variety. The characters move into a new house or new office. They gain or lose wealth.

The writing staff is similarly turned over. Usually at least one or two of the original writing staff ask to leave, feeling they are "burned out" and have little more to contribute. New writers with fresh viewpoints are brought in, and extensive discussions to find interesting new directions for the series take place.

At this critical three-year point, it is not uncommon for even the creative producer who initiated the show to leave or at least to dislocate from the everyday work environment.

The Line Producer

Producers who are nonwriters are called *line producers* or *nuts-and-bolts producers.* Their domain is the physical production itself and the quick solution of the problems that arise at every moment during production of a series.

In the early days of television, when color was a dream, and cable and videotape did not exist, production problems were relatively rudimentary. All shows except variety programs were 30 minutes in length. One producer could adequately serve all the functions necessary to put a show on the air.

By the late 1980s, however, television production demanded more sophistication and expertise. Half-hour comedies were videotaped for live audiences or shot on film like minimovies. Hour-long dramas featured location shooting, shifting color palettes to suit moods, stereo sound, and special effects. It became an impossible task for a single producer to handle it all. The solution was to hire a staff of producers with different expertise. The producing team could number two to five, including line and creative producers.

Since nomenclature can be easily misinterpreted, it is essential to stress that line producing can be a very creative endeavor. A good line producer has enormous influence over the style, look, and production values of a show. A strong line producer can deliver a superbly crafted program that is aesthetically comparable to a motion picture costing millions of dollars more. A weak producer can maim a show to such an extent that no writing or acting talent can overcome that liability.

The line producer oversees all aspects of the physical production of a show. Included in these responsibilities are selecting department heads, hiring key crew staff, scheduling production, delivering the show on budget, making decisions about location shooting, supervising editing, and supervising postproduction activities.

The line producer chooses the heads of important production departments, notably the unit production manager, first and second assistant directors, director of photography, and the key wardrobe, art direction, and set design heads. The specific responsibilities of these and other crew members are detailed in Chapter 4.

HOW THE WORKPLACE DEFINES THE ROLE OF THE PRODUCER

Role of the Producer in the Studio Environment

In the studio environment the producer is abetted and supported by the studio system. This has distinct advantages and disadvantages.

On the positive side, producers are freed from financial negotiations and complex contracts with banks and other funding organizations. Since the studio provides the financing differential between the network license fee and the cost of production, the necessity of budget control is lessened.

The studio carefully monitors costs and insists on stringent adherence to budget. It enforces the decision to cut production costs if a project grossly exceeds expectations. However, the studio does have "deep pockets." It has the ability, within reason, to absorb overages, allowing the producer to concentrate on the creative aspects of delivering the best possible show as well as completing a project.

The studio is also an effective ally in selling and maintaining programs on the networks' schedules. Studio executives have close working relationships with each of the networks, and therefore are aware of programming needs and desires. In addition, a successful studio, producing several "hits" for a network, has undeniable leverage.

Barry Kemp, producer of _Coach,_ was not hesitant in expressing his views on the matter:

> The first critical decision is, "Is this the show I want to devote my time to?" The second decision is where to take it. You want a network that will be excited about the idea and excited about you. . . . The importance of where to take a project is sometimes underestimated. One of the reasons you elect to enter into relationships with studios, versus having your own little independent place, is that studios can provide [pragmatic] feedback. They have the experience to "read" networks, and know who's got what in development. They'll know the best place to take [a specific project].[4]

There are also some disadvantages for a producer to weigh before associating with a major studio. First, if a series is hugely successful both on the network and later in syndication, the profit is similarly gigantic—and most of it goes to the studio. Only the well-established studio producer will participate in these dividends, and then only to a small degree. In return for taking the large financial gamble, the studio is sure to retain most of the profits.

There have been a number of well-publicized lawsuits in which actors and writer-producers have sued their former studios in an attempt to receive what they felt was their contractual and appropriate share in profits. For the younger, newer executive producer it is not a problem; he or she rarely is able to coerce a studio into giving profit participation at any level.

---

[4]Quotes in this chapter attributed to Barry Kemp are from personal communications in 1989.

Role of the Independent Producer

If an independent producer does not choose to associate with a studio, he or she must be able to obtain the enormous funds needed, not only to produce, but also to cover the deficit between network license fee and cost of production.

Once the financing is obtained, the independent producer has direct control over the finances. He or she must constantly monitor expenses and parsimoniously dole out funds, making sure that there is enough money to complete production.

A studio producer knows that the studio has deep pockets and will always pay for unplanned expenses. The independent producer has no such backstop. Marcy Carsey and Tom Werner, producers of *The Cosby Show*, mortgaged their own homes to pay for deficits in the first few years of series production.[5]

While it is common for independent producers to produce television movies and even miniseries, the independent series producer is rare. For drama programming the independent producer is virtually extinct. The reason is principally financial.

In 1989, the cost of a network program frequently topped $1,300,000 per hour, and deficits could run into hundreds of thousands of dollars per episode. The producing organization must bet on a series' success (not a good gamble in that environment) and then wait for three to five years for its syndication sales to accrue. Such a large financial obligation makes both financing sources and networks wary.

Due to the heavy financial obligations—on top of the difficult producing workload—many smaller independent producers seek partners. One partner usually deals with the business and financial aspects of the production, while another devotes full time and energy to the production itself.

Larger independent production organizations, like Stephen Cannell Productions, Aaron Spelling, and Charles Fries, form their own ministudios, hiring specialists to handle the financial aspects of production in order to free executive producers to devote their expertise to the tasks of producing itself.

---

[5]"Carsey-Werner: The Little Programming Engine That Could," *Broadcasting* (July 18, 1988): 60.

3

The Responsibilities of a Producer

DEVELOPMENT RESPONSIBILITIES

Series Concepts

Creative producers often function in the dual capacity of writer and producer. They come up with ideas for new series, creating characters and situations that are appealing and produceable. The *concept* usually outlines an interesting locale, occupation or situation, and characters who will clash in some inherently funny or dramatic way. In its early stages, concepts introduce the settings, potential story arenas, main characters, and ambience.

Producers talk through their concepts with studio heads or network executives to secure interest. They have discussions about potential casting of the lead characters, length and scope of the pilot story, and the potential for interesting a network in the series, along with an analysis of possible respectable time slots on the network's schedule. Armed with this information, the producer can further develop and refine characters, settings, and situations—or abandon the concept for the time being.

It is not unusual for producers to work on several different ideas simultaneously. Given the erratic nature of the marketplace, different ideas augment the chances of hitting some appropriate combination of creative output and network needs. The marketplace for new series reflects the shifting trends of programming priorities at the networks, cable companies, and stations. Those needs change from network to network, from season to season, and from executive to executive. The authors' previous book, *Primetime: Network Television Programming*, explores the process of series-concept development, and the dynamics of the interrelationship between producers, network management, and studio executives.[1]

If they do not do their own writing, producers do suggest ideas and give feedback to writers. Due to the creative nature of storytelling, each individual approaches the development process differently. Some of the most successful writers in television wait for an idea to emerge from their subconscious. In literature, film, and television, some writers confess they write the story as it unfolds in their "mind's eye." They have no idea where the story will go or how it will conclude. Among those who work this way are popular author Elmore Leonard and Don Bellesario, who created *Magnum, P.I.*

On the other hand, some creators are very structured. They outline a potential story and examine it thoroughly before they begin writing. Barry Kemp, creator of *Coach*, falls into the latter category. In the upcoming case study, he reveals that he was thinking about the concept for *Coach* for two years before he presented it to the network. He needed mentally to test its endurance as a series concept to himself.

Story and Character Development

For most writer/creators, the development process consists of a synthesis of concept and character. Ideas in television are abundant and by themselves are almost meaningless. Ideas have to be formed and structured to be workable. What is crucial is the merging of ideas with characters. Consequently, with rare exception, television is a character-driven medium. The idea of television cops working on vice was not new. It had been suggested, tried, and rejected many times. It was only after Tony Yerkovich set it in Miami and created the characters of Crockett and Tubbs, and Michael Mann contributed its characteristic style, that *Miami Vice* became successful.

Character development in comedy is as crucial as it is for drama. Many of the preeminent comedy writer/developers in television share the view that characters in crisis are prime for comedy. Garry Marshall, creator and producer of shows such as *Happy Days*, *The Odd Couple*, and *Mork and Mindy*, believes that the essence of good comedy lies in character distress. He used to coax his own staff writers to think of the most painful

---

[1]For sample series concepts and detailed discussions of how they are developed in the network marketplace, see Richard A. Blum and Richard D. Lindheim, *Primetime: Network Television Programming* (Boston: Focal Press, 1987), pp. 63–121.

or embarrassing moments in their lives. Then he encouraged them to explore those moments in comedic tones.

A great deal has been written in psychological context about comedy, the need for it as emotional release, and the theories behind the construction and execution of successful comedy.[2] It was Aristotle who first wrote about the audience's need for an emotional catharsis. In our own time, the medium of television provides its own rules and constraints, and comedy producers must be familiar with them all.

Pilot Scripts

The development of the pilot script occurs in different stages. The producer must first decide on the appropriate length, the format, and the production values that are right for the show. Then the writer (or the writer/producer) creates the first draft that is seen and evaluated by executives. The script may be revised any number of times to reflect the needs and reactions of studio and network executives. Supervisors may note problems or make suggestions to improve character appeal, dialogue that is confusing, or scenes that need better pacing. Research and legal departments point out potential problems concerning the use of names, places, and items used in each scene.

The script has to be written according to the production format and length decided by the producer, with traditional act breaks for the story to unfold.[3] In videotape, or other situation-comedy formats, the half-hour script can be up to 45 pages in length. The sitcom format is double spaced, relatively sparse in scene description, and abundant with dialogue. The script is broken down into scenes within each act. If the script is written to be produced on film, it has a one-minute-per-page count. In other words, a 60-minute show will have about 60 pages of script. The film script is single spaced and includes detailed descriptions of the set and atmosphere, as well as detailed character descriptions and dialogue. (See the scripts in Appendixes A and B.)

Deciding on the Length of the Pilot

The decision to shoot a one-hour, 90-minute, or two-hour pilot ultimately impacts on the show's projected revenues. If a drama script is

---

[2]For a history of comic tradition, see David Grote, *The End of Comedy: The Sitcom and the Comedic Tradition* (Hamden, CT: Shoestring Press, 1983).

[3]For a sample act structure in a half-hour situation-comedy script format, see Appendix A: *Coach*. For act structure in one-hour film script format, see Appendix B: *Law and Order*. For a discussion of the process and techniques of writing TV film and situation-comedy scripts, see Richard A. Blum, *Television Writing: From Concept to Contract* (Boston: Focal Press, 1984).

two hours, it can be formatted like a movie and can be sold to pay television and videocassette marketplaces. The producer can gain substantial financial assistance in covering the deficit—the difference between the network license fee and the cost of production. (The *license fee* is the amount of money negotiated per episode for the right to air the show. It is never enough to cover the cost of production.)

Networks also allow pilot programs to be sold abroad. Until recently, the monies received from foreign sales have been insignificant. In the past few years, however, this situation has changed radically. Foreign revenues can be significant for producers. But for this to work, the pilot must be formatted as a movie and shot at movie length.

Some networks resist the two-hour pilot. CBS and ABC are reluctant to produce two-hour pilots on the grounds that the projects suffer creatively. The pilot premise seems stretched beyond the limits of dramatic credulity in a two-hour version of the show.

Without the supplemental revenue, the one-hour pilot is a difficult financial risk. The compromise, the 90-minute pilot, remains a rare item. The producer has to shoot additional footage to bring it to a length suitable for cassette or foreign consideration as a movie. Additionally, the networks find it difficult to schedule 90-minute shows for broadcast.

The syndication marketplace for reruns of one-hour series in recent years has declined substantially. Studios and production companies cannot afford to produce one-hour shows at a large deficit when they know costs might never be recovered. The networks, with a declining share of audience, have become intractable in their negotiations of stringent license fees for all shows.

BUDGET RESPONSIBILITIES

The Pattern Budget and License Fee

In 1990, the costs of producing a one-hour pilot film could exceed $3 million, and the cost of producing a one-hour filmed episode of a TV series at a major studio commonly exceeds $1.3 million. (See Figure 3.1.) When a producer works for a studio, the studio dictates the actual amount available for production, and there is little, if any, chance to change it. As a result, most producers who work at studios have—at best—a sketchy understanding of financial details concerning their shows. It is not uncommon for the show's executive producer to be unaware of the license fee paid by the network—or the amount of money the studio is adding or subtracting from the base.

Studios are notoriously closed mouthed in this regard. Producers are simply handed a *pattern budget* and told they cannot exceed the

MCA TELEVISION/ESTIMATED PRODUCTION COST REPORT

FIRST REPORT

Production Number: 62210	Series:	Title:	Episode Number: 3	Date: TUE August 12, 1986

Director:	Pattern: 1,231,018	Budget this show: 1,231,006	Current (under) OVER Budget 2,240

	Est Final	Hours Budget	Hours Worked	Pages Sched	Pages Shot
1ST RPT	1,233,246	80.0	74.3	48 6/8	48 6/8
5WK					
12WK					
EST FIN					

FIRST REPORT - COMPLETION OF PHOTOGRAPHY

Remarks:
RATE CARD BUDGET. BUDGET INCLUDES WRITERS' SALARIES AT $6,419 OVER PATTERN.

SHOOTING PERIOD 08//01/86 - 08/11/86.
08/12/86 - 1ST REPORT - ADJ. $2,240.
OVERAGES DUE TO:
- Locations - Set watch and harbor warden - 2,438.

STATUS:
COMPLETED PRINCIPAL PHOTOGRAPHY ON SCHEDULE

$2,240 - Over budget
$2,228 - Over pattern

Hours budgeted - 80.0
Hours worked - 74.3

THESE ESTIMATES REFLECT PRODUCTION SHOOTING COSTS ONLY AND ARE PREDICATED UPON ALL POST PRODUCTION, GROUP AND AMORTIZED COSTS ADHERING TO BUDGET

Figure 3.1 Sample daily production-cost report for an hour-long action TV series. Note the pattern, episode, and estimated budgets and the differences between them.

amount stated. It is the producer's responsibility to make the show for the quoted dollar figure. If he or she cannot squeeze the project into the allotted budget, then the project may be postponed until costs can be reduced, or it may be cancelled altogether.

The major studios are not arbitrary in deciding the pattern budget for a project. Since the network license fee never covers the full cost of production, the studio business-affairs executives decide on an individual basis how much to deficit finance a show. At minimum, studios will take the network's license fee, add projected foreign sales, and possible video cassette rental revenue in determining the basis for a pattern budget. Then, depending on the project, they will risk spending even more money.

The amount of deficit spending is dependent on the studio's enthusiasm for the project and its evaluation of the show's potential success. Since the studio, understandably, does not want to be accused of favoritism among producers, it strives to keep the actual figures highly confidential.

Budget-Cutting Strategies

Television producing is a very expensive business. Every shooting day for a pilot could cost upwards of $50,000 for crew and equipment alone. For that reason, keeping a show on budget is critical. The producer and production manager analyze costs that are above the line and below the line. *Above the line* refers to all creative costs—producer, writer, director, actors. *Below the line* refers to all technical costs. See Figure 3.2.

A producer must find ways to reduce costs without sacrificing the quality of the show. Some strategies that can be utilized to achieve that goal are:

- If a script calls for too many locations, the producer can consolidate the location requirements. The logistics of moving from place to place cost time and money and crew time adds up quickly. A location manager can scout for one location that can double as another. (Sometimes when scenes are shot from different angles, it will look as if different locations are in use.)
- If the production is scheduled for summer shooting, and the script calls for many night scenes, production costs will escalate waiting for the sun to set. The producer can adjust the balance of scenes by altering the day or night requirements in the shooting script. This simple rule can save a great deal of money: plan to shoot more day scenes in the summer, night scenes in the winter.
- The producer should consider shooting the show in a "right-to-work" state, where nonunion (and therefore lower-paid) crew people can be hired. In the case of *Law and Order,* this option was not a viable

alternative. The producer wanted to shoot in New York, and all the states in the Northeast are heavily unionized.

• The producer needs to compile the most efficient shooting schedule. A skillfully planned production schedule keeps the show's cost tightly under control.

SCHEDULING RESPONSIBILITIES

Half-hour comedies can be taped or filmed in one night, with post-production taking about a week's time. One-hour dramatic shows require much more time for production and postproduction. A typical production schedule for a one-hour filmed pilot is 10–14 shooting days. Post-production can take much longer.

Scheduling falls under the aegis of the line producer. If the schedule is too loose, time and money are wasted. If, as happens more commonly, the schedule is too tight, the production runs overtime and the unionized members of the craft guilds are compensated in kind. Overtime production can quickly run into hundreds of thousands of dollars.

An effective schedule is vital in film production. It equates directly with money. The longer the schedule, the greater the cost. A full-scale, traditional, unionized television production costs about $40,000 per day (as of 1989). Three- or four-camera videotape shows are simpler, since they shoot a complete episode in one evening before a live audience.

The line producer, working with the unit managers, assistant directors, director of photography, and director, evaluates a production schedule like a battle plan. Filmed television production, like motion pictures, is never shot in sequence. Consequently, the producer needs to analyze the structure and needs of each scene. To help build a visual model of those needs, each scene is placed on a narrow vertical cardboard strip, which identifies the scene number, the location, the time of day, and the cast members required. These strips are designed to fit onto a specially prepared travelling schedule display, simply called *the board*. The strips can then be moved about like pieces of a jigsaw puzzle until the optimum schedule can be realized. That schedule contains the least number of production days, with reasonable work done each day.

Producer John Stephens explained the process he undertook for scheduling *Simon and Simon:*

> We make up a preliminary board, then go over the whole schedule, from day one, with the director. Then we go back to my office, and get the writers over. We discuss physical changes we want to make within the framework of the show. [The idea is] to make the show work for us, within the schedule and the budget.[1]

[1]Quotes in this chapter attributed to John Stephens are from personal communication in 1990.

UNIVERSAL CITY STUDIOS, INC.
PRODUCTION BUDGET

Scope:

Neg. Ft.: _____   Budget Date: _____

Series (Production) Title   Episode Title   Production No.

Producer   Director

Principals

SHOOTING SCHEDULE

Start Date	Finish Date	Production Est. Days	Production Act. Days

Days	REHEARSE	STUDIO			LOCAL LOCATION	DISTANT LOCATION	TRAVEL	IDLE		HOLIDAY	TOTAL
		STAGE	B/L\T	PROCESS				LAYOFF	SUNDAYS		
1st. Unit											
2nd. Unit											

COMMENTS

ACKNOWLEDGED

Approved for Production _____   Date _____

Figure 3.2 Sample production-budget form for Universal Studios. Note the items considered *above* and *below* the line costs.

Production Budget -

ACCT NO.	DESCRIPTION	PAGE NO.	BUDGET	
801	Story & Other Rights	2		
803	Writing	2		
805	Producer & Staff	2		
807	Director & Staff	3		
809	Talent	3		
810	Fringe Benefits	3		
TOTAL - ABOVE THE LINE				
811	Production Staff	4		
813	Camera	5		
814	Art Department	6		
815	Set Construction & Striking	6		
816	Special Effects	7		
817	Set Operations	8		
819	Electrical	9		
821	Set Dressing	10		
823	Action Props	11		
825	Livestock & Picture Vehicles	11		
827	Special Photography	12		
831	Wardrobe	13		
833	Makeup & Hairdressing	14		
835	Sound (Production)	15		
837	Locations (Local & Distant)	16		
838	Video Tape (Production)	17		
839	Transportation (Studio)	18		
841	Film (Production)	19		
845	Sundry & Tests	19		
847	Second Unit	20		
848	Insert Shooting	20		
TOTAL - SHOOTING PERIOD				
851	Editing & Projection	21		
852	Video Tape (Post Production)	22		
853	Music	23		
855	Sound (Post Production)	24		
857	Film & Stock Shots	25		
859	Titles, Optical, Inserts	26		
TOTAL - COMPLETION PERIOD				
861	Insurance	26		
863	Fringe Benefits	27		
866	Unit Publicist & Stillman	27		
867	General Expenses	28		
TOTAL - OTHER				
TOTAL - BELOW THE LINE				
TOTAL ABOVE & BELOW THE LINE (711)				
INDIRECT COST				
GRAND TOTAL				

PRODUCTION NO: EPISODE NO: DATE: PATTERN TOTAL:

Figure 3.2   *(continued)*

PREPRODUCTION ACTIVITIES

Casting

All television networks stipulate in their contracts that they have the right of final approval over the casting of all lead and continuing roles in a television series. The casting process can easily stretch into days and weeks.

In any pilot show, the casting process is crucial and often marks the difference between success and failure. The list of "right" casting decisions in television series is memorable: Peter Falk, Don Johnson, Bruce Willis, Angela Lansbury, Michael J. Fox, to name just a few. The list of "wrong" casting decisions is longer and easily forgotten. Few people, outside of the unhappy creator/producer, remember the brief life of these projects.

Networks sometimes turn to the controversial Performer Q (or TVQ) measurement, which ranks familiarity and popularity of actors, among a statistical sample of television viewers. Using that survey, executives can determine the most popular stars and may influence producers to use those actors in their shows. Producers often bristle at the use of Performer Q's, since it tends to limit their choices, and impinges on their freedom to choose the best actors for the roles.

Lead Actors

"Stars" are not likely to go through the open call or general audition process. Actors who have achieved a certain status in the industry are contacted through their agents and are invited by producers to private meetings. In those meetings the role is discussed, and the actor can voice enthusiasm or doubts about playing the role. If there is mutual interest, and if the actor is available, contractual discussions begin.

When a studio has network approval for an actor, there may still be unresolved negotiations. The actor's agent might have additional financial demands and any new demands must be approved by the network and studio. The producer—working from the pattern budget—must then find ways to reduce expenses elsewhere in the allotted budget.

If a deal between the star and the studio cannot be resolved, the project might be postponed, until another actor is found.

Secondary Roles

For casting of secondary characters, producers rely on the expertise of casting directors. The process begins with a meeting among the producer, the casting director, and the director. They discuss the physical and emotional qualities desired for each role. A list of all possible candidates is compiled, various agents are contacted, and availability of prospective actors is determined.

Actors who are available are sent a few pages of the script, focusing on their proposed character. They have the opportunity to practice for the role; then they come to the producer's office for a reading. Actors who are not contacted by the casting director also have an opportunity to try out. There is a publication for actors and talent agents, *The Breakdown Service,* which lists all productions in the process of casting. It identifies the producer, casting director, roles being cast, and physical requirements desired by the producer.

Readings

Readings by actors for the various roles are the first opportunity a writer/ producer has to glimpse what the finished product might be like. The reading is held in the producer's office—actors do character dialogue and the casting director plays other parts. Actors try to ignore the reality of producers and their associates scrutinizing their performances. Mental and written notes are acutely taken. It is a most unnatural situation.

The casting process progresses methodically. The producer may have prospective actors return several times, advising them how to strengthen their performances. Finally, after narrowing the list to five or six for each role, a casting meeting is scheduled with studio executives.

At the studio, the number of people attending readings escalates considerably. Among the participants are the head of studio casting, the assigned casting director, the head of the television division, the studio development executive, and key members of the production team, including the line producer and director. The finalists are then asked to repeat the performance they gave for the producer.

After all the readings, the assembled group discusses its reactions. Sometimes there are several good choices and everyone is pleased. Occasionally one actor is so superior that no second choice is needed. Frequently, no standout performer is found, and the casting director must continue looking for suitable candidates.

If there are several good choices for a role, the business-affairs department at the studio is asked to contact the agents and make a *test-option contract* with each actor. This initiates a hold on the actor for a short period of time (usually 10 days). During that period, the actor cannot accept work on another project. The actor's remuneration for playing the part in the pilot and in the series is agreed upon. It is only after the successful conclusion of this negotiation that an actor can be taken to the network for final approval.

Network Casting Sessions

The network casting session is similar to that in the studio, except it has grown even larger with the inclusion of network casting and executive personnel. At ABC and CBS there are screening rooms arranged with spotlights for readings, to accommodate the audience.

The finalists for each role are asked to read for this intimidating group. If they can manage to keep their knees from shaking and their tongues from twisting, and if they can remember the lines, they now have a good chance of landing a lucrative role in a potential hit television series. The pressure is enormous, both on the producer and the cast. A mistake here is usually nonrecoverable.

When a producer and studio decide to bring in only one actor for a part, it is a demonstration of complete faith, an affirmation that the actor is perfect for the role. However, network executives may feel they are being excluded from the casting process, and a choice is being foisted on them. If they do not totally concur with the producer's judgment, they may reject the selection, demand more choices, and refuse even to reconsider the actor at a later date.

PRODUCTION FACILITIES

Sound Stages and Locations

The producer must decide whether to shoot on the sound stage, on location, or, more commonly, on a combination of both. The studio sound stage is the more traditional approach to efficient production. Given a stage, virtually all facilities can be controlled—sound, lighting, and camera moves. Shooting on location may seem more practical, but it invites the unexpected, from weather problems to unforeseen production difficulties.

Format Choices

Technical Requirements—Tape Versus Film

Situation comedies are produced in one of four formats: single-camera film, multi-camera tape, multi-camera film, and block and tape. Since the format has a profound effect, not only on the look of the show, but also on the structure of the script and the scene locations, it is an important decision that must be made quickly and decisively. Each format has advantages and disadvantages, all of which must be weighed for the specific project envisioned.

Single-Camera Film. This is the most expensive process. A single-camera film show is produced exactly like a miniature movie or one-hour television drama. That is, it is shot out of sequence with a film camera. There is a master shot of each scene, followed by close-up coverage taken from several different angles. It is then assembled by the editors in traditional film fashion.

Importantly, because it is shot like a movie both on stage and on location, it is not possible to have an audience present. Consequently, there is no immediate feedback for actors and directors. The director leaves *holes* (silent moments) in the dialogue or action, where everyone hopes there will be laughter. Frequently, of course, an artificial laugh track is added later. Producers and audiences usually find this contrived and irritating. When watching a scene that takes place outdoors and hearing an audience laughing uproariously, one cannot help but note the incongruity.

Perhaps the most famous single-camera film comedy was *M.A.S.H.* For most of its long run, *M.A.S.H* had no laugh track.

Multi-Camera Tape. In this application, the permanent sets are constructed on a sound stage facing audience bleachers. Room is provided for one of two "swing" sets needed for each new episode. The show is rehearsed like a stage play for four days and then videotaped on the fifth day, using three or four cameras, before the live audience. While there are starts and stops for scenery and wardrobe changes, and a scene may be repeated if there are actor flubs or technical errors, the show is presented in continuity for the attending audience.

Often there is a live audience for both a dress rehearsal and the actual performance, and both are recorded. The producer and editors can then compile the best final show from both performances.

The list of successful three-camera tape shows is long, including *Roseanne, Cosby, Family Ties,* and the classic *All in the Family.*

Multi-Camera Film. The procedure for three- or four-camera film production is the same as for videotape, except that film cameras are substituted for video cameras. The disadvantages are that the director and audience cannot see exactly what each camera is recording during the performance. The advantages are that, in the postproduction process, the producer can choose between any of the different camera angles at any moment. Also, many producers prefer the look of film, as opposed to video, for the finished product.

Of the many comedies recorded on three-camera film, *Cheers* and *Newhart* are some examples.

Block and Tape. With this procedure, multiple videotape cameras are used like film cameras on a sound stage. There is no audience, so the sets are physically located in whatever manner is most conducive to production efficiency. Individual scenes are usually shot as a whole—from beginning to end—similar to multi-camera film or tape shows. However, the whole show may not be recorded in continuity (that is, from beginning of show to conclusion).

Block and tape has the disadvantage of the single-camera film technique—no audience response for director or performers. It is usually chosen either for production-cost efficiency or because some member of the cast cannot be depended on to perform well in front of a live audience. For example, shows that use animals or small children may prefer the block and tape approach.

The block and tape technique is least favored for production of primetime shows. It is commonly used in the production of daytime soap operas, and low-cost comedies produced for the first-run syndication market, such as *Small Wonder.*

The Production Meeting

The production meeting is an essential staff meeting of the heads of all production departments, including props, wardrobe, camera, lighting, extra casting, set decoration, and makeup. The meeting is run by the director and the producer assists.

In that meeting, the script is evaluated—page by page—with each department confirming its understanding of what is needed, mentioning potential problems, and asking questions if anything is unclear.

Rehearsals

A *table reading* is the reading of the script by the principal actors, with several supporting players joining the session. While it is mandatory for actors in a situation comedy to have a table reading, it is not always done for dramatic action shows. Nonetheless, experienced drama producers consider a reading invaluable. As dialogue is played out, it allows the producer and director to get a sense of the show, and it gives the actors an opportunity to raise any questions or concerns they may have before they are on the set.

Blocking is the process in which movements for actors and cameras are determined. In the blocking rehearsal, each scene is carefully rehearsed. Exact positions for the actors are marked with pieces of tape on the floor. If actors move from point *A* to point *B*, those positions are designated exactly. The same is done for each camera. The procedure is simple but tricky. Actors and camera operators must be precise in hitting their marks or the shot will not be properly composed and part of the actor's face may be out of frame. The lighting is also set according to the marks so if actor or camera are out of position, lighting will not be correct. Actors must be adept at making these predetermined moves at predetermined moments appear—like dialogue—convincing, natural, and spontaneous.

POSTPRODUCTION ACTIVITIES

Editing and Postproduction Supervision

Off-line editing is used in videotape for the initial editing process. It is a quick and dirty assembly of the different sequences, the equivalent of a rough cut in film technology. Every shot has time codes in boxes running at the bottom of the screen so that the editors can find and pinpoint a moment down to a fraction of a second. The quality of the off-line image is indifferent, however. It is often noisy and the color and sharpness can change radically from shot to shot. Like the rough cut of a film, however, which uses a cheap, quick, and untimed print, it does the job.

During the postproduction phase of a one-hour film, the film must be edited, encompassing multiple versions of the show. All the optical effects must be ordered from the processing laboratory, including fade-ins, fade-outs, wipes, dissolves, and superimposed credits. Sound-effects editors must find or create the necessary sounds for the final program. Foley technicians recreate exact sounds that must synchronize to the film, such as footsteps and door openings and closings.

If dialogue was obliterated by outside noise during production, it must be rerecorded so that it can be understood, and it must be timed to fit properly into the original scene. During postproduction, actors are called back to the sound stage for ADR work. The actor repeats the needed dialogue in a sound studio, and it is synchronously substituted for the flawed original.

Finally, all of the dialogue tracks, sound effects, and music must be mixed together on a dubbing stage to make a final composite sound track for the show.

Meanwhile, the film negative must be matched and cut to the final edited version, and color-corrected prints of the film must be made and composited with the sound track. Ultimately, the film must be the correct length for broadcast and be formatted to comply with the network's policy on the placement of commercial breaks. It is a detailed and intricate process.

Music

Music must be composed or found from a music library. During pilot season, there is usually not enough time to compose and finish a music score. For theme music, a temporary sound track with library music is commonly utilized.

Editing on Video and Film

Traditionally, filmed television programs have been shot on 35mm film. There have been a few occasions where 16mm film was used, mostly for economic reasons. In the past several years, a number of systems for editing film on videotape have emerged. While varying in sophistication and capability, the basic procedure is the same. The original film dailies are transferred either to videotape or laser disc. The editor, working first with the director and then with the producer, sequences and compiles the scenes on videotape to produce various versions, or *cuts,* of the show.

Working with videotape or laser disc, the editor has almost immediate access to all the film material. In the traditional film-editing process, the director and producer view the editor's assemblages of the show on a Moviola, Kem, or similar film-editing machine. When changes are suggested, the editor must re-edit the work-print film. If the director or producer wants another take or angle of the scene, the editor must look through cans of film to find the desired moment, and physically splice it into the reel. Each revision, therefore, can take hours of time.

In the video-editing system, all the takes and angles are recorded on videotape or video disc, so the director and producer can instantaneously see the effect of changes. Like a word processor, the video work picture remains extremely flexible and can be modified instantly to suit varying tastes and needs. Different rough-cut versions can also be quickly produced and saved.

Each editing system—film and video—offers distinct advantages and liabilities. However, a producer must commit to one or the other for the completion of the show. The decision is irreversible.

Main Titles

Numerous small companies are set up to produce main-title sequences for motion pictures and television series. They have particular expertise with special effects and optical processes. For that reason, many producers find it convenient to use one of these companies to design and produce the main titles. This is especially true for situation-comedy producers, who shoot the series on videotape and are confined to a sound stage. The title sequence is usually produced on film, using exterior locations.

4

How the Producer Functions with Others

In television, the producer is the key decision maker, the captain of the production ship, overseeing every aspect of the operation. During each phase of production, there are clear lines of authority. The executive producer is in charge of all creative and technical personnel, including the line producer, writers, lead actors, casting director, and production personnel and key crew members. But the producer also has to report to his or her superiors, the "admirals" who sign the paycheck. Those higher authorities are the executives at networks, studios, and production companies.

How the producer relates to all those people can make or break a production. In this chapter we will explore the dynamics of those critical relationships.

PERSONNEL SUPERVISED BY THE EXECUTIVE PRODUCER

Line Producers

Among the first people hired by the executive producer of a new show is the line producer. He or she is responsible for the day-to-day management of the show and supervision of the production unit. The executive producer must have complete faith in the abilities and expertise of the line producer, who works closely with the creative producer in realizing the needs of production.

Writers-Creators

As we have seen, creative producers have usually been writers themselves. They help shape the creative content of the story, script, and series—and may even write the pilot script. The work of the staff writers and freelance writers will, no doubt, be rewritten by the creative producer.

During network meetings, the executive producer receives suggestions about the show's creative content; he or she must defend the writer's perspectives. Ideas are exchanged about the show, in the form of *notes*. A network executive may want to change the thrust of a particular story, or may suggest changes in characters or settings. If the producer wants to defend a particular character, relationship, or point of view, that concern must be aggressively argued. It is not uncommon for major changes to be suggested and debated, with eventual compromises reached. Once agreement is reached, the network expects to see those changes implemented.

Notes are the most common basis for discussing potential story and script changes with the writer. In dealing with writers and creators, the executive producer must convey the precise problems in story plotting, character development, dialogue, production logistics, and other network needs.

Every producer has his or her own way of dealing with creative changes requested in network notes. Producer Garry Marshall tries to find the meaning behind the notes, rather than taking notes literally: "I usually try to do what they mean, not what they say. If I did what they said, I would be selling shoes. Most of them [network executives] aren't writers or directors. They don't say things in your terms, so you have to figure out what they are saying, and do it yourself."[1]

Other producers take the network line literally and try to resolve problems in subsequent meetings with the writer. Notes are exchanged, and the writer is sent back to revise according to the new wishes. The producer reviews all the rewrites and sends the final draft to the network executives for final approval.

Every producer relies on the creative skills of writers to overcome network obstacles and develop qualitative, produceable shows. John Stephens has great respect for the writer-producer, and relies heavily on

---

[1]Horace Newcomb and Robert S. Alley, *The Producer's Medium* (New York: Oxford University Press, 1983), pp. 245–246.

the expertise of writer-producer teams. In *Simon and Simon,* he tried not to interfere with the actual task of writing the script. His working relationship with writers was intentionally meant to inspire creativity: "The main thing was to get them to be creative."[2]

Even a show that has been on the air for years requires a good deal of rewriting. To help maximize creativity, and minimize rewriting, John Stephens reviewed episodic scripts for potential production problems, rather than creative content changes: "If an idea simply can't be done within our schedule and money, I'll suggest practical changes. Instead of seven hotels, let's use three hotels. Things like that. When I get the first draft, I'll go over it with the writer-producers in detail."

Lead Actors

Casting is an area of major concern for producers, production companies, and networks. The producer hopes that networks will not have totally different perspectives about the lead characters. However, pilots have been postponed and even cancelled because the network and producer could not agree on the casting of the lead actor.

Sometimes producers can insist on the casting of an individual for the lead role in a pilot and win the battle. They frequently lose the war, however, if network executives remain dubious and are reluctant to order the series. There are notable exceptions, of course. Brandon Tartikoff of NBC agreeably admits that he was doubtful about the casting of Michael J. Fox in *Family Ties.* Harvey Shepard, then head of programming at CBS, first rejected the idea of casting Edward Woodward as *The Equalizer* because of the concern that British actors would not "work" on U.S. television. After seeing a casting test, however, he changed his mind and approved the decision. Similarly, NBC executives were initially reluctant about the casting of Don Johnson in *Miami Vice.*

The situation is somewhat different in the casting of TV movies. While pilots for series, especially dramas, are usually cast with new or little-known actors in the lead roles, TV movies look for "name casting" to enhance their tune-in appeal.

One of the tools used by the networks is the Performer Q, which is derived from a ratings index (TVQ) that measures popularity and familiarity of a star. A high-scoring actor on that list is likely to win a part over hundreds of his or her counterparts, and over thousands of others not listed. The Performer Q is considered highly controversial.

Some years ago, the prolific writer-producer team of Richard Levinson and William Link recalled with dismay their attempt to cast Dustin

---

[2]Quotes attributed to John Stephens in this chapter are from personal communication in 1988.

Hoffman in their television film, *The Execution of Private Slovik.* They contacted Hoffman, who was keenly interested in playing the role. But NBC was lukewarm, at best. They felt Hoffman was a motion picture actor, not a television star. Moreover, his earlier film *John Loves Mary* had aired on the network and hadn't done well in the ratings. Accordingly, Dustin Hoffman was considered a minor player who didn't have a television following. The producers were outraged. Embarrassed, they called Hoffman's agent to apologize, saying the shooting schedule would conflict with Hoffman's next feature, *Lenny.* The producing team offered a darkly amusing look at the frustration producers endure in the complicated process of network casting:

> What complicates things even more is that while Actor "A" may be in great demand at ABC, CBS won't approve him, and NBC doesn't even know who he is. All of which would be a matter of amusement if it were not for the fact that the network has, at a minimum, "consultation rights" over casting, and, at a maximum, full rights of approval, particularly when it comes to the casting of pilots. Producers must often submit lists of five or six actors for every part to a network executive, who presumably consults the entrails of small animals and then circles the one or two—or none—who are acceptable.[3]

Casting Directors

In the realm of casting, producers do rely on the expertise of casting directors, who may be associated with a studio, the network, or independent companies. For a television series there may be a "precast" meeting with producer, director, and casting director. At that session, they informally discuss actors who might be right for certain parts. Sometimes parts are actually cast from those early sessions.

Producer John Stephens points out the importance of the director's opinion in those casting sessions: "The other producer and I may argue about an actor, but in the final analysis, it's the director who must get something out of that actor. For that reason, we'll never override the director."

Key Crew Members

There are so many different people involved in actual production that their roles are often confused or overlooked. We asked John Stephens

---

[3]Richard Levinson and William Link, *Stay Tuned: An Inside Look at the Making of Prime Time Television* (New York: St. Martin's Press, 1981), p. 37.

to analyze the producer's crew needs. First, he outlined the importance of matching the crew to the needs of the cast, and then he differentiated hiring a crew for pilot production versus episodic series.

> You have to cast the crew to a particular show. In *Simon and Simon*, it was not an ensemble show. It's about two guys. Those actors are on the set virtually twelve hours a day, five days a week. I've got to keep them happy. I've got to give them a [crew, and working] atmosphere that will benefit that goal.
>
> For a pilot, you're going to live with the cast and crew for four or five weeks. You want the very best person in [each crew position]. You don't have time to train anyone. If there's an attitude problem, you can live with it because you need an absolutely superb craftsperson to do the best job. In a few weeks, they'll be gone.
>
> In a series you're dealing with the same people day in and day out. You spend more time with them than with your own family. So, everybody's got to get along. I make sure there are absolutely no prima donnas. None. All acting has got to be in front of the camera. I never want any acting behind the camera. None!

If one were to build a hierarchy of key crew people, it would look like this:

> *Unit production manager*
>
> *1st and 2nd assistant directors*
>
> *Cameraman or director of photography*
>
> *Script supervisor*
>
> *Art director and set director*
>
> *Wardrobe and makeup*
>
> *Transportation coordinators*
>
> *Studio location manager*
>
> *Stunt coordinator*

To provide a real-world view of these positions, we asked Mr. Stephens to guide us through the specific functions of each member of the production team. His commentary and analysis typify the way producers perceive and utilize their crew members.

Unit Production Manager (UPM)

John Stephens ranks the unit production manager as the most important staff person in the crew. The UPM is responsible for maintaining the budget. On the set, he or she must keep everything running smoothly, "and be the catalyst between the crew and the creative staff. At this studio [Universal], the unit production manager must also keep the studio happy."

When the crew has problems, it's the UPM who hears about it, and who must resolve the difficulties intelligently. These are the typical predicaments: "Why can't we have extra lights? Why can't we have extra grips, extra electricians for that set?" The unit manager must consider what is going to be gained by either granting or denying those requests. The skill lies in knowing where to spend money, and how to spend it wisely.

The unit production manager's responsibilities extend beyond budget. Stephens feels they must have "absolute, complete dedication," and be "willing to work twenty hours a day, seven days a week." He expects them to be decisive and knowledgeable. "I want them to make all the decisions. They know they're not going to be second-guessed. That's the biggest part of their job—making decisions."

1st and 2nd Assistant Directors (ADs)

Directly under the line producer is the 1st assistant director. John Stephens outlines the responsibilities of this key staff person: "The 1st assistant director has got to know exactly what the company wants, and be the middleman between the director and the company." ADs must be responsive to the director on the set, as well as to the needs of the production team.

The assistant director must know enough about the production to make independent decisions on the set. "It's the AD who decides if we should go into meal penalty, or if we should get a [different] shot and move to a location. AD's have to be 'up' [personalities], and work as part of the team."

The 1st AD needs a 2nd AD to help in the chain of command. " 'We have two shots left in this sequence. For the next, we'll need those five actors. Get them ready.' It would be impossible for the 1st AD to leave the director's side, so the 2nd AD sets it up."

The 2nd AD is the first person on the set in the morning. He or she must be at the first makeup call to be certain all necessary cast members are present.

Cameraman or Director of Photography (DP)

Another essential individual is the cameraman or director of photography. As Stephens points out: "The cameraman sets the pace for the entire show. Directors come and go, but the cameraman is constant."

In episodic television, the DP has increased in importance. Directors can rely on their stability and expertise. "In the old days the 1st assistant director ran the entire set, established the pace. Now, the cameraman really sets the pace because most directors in episodic TV are as fast as their cameraman. . . . When a director comes in to do your show, the first thing asked is, 'Who is your DP?' They never ask about the 1st AD." Directors have become dependent on directors of photography for their best day's work [shots and lighting].

The director of photography usually has a key "gaffer," who is the chief lighting electrician, and a "key grip," who moves the equipment. Stephens explains: "Most DP's in this business have a steady gaffer and a steady key grip. That means that, once the setup is given, a good DP with a good crew does not even have to say, 'Do this, do that.' They're already in motion. They know exactly what to do."

The director of photography also informs the crew when the scene is ready to be shot. "Until you hear those magic words, 'We're ready,' everybody is standing around, waiting." The crew is dependent on the DP to let them know when the camera's ready to roll.

If a location is needed, the DP sees the location ahead of time and evaluates its effectiveness. As Stephens notes, the DP can spot things that might be elusive to others: "The DP can tell you if you're making a mistake. 'It's all outside. We're going to lose the light at such and such a time.' Even a unit manager could miss that. The director could miss that. But the cameraman, director of photography, absolutely can tell you that."

Camera people have different styles. Some are known for their crisp, clear setups and shots. Others are known for mood and style with low-key lighting. The match for the show is important. According to Stephens, "It's got to be consistent with the style established for the show, to maximize the talent involved."

Script Supervisor

The script supervisor keeps track of every detail occurring during production, from shooting of scenes and angles to timing of the segments. He or she knows exactly how many pages are to be shot each day and scrutinizes the production schedule.

It is important for the script supervisor to be acutely aware of timing problems. If the length of the production is running too long, or for some reason the show is going to finish short of the network's specified running time, the producer and director decide where to trim or how to add.

John Stephens illustrates the importance of his script supervisor on filming of *Simon and Simon:*

> This person is vital. We're going so fast, often working with two cameras. We have to keep track of what both cameras have. All of

a sudden we're on a close-up of Jamison, or a two-shot of Jamison, and the script supervisor says: "Wait a minute, you already have that." She's the only person who actually knows all that. The camera people may argue, but she has it right in her notes.

Those notes go to the editor for use in the selection of angles and scenes in the edited show.

Art Director and Set Director

The art director and set director are important to the look of a show. They usually work closely together, and as Stephens succinctly puts it: "They must be a good team."

When the major part of a show is produced inside (on a sound stage), the art director predominates. The set requires more attention to color and tone than construction. Conversely, when shows are shot on location, the set decorator predominates. There must be more focus on creating and dressing credible exterior locations.

As Stephens explains: "On *Simon and Simon,* the set decorator is a little more important because we have so many locations. We will simply go into the location and shoot it. If we want it dressed, the set decorator must have his crew there before we even start moving the lighting. It's got to be set for us to see before rehearsals."

Wardrobe and Makeup

The responsibilities of wardrobe depends on the needs of the show. In a period piece, the wardrobe is carefully researched and prepared with great attention to detail. In a contemporary show, the work is less intense but is still vital to the look of the show and the actors.

John Stephens highlights the relevance of wardrobe in a contemporary series: "In a modern-day show, we want the best people to help dress the actors . . . [In a show like] *Simon and Simon,* we have the same gentleman that does the Angela Lansbury show *[Murder, She Wrote],* and he's won Emmys. He's been with our show for years, and he's a big help."

The makeup and hair personnel are also important to the everyday operation of the production. Stephens notes that most makeup and hair dressers know how to relate to actors. This can have its good and bad elements: "This is the first person to talk to the actors once they get into makeup and hair. I don't want anyone gossiping. I don't want anyone bad mouthing anyone else on the set."

He is adamantly opposed to guest stars hiring their own makeup people:

> In no way will I have stars bringing in their own makeup and their
> own hair stylists. In a movie of the week it's different, because that's

part of the actor's contract. But in episodic television, everyone must work together as one. I'll always turn down requests for outside makeup and hair people. We've had our makeup and hair staff for seven years. The only time I didn't stop the request was when I was a unit manager, and Henry Fonda insisted on his own makeup man. I remember thinking, "I won't do that," but I wasn't about to argue with Henry Fonda. Since then, I've turned down those requests, and the guest stars usually go along with it. It's counterproductive for a show to have a guest star come in with a single makeup person. Everybody else is working on six different actors, and the makeup person for the guest star is doing one person and then does nothing. I've always tried to stop that.

Transportation Coordinators

For a production that moves around a great deal, the transportation coordinator is crucial. Stephens assesses the position as follows:

> I want a young, eager person that reads scripts and gets involved. I want the coordinator to feel involved, make suggestions. He should realize he's just as important as anyone else. There's been a problem with people treating the drivers as nonprofessionals: "He's just a driver, what does he know?" But our transportation coordinator gets involved in everything, suggesting the types of vehicles that should be used in certain scenes, even suggesting colors of vehicles. He also suggests locations.

When a production makes a move from one place to another, the schedule is affected by the organization and speed of the coordinator. "He's got to be organized. He also has to have all the maps drawn for the locations, run all of his people to the site locations, and make sure everybody else is coordinated. So it's an important job."

To John Stephens, everyone has an important position on the crew of an episodic television show. "Even service people are important. They've got to make good coffee, make sure there's donuts, eggs, things like that for the crew. Make sure the dressing rooms are cleaned up when the actors and actresses get there."

There's no such thing as a small job in the difficult, costly, and time-conscious demands of television production.

Studio Location Manager

At studios, the producer has access to a location manager, and when the production moves around a lot, this person can be particularly helpful. The job of the location manager is to coordinate different elements of the production for the production company. He or she serves as the coordinating center for the art director, set decorator, and transportation coordinator. This individual also makes sure that location choices are feasible.

Stephens appraises the position this way: "A great location manager can actually suggest schedule changes to you. Sometimes they've got ideas that are really creative and inventive. They can save you a lot of time and money. We prefer to find location managers like that. But it isn't that easy."

This is how he puts it into perspective:

> If you get your scripts ahead of time, a number one priority in television, you can get the location manager in your office and say, "Here's what's coming up in four weeks—start looking." The main problem with location managers is not really their fault. They're often not given specific directions. They're simply told, "Go ahead and do this." Sometimes they're afraid to ask questions, and sometimes the person giving directions isn't explicit.

It was Stephens' opinion that location managers have limited career opportunities, which makes it difficult to find good ones: "Once you're a location manager, where do you go? It's pretty tough for location managers to climb up. They are members of the Teamsters, so at least they've got benefits."

Stunt Coordinator

The importance of the stunt coordinator is tied directly to the actual needs of the show. In an action series like *Simon and Simon,* the needs are considerable. As the producer explains, "We have one of the best stunt coordinators in the business—Gil Burton—because we have quite a few stunts on that show. . . . The stunt coordinator has to be a diplomat. He's got to know what the company wants, and he's got to really have the confidence of the stars."

As producer of the show, Stephens goes over the proposed stunts in a meeting with the stunt coordinator and accommodates any changes necessary.

> We discuss exactly what we want in a production meeting with Gil Burton. Then he'll go out and look at the location. He can overrule locations if he thinks they won't work. "You want these cars to crash through this door, but there's no door here. And when the two guys are coming down the skylight—there isn't any skylight. So what about that place over there?" Then we'll turn to the set decorator and say, "What could you do? Could you give me some crates? Can you do something else to make it gel?" And it actually does gel.

The work of the stunt coordinator involves a great deal of preparation and organization. Building the confidence of actors is also crucial.

> It's vital for the stunt coordinator to be so organized that by the time the actors get there in the morning, everything is set. You seldom want to start the day with a stunt. But the first thing you want is to get the stunt coordinator and actors familiar with the entire stunt. They'll work out any changes they feel necessary. It has to be worked out by the time the camera crew gets there, so you're ready to go.

It is helpful in episodic television if the stunt coordinator is a member of the Director's Guild of America, so he or she can direct a second shooting unit, if necessary. Sometimes, the stunt coordinator is the only one who can do that, especially if the director is not action-oriented.

As a parting analysis of the role of the stunt coordinator, John Stephens notes that the stunt person is usually highly motivated:

> Everyone in their jobs is motivated, but I think the stunt coordinators want to do a lot more than necessary. The reason is that more sitcoms are taking hold, and the [stunt coordinators] are working less. It's as if they were waiting in the wings, vowing "Here's my chance, and I don't want to blow it." They're also members of SAG [Screen Actors Guild], so there's a little bit of movie actor in them.

RELATIONSHIPS WITH SUPERVISORS

Studio Executives and Production Supervisors

A producer must not only battle the whims of the network, but he or she must also manage the demands of his or her own studio. Studio executives are closely connected with every major decision, from story and script content to casting. Studio heads are responsible for overseeing pilot development, pilot production, and every episode of every series they have in production, regardless of network.

The relationship of the producer to the studio is a mercurial artistic-managerial one, complicated by the practical demands of the production company. A production entity is in business to maximize profits and to watch economics carefully. Producers must work within that reality and deliver the best show for the least expenditure.

As explained earlier, the producer may not even know the actual budget, but may be working from a pattern budget. For any number of reasons, production costs may escalate into the stratosphere, creating impossible friction between the producer and the studio or production company.

When Steven Bochco was at MTM, his fights with management over budgets became legendary. He encountered unending budgetary crises on *Hill Street Blues.* This is how he recalls it:

> It wasn't a fun show to make. We were at war every single day. We were doing something we had no business trying to do, making 48 minute movies in seven, eight days. And of course, MTM hated us, because they thought we were spending them into oblivion. Though I maintain to this day that it was one of the most responsibly produced shows in the history of television—given what we were able to put on the screen for the amount of money we spent. But it was a runaway train. At all times.[4]

Bochco was fired from MTM, and moved to Twentieth Century Fox with a more produceable concept, *L.A. Law.* He felt that kind of series would be more manageable under the pressure of studio financing. While *L.A. Law* utilizes a large cast, as did *Hill Street Blues,* it does not require any action sequences, which can be expensive and time consuming. Also, scenes are set in rooms on sound stages, which are easier to control for production costs. As Bochco put it: "I was highly sensitive to [budget problems] because I got my brains beat out when I was fired by MTM."[5]

Responsible production management is just one aspect of the producer's responsibilities within a studio structure. There is also the behavioral factor of dealing with the wishes of upper-level management, writers whose work must be rewritten, directors, actors, and the entire crew, who must work closely together in a disciplined production environment.

Network Program Executives

The network is the pivotal juncture for moving a project from development into production and onto the air. Since networks commit large sums of money (though never enough to fully finance the production), they insist on creative rights in contracts with producers. That is the bane of existence for many producers and the source of significant creative and managerial conflicts.

Networks have approval rights over every major aspect of the show, from the story and first-draft script through final script revisions. They

---

[4]"Stephen Bochco: Dialogue on Film," *American Film* (July/August, 1988): 16.
[5]Ibid, p. 17.

also have final say over key series staff, actors in continuing roles, and directors of pilot shows. Their imprint is on every major creative concern.

Given the financial commitments and scheduling needs of a network, it would seem that the executives would be consistent in their approach to producers. Not so. Network management is notorious for offering contradictory messages and unclear signals.

Almost every producer has a harrowing tale of survival through the barrage of network responses to their shows. When Marcy Carsey and Tom Werner created *The Cosby Show,* they offered the network a very attractive package, including Bill Cosby, writers Ed Weinberger and Michael Leeson, director Jay Sandrich, and a top crew. When they pitched the idea, they battled network indifference at every turn. As producers, they believed in the concept of quality comedy. The network insisted the genre was dead. Carsey recalls: "I can't tell you how many people told us how this will never pay off, the idea was not glitzy enough, that comedy was dead. You just have to put blinders on and do what you have to do because you believe in [it]."[6]

Norman Lear had difficulty getting his classic comedy series, *All in the Family,* past the network approval process. Initially, ABC turned down the concept as too controversial. CBS accepted it, but wanted to make changes. Lear had just finished a motion picture for United Artists *(The Night They Raided Minsky's),* and was offered a three-picture contract by that studio. He told CBS executives that he wouldn't do the series if changes were required. He had a safe place to go: "I wanted to do *All in the Family,* but if I couldn't do it the way I wanted to do it, then I could accept United Artists' proposition. . . . So I won every major battle [with the networks] on that first one."[7] He continued battling with the network well into the 16th week of the show, when the ratings first started to pick up. The battles were over substantive issues, including story content and character development.

Steven Bochco encountered a similar situation with NBC and *Hill Street Blues.* His recollection of the inception of the series concept, which he created with Michael Kozoll, is informative:

> That show came out of a process that I think typifies television at its best: It was a genuine ensemble invention. . . . NBC made it click when they said Fred Silverman wanted a television series like *Fort Apache: The Bronx.* Of course, they didn't flat out say "Steal," but you never have to actually utter the "s" word in television— everybody knows what you're doing.[8]

---

[6]"Carsey-Werner: The Little Programming Engine That Could," *Broadcasting* (July 18, 1988): 61.
[7]Newcomb and Alley, *The Producer's Medium,* p. 187.
[8]"Steven Bochco, *American Film* (July/August, 1988): 16.

He copied the style of *Hill Street Blues* from a project called *The Police Tapes,* which was shot in the South Bronx, in black and white. It conveyed the feeling and illusion of a "random event." NBC offered Bochco and Kozoll a deal on the series, but the producers held out for creative control: "We finally agreed to do the show under one condition: that they absolutely leave us alone. And they agreed. Which was pretty surprising, but . . . they needed a pilot desperately."[9]

Despite the erratic nature of network decision making, producers must wade through the network executive sphere, trying to second guess what the network really wants. If producers have strong track records, they may be able to grapple some control from the networks. For the record, however, the network has the last word on creative rights in story and script, production, and compliance with broadcast standards.

Dealing with Studio Heads and Network Program Executives

A metaphor constantly quoted in Hollywood is that "a camel is a horse designed by committee." It is difficult if not impossible for a producer to ignore the input of network program executives and studio heads.

After the pilot script is written, network and studio executives set up meetings with the producers to comment on the script and suggest changes. These notes sessions are always a source of tension for the producer since networks and studio notes often contradict each other. Often these notes tend to round the corners, make the edges duller, and generally soften television concepts. At times, if taken too literally, these suggestions diminish a project's originality and therefore its distinctiveness and chances of success.

The producer is placed squarely in the middle. As buyer of the show, the network pays most of the production cost, and its acceptance of the program is vital. If displeased for any reason, the network can abandon the project by cancelling it or placing it in an unpopular time period. The studio, on the other hand, is the producer's immediate boss. It has the producer under contract and disburses the weekly paycheck. The studio's financial interest is substantial. It is responsible for paying the difference between network license fees and the actual costs of production.

Clearly the producer is indebted to both studio executives and networks. However, he or she must not let those suggestions—and sometimes outright demands—destroy the vision of the show. There must be

---

[9]Ibid.

a careful, deliberate negotiation about dealing with network and studio notes.

Producers find their own way of dealing with the exacting nature of these note sessions. This is how Barry Kemp manages the situation:

> Generally, I don't respond positively or negatively to notes right off the bat. I usually say, "Let me think about it." Because I always go back to evaluate [this critical point]: "Is there a compromise in there that affects the initial vision?" If not, then, if someone feels strongly about [the change], and I don't mind it, I'll try to incorporate it. Ultimately, if I reject it, it's because I do think it somehow compromises the vision. I have thought about a show for so long [I know it better than anyone else] . . . I can quickly evaluate whether those changes will throw the idea off.[10]

He described a typical confrontation, after creating a comedy series, *The Popcorn Kid,* for CBS. That short-lived series featured a young man working at a movie theater in a small town in the Midwest. The concept was to show the time in a young person's life without parents around.

> When I produced *The Popcorn Kid,* CBS wanted me to show the kid with his parents. I said, "You knew from the very beginning . . . the one thing we wanted to do was show that time in a young person's life—after school, before they went home. It's the one time of day— the one time of life—that had never been shown on television. If we compromise that, we have taken what I thought was special about the show, and we've bastardized it." I don't care if [the show initially] gets two or three ratings points higher. In the long run, [that kind of change] will diffuse the show and make it less clear. It's a quick fix which will ultimately hurt the vision.

Before delivering a pilot to the network, major studios often test their pilots with audiences to gain insights into the show's strengths and weaknesses. Each network tests every pilot, so many studios prefer to test their own pilots in rough-cut form. That process allows time for last-minute changes, if necessary. Pilot testing gives the producer information that can be helpful in fine tuning the picture, in the last stages of post-production. It also provides the producer and the studio with a preview of what the network research report might say. If a lead character is perceived as too negative, or the show does not appeal to the right audiences, there is still a chance to tighten the show before delivery.

Sometimes the networks will use information derived from their

---

[10]Quotes attributed to Barry Kemp in this chapter are from personal communication in 1989.

test to require changes in the show—from character relationships to title changes. The producer and the studio argue the issues, offer appropriate compromises, and promise to comply in some way to get the show on the air.

THE KEYS TO SUCCESSFUL PRODUCING

Decision Making: Setting Priorities and Choices

The critical quality required for any producer is the ability to make decisions quickly and decisively. There may be hundreds of decisions to be made, some major, others seemingly inconsequential. Each can have a marked effect on the final project. Each must be prioritized, or discarded, accordingly.

An experienced producer quickly decides which of the vast number of choices might help, alter, or destroy a project. Those decisions range the gamut from script and character changes to casting lead actors and secondary roles. They encompass choices for production requirements, from sets and locations to film and videotape formats. They involve creative, technical, managerial, and financial choices at every turn.

Each can have enormous impact on the show's eventual quality and atmosphere.

Dealing with Compromises

An experienced television producer is always willing to accept input from executives and subordinates. He or she must be able to reconcile divergent points of view and quickly reach acceptable resolutions.

When network and studio executives differ over important perceptions of script content, casting, or production needs, the producer is caught in the middle. He or she must call on the skill to compromise personal vision against the realities of studio and network demands. It can be a complicated balancing act.

When the producer is also the writer of the teleplay (as is the case with *Coach* and *Law and Order*), changes are especially formidable. A writer/producer has a definite vision of each character, each line of dialogue, each scene in the show. When others try to change the vision, there is inevitable confrontation.

It is sometimes easy to play Mr. Nice Guy, agreeing to all compromise, but the price may be too high. As Barry Kemp points out:

You always walk a fine line between being perceived as too difficult or . . . as a great guy who's willing to compromise but never deliver a great show. Every single time you come up with a show, someone's going to request something that in your heart you think is wrong. The path of least resistance is to go with their request. . . . But what ultimately happens is—they will hate you for not standing up for your [convictions]. You're not doing your job as a producer if you don't follow through on your instincts and honest beliefs.

Maintaining Integrity of Artistic Vision

Maintaining integrity of vision is a producer's most difficult task, particularly when there are others who hold positions of power in the network or studio hierarchy, and do not have as clear a vision of the project. Some of a producer's most vexing moments involve compromises with those individuals.

In defining successful producing, Barry Kemp points to the importance of maintaining clear intentions from the start.

The key to producing is knowing what it is you want. If you stay clear about what you set out to do, you can't guarantee the commercial success of a project, but you can always guarantee the quality of a project. To me, if the intent is clear, and it is executed clearly, your chances of success jump a hundredfold. If your vision is off, or you don't know what you are trying to communicate, you'll have a show that technically looks fine, but [has] no substance to it. No heart to it. And it will look empty.

In the following chapters you will see how Barry Kemp, the writer/ producer of *Coach,* and Dick Wolf, writer/producer of *Law and Order,* worked within these parameters, setting a singular vision for their shows. Their decision-making skills—and the art of negotiating compromise— were called on from the start, and built relentlessly through development, production, and postproduction phases. In each case, the final project reflects their decisive choices and compromises, as well as the producers' initial artistic vision.

A Case History of a Situation Comedy, *Coach*

5

The Development Process

THE CONCEPT FOR *COACH*

Coach Hayden Fox heads the athletic department at Minnesota State University. In his early forties, with a perennially losing football team, he recognizes, but is not willing to admit, that the forward progression of his career has ended. His only hope is to meld the disparate team into an effective unit. His only assistance in this task are the assistant coaches, Luther and Dauber. Dauber is also a member of the team and holds the record of being a student at the university for the most number of years.

Coach Fox has been divorced for many years and has had little if any contact with his daughter, Kelly. Recently, he has developed a relationship with Minneapolis newscaster Christine.

In the pilot story Coach Fox learns that his daughter is entering Minnesota State as a freshman. He feels uncomfortable as a father but desperately wants to reestablish a relationship with her. At the same time, he feels awkward about exposing Kelly to his emerging relationship with Christine.

THE DEVELOPMENT OF *COACH*

The origin and development of the situation comedy *Coach* is representative of the process by which many producers function. The development process spans the gamut of decisions that producers face, from series concept and characters, to casting, set design, and production planning.

Barry Kemp, creator, writer, and executive producer, permitted us to chronicle *Coach* from inception through production. As each problem arose, he shared his thoughts, concerns, and decisions with us. While each project is distinct—with circumstances, situations, and problems unique unto themselves—the results represent a working model of one successful producer's creative and critical thinking process.

Mr. Kemp graduated from the University of Iowa, with a degree in Speech and Dramatic Arts. In Hollywood, his career has progressed from writer and executive script consultant on the hit comedy series *Taxi* to creator and executive producer of the *Newhart* series. He was creator and executive producer of the comedy miniseries *Fresno,* the comedy series *The Popcorn Kid,* and *Coming of Age.*

As one of the United States' most prolific comedy producers, Mr. Kemp accepted a contract in 1987 to provide exclusive services to Universal-TV. In that year, ABC-TV, trying to extricate itself from third place in the ratings, was searching actively for new creative talent. Then ABC's vice-president of comedy development, Stu Bloomberg,[1] Barry Kemp, and Universal met about the possibility of Kemp developing a new comedy series. The result was *Coach.*

CONCEPTUALIZATION: THE BEGINNING OF THE DEVELOPMENT PROCESS

Coach was one of several shows Barry Kemp had been thinking about for some time. It was conceived as a situation comedy centering around the psychological and professional problems of a divorced, middle-aged football coach in the Midwest.

Like most writer-producers, Kemp had been privately working on many different concepts for potential television series. His first rule of thumb was to be personally committed to the idea. He knew the development process would be long, and the time commitment prolonged, for any project that proceeds:

> I have to be excited about the concept, because the job's just simply too hard to do if you're not excited about it. Peripherally I'm excited when I find out I've got an idea that also works at 8:00 P.M. [the time period where network demand is greatest]. . . . But if I had

[1]Currently executive vice-president, ABC Entertainment, with responsibility for developing and supervising all ABC series—comedy and drama.

an idea that I thought was perfect for 8:00 and I wasn't [personally committed] to it, I simply wouldn't do it. . . . [The most intriguing prospect for me] is to get a show on the air that I [believe in], and people [react instinctively to it], "Wow! That's kind of different. That hasn't quite been done this way."[2]

Barry Kemp worked on the concept of *Coach* for nearly two years to test the endurance of the concept.

I need at least six months [to think about an idea]. . . . I would say an average would be a year. I first got the idea for *Coach* almost two years ago. I started thinking about it before we started shooting *Fresno,* and made notes on it back then. . . . It takes me [that long] to know if I'm still going to be interested in it. . . . I have [many] "notions." People throw a lot of notions at me. [Some of them] may initially spark my imagination. . . . But if I'm still interested six months after I hear it, then I think there's something really there. Most of the ideas fall by the wayside. There's just not enough [substance] to support them. But if I'm still excited after six months, then I know that I can do that as a series.

In his initial development of *Coach* it was his conceptualization of the central character that intrigued Barry Kemp the most. He wanted to examine the personality of an ambitious man and the ethical problems faced by that character. He felt those attributes could be identifiable for audiences.

I wanted to explore the personality of an ambitious man, a highly motivated man . . . and put him in the Midwest. He is a man who is a superstar in his community. But he knows his community is small. He knows he's not a big fish in the [national] pond. And that is something I think every person with ambition will relate to . . . the daily moral dilemmas that confront achievers: "Do you take short cuts to get there? Or do you walk the straight and narrow, [knowing you] may never get there following that path?" The coach does what most of us would do. He hits and misses. He sometimes takes the short cut, sometimes the straight and narrow, and he's never totally right.

The ethical dilemma of the coach became the backbone of the series concept. Kemp wanted viewers to identify with the daily dilemmas faced by the featured character. The coach was viewed in terms of "noble" traits and "tragic" character flaws:

---

[2]Quotes in this chapter attributed to Barry Kemp are from personal communication in 1988.

Here's a person who philosophically is starting to come to terms with understanding those choices in his life—and realizes that he doesn't always make the right ones. What's noble about the guy is that at least he's reached a point where he has started to identify it. What's tragic about him is that he can't help himself from sometimes wanting the [ends to justify the means]. . . . Sometimes he uses people to get there, and he doesn't feel good about that.

Barry Kemp examined the inner life of the character, almost creating a psychological profile. He analyzed what the character would think about his life and position but would never reveal (except, perhaps, in therapy).

This guy is a little fragile. Conceptually, he's in his late forties. He has spent all of his life believing that he is on some kind of ascending ladder, career-wise. Every move has been a move up. Now he's beginning to realize that [there may not be many other career steps]. Now that he's gotten to a bigger school, he hasn't performed in a way that has brought national attention to him. He's been at this same level for five years, and he's starting to have doubts about whether this is the last stop. If it is, he may have to work just as hard just to keep treading water. And that's starting to frighten him. He also knows that all of his charisma, and everything he'd relied on all these years, will [diminish] as time goes on. . . . He's started to question whether he's got enough substance to withstand that.

Kemp's reasoning was of special interest. He wanted to find a common base for character identification with audiences—including women who might otherwise not be interested in a sports setting. He wanted the widest possible audience to empathize with the personal angst of this man:

Even if they don't relate to the coach's [problems] personally, people will identify with his fears. They will understand [his dilemma]. I think when they see the guy struggling with it, they'll start rooting for him. They'll root for him to make the right decision, and hurt when he doesn't. So, it is by nature, by design, a sort of microscopic look at a complex personality, but a personality which has some roots in all of us.

If this all sounds very dramatic, it is purposeful. Sounding almost Aristotelian, Barry Kemp believed that "placing drama in a comedic setting permits laughter, and releases a certain tension, keeps it from being unrelenting." He applied that theory to the character of Coach:

> For all of the serious implications about [the coach's] personality, it
> should be tempered with the realization that fears and ambitions
> aren't the most important things in life. Ultimately, I think that's
> what he learns. Those very foibles of his, the very things that he
> worries most about—make us laugh. As much as we hurt for him,
> we also gain perspective.

When the concept of _Coach_ was presented to ABC, the lead character was intricately discussed. All agreed that the comedy potential was
strong. The next step was script development followed by pilot production.

DEVELOPMENT: THE PREPARATIONS FOR ACTUAL PRODUCTION

With the project approved by ABC, Barry Kemp began writing the pilot
script. The script had to reflect the basic character conflicts and demonstrate the coach's quirks, conflicts, and interrelationships. In a half-
hour script, the entire backstory (character exposition) needed to be
explained, and the ongoing major conflicts set up.

In fact, the pilot script accomplishes all those goals. (See Appendix A for the final draft script.) The storyline conveys the coach's concern
for his daughter, played against his midlife angst. The script also estab-
lishes the coach's tumultuous relationships with his girlfriend Christine,
his slightly odd friend Luther, and perennial student Dauber.

While still in the process of writing the script, other problems arose,
needing immediate attention. Some of them would ultimately affect not
only production but the look of the show, and its chances for success.
Those concurrent problems included: casting, establishing setting and
atmosphere, and choosing tape versus film format.

Casting

Preeminent among the problems was the choice of actor to play the role
of Coach Hayden Fox. The producer was acutely concerned about finding the right person for the lead character:

> Needless to say, we can be wrong in casting any character in the
> show—except for Coach. We can't make a mistake there. That's the
> one place we have to be infallible.

He was also concerned about the customary network pressure to
use familiar names in lead roles. He thought the network might impose

lead actors based on their use of TVQ (Performer Q) scores. Kemp's reaction to the use of popularity measurements in casting the role of Coach was typical of most writer/producers.

> [A star with a high TVQ] will get people to tune in the first week. . . . But if he's wrong for the role, the public will know within 22 minutes and you'll never get them back again. So I'm much more concerned that we have the right guy, even if the first week we finish 50th [in the Nielsen ratings]. Eventually, word of mouth and time will prove that we've got the right guy.

His concerns about casting were paralleled by the need to define and distinguish the look of the set.

Setting and Atmosphere

While completing the pilot script, Kemp began the process of assembling the key staff for the show. As writer-producer, he was especially concerned about finding the right texture and setting for the program. His art director, Tommy Goetz, was particularly helpful in that regard. This is how the setting evolved for the *Coach* pilot:

> One of the first people I needed was the art director, Tommy Goetz. . . . We talked about the atmosphere, what the show would look like. First we decided "tape" or "film" because it says so much about the kind of show it's going to be. We started talking about it color-wise. Is it going to be a dark show? Is it going to be a bright show? We started seeing *Coach* in terms of a Fall show. Football is a Fall sport. There's a smell in the air—in the Midwest in September. It's a smell of a college football Saturday, and the sound of the crowd.
>   We decided upon Minnesota. We have the change of seasons. We can sell that. . . . We wanted to put him in a cabin. Let's put him on a lake. We started selling his environment—what's special about where this guy is? We could have taken any TV living room and any TV office, and had a very bland show. So we said, "Where does he operate?" Tommy was the one who said, "Let's put him in the basement so that we get some texture to his office. It will sell the fieldhouse. It will give us a lot of things. We'll see the pipes and we'll see all that sort of stuff."
>   My wife suggested, "If he lives in Minnesota, if he's on a lake, doesn't that give you a great view?" Because I was terrified that we were just going to have a living room. Once we established the lake, that began to establish the whole sportsman aspect of his character.

In fact, the pilot script reflects those deliberations. There are two main sets described. The coach's office is set in the basement of the fieldhouse, and is described with this kind of texture:

> The office is a collecting bin for every possible item you can make to promote Minnesota state football, including coffee mugs, glassware, lamps, wastebaskets, blankets, calendars, key rings, seat cushions, caps, sweatshirts, bumper stickers, little stuffed Screaming Eagles mascots, etc. Also prominent are a blackboard, a weight scale, a poster of the upcoming season's schedule, and a large wall hanging proclaiming "This is Minnesota State Football!"

The other major set, the coach's cabin, reflects the concern for providing a lake-front atmosphere, a masculine getaway. This is how that set is defined in the pilot script:

> A rough-hewn home on the waterfront of one of Minnesota's small lakes. It's a very masculine environment, with a large stone fireplace dominating the upstage wall of the living room, flanked on either side by large windows looking out over the lake view. . . . The open kitchen is stage left, all knotty pine and actually very cozy. The home is furnished warmly in odds and ends, but nothing is "decorated." A large mounted fish indicates one of Hayden's other passions. Except for a few things in the den, there are very few remnants of Hayden's life as a coach. Rather, this place is an escape from the pressures of the job.

With the setting defined, interrelated decisions needed to be reached about the production medium for the show.

Deciding on the Production Format for *Coach*

Having worked with the various production techniques, Barry Kemp preferred the three-camera film format, mostly for aesthetic reasons.

> I have a very difficult time personally with tape. I'm not saying I would never do a show on tape. But if I want to sell "upscale" quality to a show, and I also want to sell certain kinds of color, tones, and texture, I can't do that on tape. . . . I want the shows to be real, but I don't want them to appear as if it's being shot live. . . . I think tape gives that illusion. I like my half-tones to look like little movies. . . .

> A number of people think you have to be funnier on tape than on film. I think that's true. Tape looks live—film doesn't. A joke on tape that doesn't play [looks like] you couldn't do anything about it. Somehow the same joke on film looks more intentional: "They would have cut it if they didn't like it." There's a sense of [having] more control in film. So I like it for that reason too.

While choosing film over tape, Barry Kemp prefers three-camera technique over single-camera film. This decision stems from his attitudes about the importance of an audience for comedy performance.

> I personally like the pressure of having an audience—knowing that you have to be funny. The audience will tell you whether you are or not. . . . A live audience shouldn't dictate how you write a show, but it does let you know how an audience is reacting. It keeps you honest. It does me, anyway.

Kemp also prefers the challenge that a live audience provides. He feels it spurs him and his creative team to be innovative and to take chances. For *Coach* he purposely devised a set that would engage the audience in the production atmosphere of the show:

> I'm really interested in knowing if we can sense the presence of an audience listening, and have a slightly more intimate feel to the show. That's why the sets are—by design—not as deep as sets we've done in the past. I want to bring the show closer to the audience. I literally want to have a sense that the audience is leaning in, watching, listening to it. . . . I want to have a sense that they're watching a play unfold. The play at times is funny and at times not. It's different than doing a "dramedy," which is basically serious, with occasional light moments. . . . When we do flat-out funny moments, we want the audience to respond flat-out. In other scenes, I'd prefer they just listen.

These are only a few of the myriad decisions that required Kemp's attention in the early stages of development. Later chapters will show the impact these early decisions had on the production itself.

THE NECESSITY, AGONY, AND CONSEQUENCE OF COMPROMISE

Almost all creative and production decisions involve compromise to some degree. For example, Barry Kemp was aware of the problem in selecting three-camera film as the recording medium, but felt the ultimate advantages outweighed the liabilities.

[Three-camera film] restricts you to a couple of sets. You sometimes have to compromise performance. It puts you on your toes. It puts pressure on the cast to make sure that they deliver while the audience is there. It puts pressure on the crew to make sure they get that shot, because if the best moment of the evening happens and the camera missed it, it's gone forever. Then you have to ask, why did you do this? We went to all the trouble to bring in an audience at the risk of hurting the show in order to have the experience live, and now we've lost it because we didn't get it.

Even before producing the pilot, Kemp was concerned about compromises that network executives might impose on the series. His main concern was that the network might insist on an actor who would not be right for the lead role. That kind of compromise might destroy the integrity of his vision:

That's the one compromise that I am most concerned about making. . . . Right now I'm optimistic that we may have avoided that pitfall. . . . We don't have a [preselected] actor in mind who everyone [contends is] perfect. Also, the network is not demanding a certain kind of celebrity. So I feel optimistic that we'll all agree when we see him. If we find the perfect actor, we'll all see it.

Additionally, Kemp tried to prepare for other network reactions that could later alter the focus of the series:

If we do the pilot and test [it with audiences], I anticipate the audience will respond with warmth to the coach and his daughter [Kelly]. I think they will respond to the heat of the coach and Christine [his girlfriend]. That will cause the network, I'm sure, to come back and say the public wants to see more of the coach and Christine and more of coach and Kelly. . . . The key is to not let the network research dictate how to do the show. We put those elements in there on purpose. . . . If we lose the texture and balance, we lose our own focus. That would be a very damaging compromise.

Barry Kemp was also aware that the "sharp edge" of Coach's character might create concern among network executives. He strongly felt that the abrasiveness of the character was crucial to the point of view of the show and was therefore resolute about compromises in that area.

In the meantime, ABC's department of broadcast standards and practices responded that the first-draft script would be approved only under the following conditions: (1) that the university setting be fictitious, and (2) that "offensive" dialogue in one scene be changed or deleted. See Figure 5.1.

American Broadcasting Company

DEPARTMENT OF BROADCAST STANDARDS AND PRACTICES • WESTERN DIVISION • HOLLYWOOD

STUDIO UNIVERSAL TELEVISION   DATE February 26, 1988

CONTACT Barry Kemp   SHOOTING DATE

PROGRAM TITLE DEVELOPMENT   EPISODE TITLE   "Coach"
                                                              (1st draft 2/10/88)

The above indicated shooting script, received this date, has been reviewed by the Department of Broadcast Standards and Practices under current ABC broadcast standards.

Kindly forward such revisions as are necessary to effect the modifications requested below. If revisions are acceptable upon receipt by the Department of Broadcast Standards and Practices, no supplementary review will be forthcoming.

This review does not constitute a Broadcast Standards approval of subsequent script changes or changes in method of treatment in production. A separate screening report will be issued upon viewing the Rough Cut film. *Kindly advise me at such time as this episode is available for Rough Cut and First Trial screening. Final approval is based on viewing the completed film.*

COMMENTS (Confidential):

Pg. 1 - Minnesota State University must be a fictitious reference.

Pg. 51 - Hayden's "Even a son-of-a-bitch like me" is unacceptable. Change or delete the underlined.

Otherwise approved.

cc: Hikawa, Hadden, Baerg, Bloomberg, Fleary, Bell, file
     Sheldon Bull

                                           Roland McFarland
                                           Roland McFarland
                                           Manager, Development

---

Figure 5.1   Letter from ABC Department of Broadcast Standards and Practices covering the first-draft script of *Coach.*

Universal's research department routinely checked legal clearances for items in the script, including the names of characters, institutions, and other potentially libelous references. See Figure 5.2.

The revised script incorporated all the suggestions from the network. It set the premise for the ongoing character conflicts and adhered to the formal requirements of studio and network executives. That final draft, as approved by the network, is found in Appendix A. It served as the basis for all ensuing production deliberations.

With the script written and approved, Barry Kemp was now ready to move into production of the pilot episode.

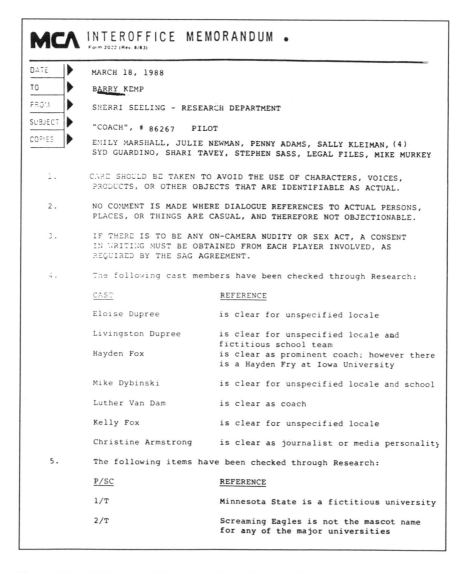

MCA INTEROFFICE MEMORANDUM ●
Form 2022 (Rev. 8/83)

DATE	▶	MARCH 18, 1988
TO	▶	BARRY KEMP
FROM	▶	SHERRI SEELING - RESEARCH DEPARTMENT
SUBJECT	▶	"COACH", # 86267 PILOT
COPIES	▶	EMILY MARSHALL, JULIE NEWMAN, PENNY ADAMS, SALLY KLEIMAN, (4) SYD GUARDINO, SHARI TAVEY, STEPHEN SASS, LEGAL FILES, MIKE MURKEY

1. CARE SHOULD BE TAKEN TO AVOID THE USE OF CHARACTERS, VOICES, PRODUCTS, OR OTHER OBJECTS THAT ARE IDENTIFIABLE AS ACTUAL.

2. NO COMMENT IS MADE WHERE DIALOGUE REFERENCES TO ACTUAL PERSONS, PLACES, OR THINGS ARE CASUAL, AND THEREFORE NOT OBJECTIONABLE.

3. IF THERE IS TO BE ANY ON-CAMERA NUDITY OR SEX ACT, A CONSENT IN WRITING MUST BE OBTAINED FROM EACH PLAYER INVOLVED, AS REQUIRED BY THE SAG AGREEMENT.

4. The following cast members have been checked through Research:

CAST	REFERENCE
Eloise Dupree	is clear for unspecified locale
Livingston Dupree	is clear for unspecified locale and fictitious school team
Hayden Fox	is clear as prominent coach; however there is a Hayden Fry at Iowa University
Mike Dybinski	is clear for unspecified locale and school
Luther Van Dam	is clear as coach
Kelly Fox	is clear for unspecified locale
Christine Armstrong	is clear as journalist or media personality

5. The following items have been checked through Research:

P/SC	REFERENCE
1/T	Minnesota State is a fictitious university
2/T	Screaming Eagles is not the mascot name for any of the major universities

Figure 5.2 MCA interoffice memo from Universal's research department on legal clearances.

```
                              -2

     P/SC                     REFERENCE

     5/A                      East Texas is real, suggest changing to
                              South Texas

     8/A                      Fred Webb is clear for unspecified locale
                              and fictitious school

     9/A                      ref. to Gatorade is casual and not deroga-
                              tory, but network might object to the
                              free advertising

     9/A                      Tommy Jordan is clear for Miami

    10/A                      Jimmy Johnson is the real coach at Miami,
                              suggest deleting ref.

    12/A                      Beth Fox is clear for unspecified locale

    30/C                      Downtown Hotel - if named, please clear
                              with Research

    30/C                      magazine stand - avoid i.d. of copyrighted
                              publications

    31/C                      magazines - as above

    35/D                      bottle of red wine - avoid i.d. of trade-
                              marked product

    49/E                      team in Chattanooga is clear, as it refers
                              to intramural team at unspecified school
```

Figure 5.2   *(continued)*

6

The Production Process

Once Barry Kemp delivered his pilot script to the network, the production process began. Like most experienced producers, Kemp was prepared to deal with problems, but there was no way to predict exactly what those problems might be. That is the most common and unnerving aspect of producing—dealing with the myriad problems that arise unpredictably on each day.

The following chronology serves as a working example of the kind of unforeseen problems faced by producers of any pilot. The log begins shortly after the pilot script, written by Barry Kemp, was delivered to both Universal Television executives and ABC-TV program executives. The log continues throughout the nine-week period of production. The show was scheduled to be filmed on April 13, 1988, and the completed pilot was to be delivered to ABC on April 30, 1988.

THE PRODUCER'S DAILY ACTIVITIES

Wednesday, March 2, 1988

After delivering the pilot script to the network, Barry Kemp hopes for a prompt response. He is concerned about an impending strike by the Writer's Guild of America, which could impinge on his ability to revise the script. Still awaiting the network response, he and his associates consider possible script changes that are needed.

He is also concerned about dual demands on his work schedule. In conjunction with writer/producer Emily Marshall, he has just launched a new show for CBS, entitled *Coming of Age*. Production of that series will overlap with the production of *Coach*. He must find the time to do both without sacrificing the quality of either.

Mr. Kemp conceived of *Coach* as a show that is unwaveringly focused on the life and attitudes of a single character: Coach Hayden Fox. For that reason, he is intensely concerned about casting. He has already contacted talent agents and has been busy listing prospective lead actors. Prominent in his thoughts are Craig T. Nelson and Gerald McRaney. Craig Nelson is well known as a dramatic actor, having played the father in the movie *Poltergeist* and the lead in the television series *Call to Glory*. At one point he was also a stand-up comedian. Gerald McRaney is the co-star of *Simon and Simon*, a series that may not be renewed for an eighth season.

As is customary for actors of his stature, Craig T. Nelson will not audition or "read" for the role in a general casting call. He has agreed, however, to meet with the producer privately. In that meeting, with Barry Kemp and two Universal executives, Nelson affirms his interest in the part. He feels it would be a good vehicle for him, and he would like the opportunity to do comedy again. Unfortunately, he is fighting a bad cold. Between nasal distress and nervousness, the meeting is awkward. No conclusions are reached.

Thursday, March 3, 1988

Today, casting brings in prospective actors for the important secondary roles in *Coach:* Christine, Kelly, and Dauber. In the pilot script, Christine is the coach's current girlfriend, a television reporter. Kelly is the coach's daughter, whom he has not seen for years since his divorce. Dauber is an assistant coach and is the oldest player on the coach's team. He is a very good football player but not too bright; he has been trying to accumulate enough passing grades to finally graduate.

This morning, Barry Kemp is pleased with the readings of initial actors brought in, and he is particularly gratified that his script "played" so well. It is the first time he has seen it performed by actors, and he feels the humor and characters come across nicely.

Later in the morning, he meets with John Whitman, one of Universal Studios' senior executives in production. Together they discuss possible candidates for various key technical positions. After reviewing the choices, Barry Kemp and John Whitman decide on who will function as co-producer, associate producer, script supervisor, director of photography, first assistant director, unit production manager, camera crew, and prop master.

Afterwards, producer Kemp inspects Stage 43 at Universal Studios, where the pilot is scheduled to be filmed. He wants to make sure that the sets fit properly on the sound stage. Since this will be a three-camera film show, part of the large stage will be occupied by bleachers for an audience of several hundred people. For the best audience reaction, the sets must face the bleachers and be visible to the entire audience. Unlike a three-camera videotape show, there will be no TV monitors for the audience to watch if they cannot see the stage action clearly. The blueprints are checked and approved. The construction of the sets is scheduled to begin on the following Monday.

In addition, a production schedule is issued. (See Figure 6.1.) The first reading of the entire show with the actors is only a month away—April 5th. The show is to be filmed before a live audience on April 13th. The completed pilot is to be delivered to ABC on April 30th. As changes occur in the schedule, everyone concerned will be notified.

After leaving the stage, Barry Kemp meets with Universal's program executives and with ABC programmers to hear their reactions and suggestions for the revision of the pilot script. Fortunately, the notes are minimal from the network and from the Tower (Universal executives are housed in a tall, sleek black building, hence their nickname). As a whole, everyone is very pleased with the script. Still, there are suggestions for possible changes. One suggestion is to make Christine a local sportscaster working out of Minneapolis, in order to make her contact with Coach Hayden Fox both credible and convenient.

There is also considerable discussion about whether Kelly, Coach's daughter, should move in with him at the end of the show. The network feels that such an arrangement provides opportunities for continuous interesting dilemmas. Barry Kemp does not agree. He feels it is always possible to have Kelly move into her father's house, but if that situation does not work creatively, it would be difficult for her to leave. He is also concerned that if Kelly stays with her father, it would turn the show into a familiar version of an old television series, *Bachelor Father*. He prefers that Kelly live in a dormitory but see her father regularly. While ABC is concerned, they acquiesce.

Friday, March 4, 1988

Casting auditions continue. Barry Kemp is pleased with the quality of actors arriving for readings. At the end of the sessions, he feels he has at least one strong candidate for each of the key secondary roles: Kelly, Christine, and Dauber.

The situation regarding the lead role, Coach Hayden Fox, however, is less positive. Craig T. Nelson remains a strong possibility, but there is concern about whether he can be funny enough to make the role work.

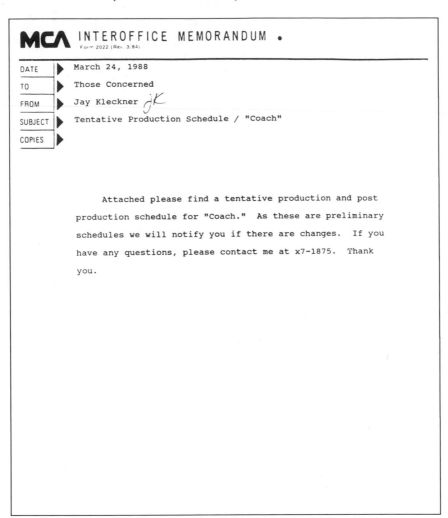

MCA INTEROFFICE MEMORANDUM ▪
Form 2022 (Rev. 3/84)

DATE ▶ March 24, 1988

TO ▶ Those Concerned

FROM ▶ Jay Kleckner *jK*

SUBJECT ▶ Tentative Production Schedule / "Coach"

COPIES ▶

Attached please find a tentative production and post production schedule for "Coach." As these are preliminary schedules we will notify you if there are changes. If you have any questions, please contact me at x7-1875. Thank you.

Figure 6.1 *Coach* tentative production and postproduction schedules.

As Barry Kemp assesses the problem, "What is interesting is that Craig Nelson seemed to completely understand it, but didn't communicate it when he went to do it."[1] Kemp learns that his other favorite, Gerald McRaney, will not be available. Surprisingly, CBS has renewed *Simon and Simon* for another season.

With the strike by the Writer's Guild pending, this may be the last

---

[1] Quotes in this chapter attributed to Barry Kemp are from personal communication in 1988.

```
                COACH TENTATIVE PRODUCTION SCHEDULE


Tuesday, April 5.......PRODUCTION MEETING  10AM ON STAGE 43
                       CAST READING        11AM ON STAGE 43
                       LUNCH AND CAST
                       PHYSICALS           12PM-2PM ON STAGE
                       REHEARSE            2-5PM


Wednesday, April 6.....REHEARSE            10AM ON STAGE 43
                       PRODUCERS' RUNTHRU  4:30PM  STAGE 43



Thursday, April 7......REHEARSE            10AM ON STAGE 43
                       UNIVERSAL RUNTHRU   4:30PM



Friday, April 8........REHEARSE            10AM ON STAGE 43
                       NETWORK RUNTHRU     4:30PM


Friday/Saturday
April 9, 10............MOVE BLEACHERS AND BOOTHS ONTO
                       STAGE


Monday, April 11.......CAMERA BLOCK        9AM
                       SHOOT CAMERA TESTS
                       OF MAKEUP, SETS,
                       WARDROBE


Tuesday, April 12......CAMERA BLOCK        9AM
                       PRODUCERS'RUNTHRU
                       WITH CAMERAS        4:30PM
                       UNIVERSAL (optional)


Wednesday, April 13....CAMERA REHEARSE     12P
                       SHOOT DRESS REHEARSAL
                       W/AUDIENCE          3:30PM
                       DINNER              5:30-6:30PM
                       SHOOT SHOW          7:30PM


Thursday, April 14.......TRANSFER FILM
                         TO VIDEOTAPE


Friday, April 15.........SHOOT MAIN TITLES
```

Figure 6.1   *(continued)*

chance to revise the script substantively. There is another meeting in the Tower, where Barry Kemp and the studio executives review the network note session from the previous day.

In the first act of the script, a phone conversation seems unclear. It is not apparent with whom the coach is conversing, although we later learn it is his ex-wife. Clarification is important, since the audience must understand his discomfort at being a father. The network would like to see that discomfort reinforced.

The scene was rewritten to address the network concerns. (See

```
        COACH TENTATIVE POST PRODUCTION SCHEDULE


    SATURDAY, SUNDAY
    April 16, 17


    MONDAY, April 18.........EDIT AT LASEREDIT
    Thru FRIDAY, April 22


    SATURDAY, SUNDAY
    April 23, 24


    MONDAY, April 25......... ON LINE AT LASEREDIT


    TUESDAY, April 26........PRELAY AUDIO AT
                             COMPACT VIDEO

    WEDNESDAY, APRIL 27......DUB AT COMPACT VIDEO     9AM - 1PM


    THURSDAY, April 28.......REMIX IF NECESSARY AT    9AM - 12N
                             AT COMPACT VIDEO


    FRIDAY, April 29.........DELIVER DUBS TO NETWORK
```

Figure 6.1 *(continued)*

Figure 6.2.) Hayden is the coach, who has just received a letter from his daughter, Kelly, informing him she plans to join him on campus. The coach expresses his uncertainty about being a "responsible" father. He confides his discomfort to Dauber, the perennial student/athlete, and to Luther, Coach's right-hand man. Note that the coach's attitude is carefully constructed to show his ambivalence. He calls his daughter long

```
                                                        12.
                                                        (A)


                        DAUBER
         Actually, I think all freshmen girls
         have to live at the market.
                        HAYDEN
         The what??
                        DAUBER
         Shaeffer Hall.  It's called "the market"
         because it's a tradition each year for
         all the jocks to go over there and check
         out the fresh...
DAUBER STOPS HIMSELF, REALIZING WHAT HE'S ABOUT TO SAY.
                        DAUBER (CONT'D)
         ...faces.
                        HAYDEN
         Oh, great.  See, this is what I'm
         talking about.  I don't want to be
         responsible for this.  I don't even want
         to know about this.
                        DAUBER
         So what are you going to tell her?
HAYDEN SCOWLS.
                        HAYDEN
         She's my daughter.  I have to tell her
         the truth.  (SADLY)  And the truth is,
         if she's coming here for an education,
         fine.  But if she's coming expecting to
                        (MORE)
```

Figure 6.2   Excerpt from *Coach* final script.

distance to convey his uneasiness, but reaches his ex-wife, who hits all the "tragedy" buttons. Hayden feels forced to declare he is more mature now and eager to spend time with Kelly. His on-camera reactions, however, show just the opposite.

```
        Revised 4/8/88                                        13.
                                                              (A)


                           HAYDEN (CONT'D)
                find a father, she might as well go

                someplace else.  (A BEAT)  Would you

                guys excuse me?  I've got to make a

                phone call.
                              DAUBER
                Sure.
        THEY BOTH WAIT FOR HAYDEN TO GO.
                              HAYDEN
                I meant you guys leave.
                         DAUBER AND LUTHER
                Oh.
        HAYDEN HEADS BOTH OF THEM OUT.  AS HE DOES, LUTHER TAKES HIM
        ASIDE.
                              LUTHER
                Listen, I know that's not going to be an

                easy conversation.  I just want you to

                know...well, I don't know what I want

                you to know.  That I know that, I guess.
                              HAYDEN
                (CONFUSED)  Thanks.
        HAYDEN TAKES A DEEP BREATH; THEN VERY DELIBERATELY DIALS A
        LONG DISTANCE NUMBER.
                           HAYDEN (CONT'D)
                (INTO PHONE)  Hello, Kelly?...Oh, Beth.

                Boy, you two sound more alike everyday.

                It's Hayden, how are you?...
                              (MORE)
```

Figure 6.2   *(continued)*

Monday, March 7, 1988

The Writer's Guild of America strike is announced. All the writers under contract to the studio are staying home, awaiting instructions from the guild leadership. Hyphenates (writers who are also producers) report to

```
Revised 4/8/88                                      14.-15.
                                                    (A)


                        HAYDEN (CONT'D)
         Oh?  What's wrong?...Yeah, well, that's

         why I'm calling.  I just got it a few

         minutes ago...Well, I was surprised,

         obviously.  And thrilled, of

         course...Beth, I don't know as I'd call

         it a "tragic" decision...
AS HE TALKS, HAYDEN NERVOUSLY PICKS UP A FOOTBALL AND TOSSES
IT IN THE AIR.
                        HAYDEN (CONT'D)
         No, I realize being a parent was never

         my long suit, but I've changed since

         then...Look, is Kelly there?  Maybe I

         should talk to her about this...Oh.

         Well, when she gets back would you tell

         her I called and let her know I-I

         couldn't be more pleased about her

         coming...No, I really am.  I'm looking

         forward to getting to be the father I've

         never been...Honestly, I couldn't be

         more excited...You be sure and tell her

         that, okay?...I will.  You, too...

         Goodbye.
HAYDEN SMILES AND HANGS UP.
                        HAYDEN (CONT'D)
         (TO HIMSELF)  There, that wasn't so

         hard.  The truth would've been hard.

                                         DISSOLVE TO:
```

Figure 6.2 _(continued)_

work. They are permitted to function solely as producers, so long as they perform no writing services during the strike. The only writing permitted by the guild during a strike are so-called "A to H" changes. These are sketchy instances related to actual production exigencies. For example, the script may refer to a specific location that is not available, and a substitution can be made.

Barry Kemp completed his polish over the weekend, addressing the Tower and network notes, and making small cuts or "trims" in the script. He reduced the script length by one-half page, which still leaves it five pages too long for a typical half-hour program. He has deliberately kept the script long. With or without a writers' strike, he can delete material during rehearsal or in postproduction.

There is another meeting with the Universal executives. In light of the strike, should they try to maintain the original shooting schedule? Universal has already been in contact with ABC, and it is everyone's choice to continue with the original plan. The first rehearsal (table reading for actors) remains April 5th. The shooting date remains April 13th.

Barry Kemp is troubled by the repercussions of the writers' strike. It will inhibit his ability to revise the script during rehearsals, a crucial period for any situation comedy. He knows that not being able to make substantive changes can hurt the project. He hopes the effect will not be too great.

As for casting the lead role, the ABC casting department suggests Wayne Rogers, Bruce Dern, Michael Murphy, and Ryan O'Neal. None of these actors has actually been contacted. They may not be available, and, even if available, may not want to work on a television series. And Barry Kemp may not want them.

Tuesday, March 8, 1988

Two more casting sessions are scheduled today, including some prospective candidates for the lead role. Barry Kemp wants to take some of the finalists for the secondary roles to the network in order to get the process moving and to focus better on the major problem: who will play the lead role of Coach Hayden Fox?

The day is also occupied in a discussion of directors. Barry Kemp has considered several individuals with whom he has worked successfully. For this pilot, he is also considering directing himself. There are pluses and negatives to that decision. On the positive side, he is clearly the individual most familiar with the material, and he has a firm vision of what must be accomplished. He also would be the most efficient director, a factor that must be considered in light of the tight time requirements for delivery.

On the other hand, an outside director would bring a valuable fresh perspective to the script, which Barry Kemp would welcome. And in light of the strike by the Writer's Guild, he would not want it misconstrued that he is skirting strike rules and implementing script changes by wearing a director's hat. Ultimately, he decides to direct the pilot. Both the studio and the network approve.

Meanwhile, construction of the set has begun on Stage 43 at Universal Studios. Kemp finalizes the hiring of an art director, associate producer, music composer, main title designer, and line producer.

Finally, there are phone calls inquiring about the possibility of using the UCLA Marching Band for the opening title sequence. Since the band is nonunion, the American Federation of Musicians must approve the arrangement. The letter shown in Figure 6.3 is drawn up by the studio's business-affairs department.

Wednesday, March 9, 1988

This is a quiet day. Barry Kemp meets with line producer Jay Kleckner to discuss other staff positions to be filled. There is supposed to be a meeting with Robert Foxworth, a possible consideration for the lead, but it is postponed.

Thursday, March 10, 1988

There are more casting auditions. Barry sees one actress for the role of Kelly who is clearly talented, but who is not his image for the character. In all, the casting session is a washout.

Friday, March 11, 1988

Barry Kemp and Jay Kleckner meet to discuss Universal Studios' operating procedure. Additionally, they evaluate the music intended for the show.

The afternoon is occupied by another casting session, concentrating on the roles of Christine, Kelly, and Dauber. Jerry Van Dyke is coming in for a meeting about the role of Luther, Coach's right hand.

Monday, March 14, 1988

A new casting opportunity presents itself. Kerry McCluggage, the president of Universal Television, has had conversations with the agents representing Burt Reynolds. They love the project and think it would be good for him. Universal is prepared to make a formidable financial offer to Reynolds, but no one knows if he is really open to working in television again (early in his career Reynolds had starred in a television cop show called *Hawk*). It is decided not to mention anything about the

MCΛ

UNIVERSAL CITY STUDIOS, INC., 100 UNIVERSAL CITY PLAZA, UNIVERSAL CITY,CALIFORNIA 91608

VIA MESSENGER

Writer's Direct Dial

(818) 777- 1948

March 17, 1988

Dick Gabriel
Assistant to the President
American Federation of Musicians
1777 North Vine #410
Hollywood, CA 90028

RE: "COACH"

Dear Dick:

This letter is to confirm our understanding in connection with
Universal's proposed use of a non-union marching band to record music
for possible use in the main and end titles of the Universal
Television series presently entitled "COACH."

Universal has selected the UCLA Marching Band for this project. Sandy
DeCrescent informs me that this choice is acceptable to the AFM.
Further, I understand and agree that AFM approval for use of these
non-union musicians is limited to the main and end titles of this
series only. Of course, the underscore to be contained in this
production will be produced strictly in accordance with the applicable
collective bargaining agreement between us.

If for any reason the foregoing does not accurately or fully reflect
your understanding of this matter, or if for any reason the foregoing
is not acceptable to you, please contact me as soon as possible to
resolve any problems.

This project would not be possible without your cooperation, which is
greatly appreciated.

Best regards,

Richard Cray
Director of Music/Creative & Business Affairs

RC/lt

cc: Harry Asher-Garfield   Barry Kemp
    Sandy DeCrescent   Jay Kleckner
    Warren Holcomb   Roxanne Lippel

Figure 6.3   Letter to Dick Gabriel, American Federation of Musicians, concerning use of the nonunion UCLA Marching Band in the opening title sequence of *Coach.*

possibility of Burt Reynolds to ABC, since it could raise expectations needlessly.

Tuesday, March 15, 1988

The company of Castle and Bryant have been selected to produce the main titles for *Coach*. They plan to shoot at the Rose Bowl using the UCLA Marching Band. They also discuss prospects for using a team mascot.

The afternoon is occupied by another casting session. The producer feels he has two to three strong candidates for Kelly and two strong candidates for Christine. He also meets with another candidate for Coach, Tom Skerritt.

Wednesday, March 16, 1988

Barry Kemp's day is occupied by more casting sessions.

Thursday, March 17, 1988

There is two and a half-hour casting session specifically for the role of Dauber, assistant coach and oldest player on the team. Barry Kemp feels that actor Bill Fagerbakke is by far the strongest candidate. A meeting in the Tower is set to expose Fagerbakke to the studio executives.

Friday, March 18, 1988

The casting process for the roles of Dauber, Christine, and Kelly reaches its climax. There is a session tentatively scheduled with ABC for the afternoon. If there is internal agreement, the finalists will be brought to the network for the final round of the competition.

Bill Fagerbakke is brought to the 12th floor offices of Joan Sittenfield, vice-president of casting for Universal. Joining her are Kerry McCluggage and other studio development executives. Barry Kemp explains he has found two or three good actors for the part of Dauber, but no one as good as Fagerbakke. Joan Sittenfield remarks that she is aware that ABC is favorably inclined toward Fagerbakke, and that he has not been seen too much on television. Furthermore, a decision is needed quickly, because he lives in New York and has to return. After the reading, there is general agreement that he should be taken to ABC.

For the role of Christine, Shelley Fabares is Barry Kemp's only choice. He and Universal executives feel that she has the part "nailed." Joan Sittenfield reminds the group that the actress has offers for other roles, and therefore a decision must be made quickly. It is decided to take her to ABC as the only choice.

A test-option deal must be negotiated with the actors. The studio casting department initiates the test option through a memo (see Figure 6.4).

There are three actresses as finalists for the role of Kelly: Clare Carey, Lori Laughlin, and Gina Kaufman. There is consensus that Gina Kaufman may be the best actress of the three, and she has excellent comedy timing but there is concern that she does not look the part and may be too old for the character. Lori Laughlin is the second choice. All agree that she is quite beautiful but there is some concern that, while she can play vulnerability very well, she is less adept at other moments. Moreover, in the opinion of the group, she does not look like the daughter of Coach Fox.

Clare Carey emerges as the first choice. For Barry Kemp and line producer Jay Kleckner, she seems like a college student. They believe

MCA INTEROFFICE MEMORANDUM ●
Form 2022 (Rev. 10/84)

DATE ▶ March 9, 1988
TO ▶ Pete Terranova
FROM ▶ Joan Sittenfield
SUBJECT ▶ COACH Test Option Deals
COPIES ▶ Ed Masket
Kerry McCluggage
Dick Lindheim
Barbara Romen
Brad Johnson
Barry Kemp
Sheldon Bull
Megan Branman

Please start Test Option Deals for the following actors.
We will be going to the network on Friday, March 18, 1988.

Christine (10 out of 13) - Shelley Fabares (Triad)

*Dybinski (all shows) - Bill Fagerbakke (Writers & Artists -
Paul Feldsher)

*Fagerbakke will be flown out of NY on Wed., March 16.

Others will probably be added, but please start these at once
because other projects are in hot pursuit.

Joan

Figure 6.4 Memo requesting test-option deals for possible *Coach* cast.

she could be the coach's daughter. They also feel she has more comedic possibilities than the others. Barry Kemp comments that Lori Laughlin is the daughter every parent wished they had, but Clare Carey seems more real. In order for the concept of the show to work properly, the coach must deal with two strong women—Christine and Kelly. To the producer, Clare Carey offers that potential.

The casting meeting is followed by a strategy session. Since Barry Kemp has only one real choice each for the roles of Christine and Dauber, he is wary about taking them to the network, along with only one choice for Kelly. What should be done about the choices for Kelly? If he takes only his final choice for each role, the network may feel excluded from the casting process, and on principle, coupled with human nature, reject at least one of the choices. But he is reluctant to take Lori and Clare to ABC, since it increases the risk that the network will insist on his second choice.

It is decided not to take either candidate to the network that afternoon. Instead, the approval process will be handled piecemeal.

For the role of Luther, Barry Kemp wants Jerry Van Dyke. But another potential problem surfaces. The producer has worked with the actor many times and is confident that he will perform the role superbly. However, he knows that Jerry Van Dyke becomes very nervous in casting sessions and does not read well. The actor just completed a strong comedic performance as guest star in *Coming of Age*, the other series Barry Kemp is producing. The producer decides to send a tape of that show to ABC, in the hope that the network will approve Van Dyke on that basis.

Finally, the internal discussion turns to the key unresolved problem—who will play Coach Hayden Fox? ABC casting has suggested Larry Pyne, who is arriving from New York to meet Kemp. Another possibility is Wayne Rogers, who may not be interested in working on a television series again; the prospect will be pursued. As for Burt Reynolds, his manager is meeting with the actor today. Kerry McCluggage hopes to hear the results of this conversation by the end of the day or over the weekend.

In the afternoon, the entire group assembles at the ABC network headquarters in Century City. Shelley Fabares and Bill Fagerbakke are introduced to the network programmers. They read for the parts of Christine and Dauber. Both are approved.

Monday, March 21, 1988

The morning begins with anxious conversations from ABC. As the shooting date for the pilot looms closer, they are increasingly worried about the lack of choices for Coach Fox.

Kemp has met with Larry Pyne. He feels Pyne is a good actor but does not have the inherent dynamic necessary for Kemp's vision of the role. Kemp has told Donna Rosenstein, ABC casting, that Pyne was too low key.

There has been no response yet from Burt Reynolds. But the producer feels he has four other good possibilities: Craig T. Nelson, Tom Skerritt, Ron Leibman, and Bruce Dern.

Part of the afternoon is spent in a budget meeting, trying to reduce the production cost. In that session, Kemp is able to trim about $50,000 from the budget, which now stands at $1,250,000 for the half hour.

Tuesday, March 22, 1988

This afternoon Barry Kemp will meet with Ron Leibman, who will read with him for the role. Afterwards there will be another general casting session.

While construction of the set is progressing, there have been some problems. It has been decided to switch to another sound stage. Because of the physical configuration of that stage and the location of the audience bleachers, it will be necessary to flip-flop the major sets. Whereas Coach Fox's cabin was originally designed to be camera right, it will now be camera left. (See Figure 6.5.)

For producer-director Barry Kemp this requires a major read-

Figure 6.5 Artist's conception of the set of Coach Fox's cabin. The artist's conception of the sets for *Coach* were modified when an alternate sound stage was required. In the final show all the sets were constructed as mirror images of the original design shown.

justment of his staging. He must rethink the entire script in terms of entrances and exits to make sure that everything still works. He is confident, however, that it will not pose a significant problem.

Late in the afternoon, Kemp has a meeting with Castle and Bryant regarding the main title sequence. They have learned that they will not be able to use the Rose Bowl on Friday. Instead they have found a college in East Los Angeles that seems suitable.

John Morris has been set to compose the music for the main title. He did the theme for Barry Kemp's miniseries, *Fresno,* and for several Mel Brooks films.

Wednesday, March 23, 1988

There is another casting session scheduled at ABC today. Barry Kemp wants to take Tom Skerritt and Ron Leibman to read for the role of Coach Fox, but the business deals between the agents and the studio are complex and have not been resolved.

At the same time, another actress arrives from New York to read for the part of Kelly. Barry Kemp brings her to the Tower for the studio executives to evaluate. It is decided to take her along with Clare Carey to ABC. The latter is still everyone's first choice.

Word reaches Barry Kemp that Burt Reynolds has reluctantly passed on the project. If he wanted to do television again, it would be a project of this quality. However, at this time he is not ready to commit. (A few months later he will agree to star as B.L. Stryker in one segment of the *ABC Mystery Movie*). The producer now talks with James Farentino, another interesting possibility for Coach.

Meanwhile, line producer Jay Kleckner is meeting with the wardrobe and set-decorating personnel. They discuss the coach's home and office set, and determine which of his clothes will have logos on them. Klechner also becomes involved in a reworking of the audience bleachers on the sound stage in order to improve audience viewing of the show.

At the network, ABC approves Clare Carey. They also approve Jerry Van Dyke for the role of Luther.

Friday, March 25, 1988

The business deals with Ron Leibman and Tom Skerritt are completed. Barry Kemp feels they are good possibilities. To simplify and expedite the casting process, and because of the caliber of the candidates, there is no separate reading for the Tower by Skerritt and Leibman. Instead several key ABC executives and studio personnel will join Barry Kemp at his office at Universal to meet the actors.

Afterwards there is general agreement that, while both are accomplished performers, neither is right for the part of Coach Fox. The week ends in disappointment.

Monday, March 28, 1988

Casting for the lead is beginning to reach crisis proportions. Everyone is becoming nervous, and there are new suggestions from the network and studio casting personnel, as well as agents learning about the opening. Meanwhile, Barry Kemp learns that Craig T. Nelson still wants the role. He has passed on a feature offered to him and will be back in town this Thursday.

The other names that seem most promising include David Rasche, James Farentino, Gary Lockwood, Jim Stafford, and George Peppard. There is also some interest in Richard Crenna. In the afternoon, the producer meets with David Rasche.

Tuesday, March 29, 1988

Barry Kemp is becoming very concerned that he may have to compromise in the casting of Coach Fox. He feels it could be devastating for the project. He has told ABC that David Rasche is just not right for the part. Richard Crenna seems like an interesting idea.

Wednesday, March 30, 1988

Kemp meets Jim Stafford, Gary Lockwood, and James Farentino. None is the perfect match of character and actor. Time is pressing—a decision must be made very soon.

Thursday, March 31, 1988

The final decision is made. An offer is made to Craig T. Nelson to play the role of Coach Hayden Fox. However, the actor is feeling uncomfortable. The offer was so long in coming, he is not sure the producer truly wants him for the part.

Barry Kemp and his key writer/producer, Sheldon Bull, have dinner with Nelson. They discuss the entire character background search and convey their thorough confidence in his portrayal of Coach. Nelson accepts the offer, and the casting is completed. (See Figure 6.6.)

Figure 6.6 The cast of *Coach*. From left to right: Jerry Van Dyke, Shelley Fabares, Craig T. Nelson, Bill Fagerbakke, Clare Carey, and Kris Kamm (playing the character of Kelly Fox's eventual husband, who does not appear in the pilot).

Friday, April 1, 1988

Relieved that he has the "right" coach, Kemp spends a few hours concentrating on his directing duties. He makes notes on the pilot script, while also dealing with normal production problems on his other series, *Coming of Age*.

Monday, April 4, 1988

In the morning Barry Kemp and Craig T. Nelson walk through the set so the actor can familiarize himself with the role and details of the set can be tailored to suit him. As a result, changes are made in the set dressings.

At lunch, the entire cast and crew meet for the first time. It is a pleasant encounter, and everyone eagerly anticipates production. But a new problem has surfaced. There is a substantial and seemingly irreconcilable difference between the studio's budget for this pilot and the dollars that ABC is willing to pay for it. The license fee cannot be agreed upon. The business-affairs executives at ABC argue they cannot afford to pay the same money for *Coach* as they did three years ago for another Universal-produced situation comedy. The two sides are deadlocked.

Without the conclusion of a business deal, ABC executives are told by their own management that they cannot attend the table reading. They ask to have it postponed. Barry Kemp, his cast, and crew are caught in the middle. He is frustrated and impatient, and cannot understand why such an important negotiation has been left to what seems the last minute.

Tuesday, April 5, 1988

A compromise is reached. The table reading of the script will be delayed from 11 A.M. to 3 P.M. to allow time hopefully to conclude the business negotiations between Universal and ABC. As a sign of good faith, the ABC comedy program executives are given permission to attend.

That compromise is important—if the table reading were held without the network, it would be denied input to the project at this crucial creative stage. It is likely that, without the ability to make suggestions and evaluate the status of the project, the network would abandon *Coach* altogether.

In the morning the production meeting takes place as scheduled. Heads of all production departments are present, and the script is analyzed, page by page, for production needs. Kemp explains to them what he has in mind for each moment of each scene.

This is followed at 2 P.M. by a meeting on stage with Barry Kemp and the cast. At 3 P.M. Stu Bloomberg from ABC and his associates arrive, along with the studio executive staff. The table reading goes smoothly. Everyone is pleased. What seemed good on the printed page is translating well into words and characters. Craig T. Nelson slips easily into the role of Coach Fox and is both convincing and funny. But the business deal has still not been closed, lending an air of tension to the proceedings.

Wednesday, April 6, 1988

The business deal has still not been closed. Rehearsal begins at 10:30 A.M. and continues until 5 P.M.

Thursday, April 7, 1988

The business deal has still not been resolved. The first "run through" of the show has been scheduled, but again ABC executives are told they cannot attend. Once more, this is a serious complication. A run through is the first opportunity to see the show "on its feet," actually performed. Suggestions, notes, and changes at this point are decisive. The inability to revise the script because of the writers' strike has already made this process cumbersome. The absence of the network at this stage could be crippling.

The run through takes place in the afternoon with only the studio executives present. The cast is understandably nervous, since this is the first time the show is performed from beginning to end. Nevertheless, Barry Kemp and the Universal personnel agree that it went well. The suggested changes are minor.

Friday, April 8, 1988

The business deal has still not been closed.

The only alteration that can be made to the script during the Writer's Guild strike is deletion. As discussed previously, Barry Kemp intentionally wrote the script too long, providing himself with a safety margin in case of the strike. Now he can take advantage of that forethought. The run through timing is eight minutes over. With Sheldon Bull assisting, they eliminate two minutes and forty-five seconds.

Barry Kemp now devotes considerable time to working with the actors individually. He gives them insights into the reasons he wrote the words, asking their feelings about the characters and the dialogue. They mutually decide what alterations in tone can and should be made. It is a comfortable process for the producer-writer-director and the cast. The improvements are noticeable in the next rehearsal.

The process concludes this day with another run through. This time the network executives will attend. Once again it seems as if the business negotiations are close to being successfully concluded, and all have agreed to behave in an optimistic manner.

This is an extremely risky procedure for Universal. If the network programmers are displeased with the run through, they can still legally walk away from the project. This could be financially disastrous for the studio. But Universal TV President Kerry McCluggage is gambling on the ability of Barry Kemp and the actors to convince the network that it both wants this show and will pay the money necessary to get it.

The run through is understandably a nervous affair, as all parties are aware of the risk. But the show is coming together well, and the performances, even at this early level of preparation, are excellent. Stu Bloomberg and the other network executives are very pleased.

The programmers from both the studio and network coalesce to insist that their counterparts in the business-affairs departments conclude an equitable contract. The business deal is finally closed.

Barry Kemp's day ends with a meeting with Mike Stanislavski, the director of photography, to go over all the camera angles he wants for the shoot.

Monday, April 11, 1988

The day is spent in "blocking" rehearsals. The blocking rehearsal is important, but it is strictly technical in nature. The ensure that the actors maintain their emotional connection with the characters, Barry Kemp ends the day working on individual moments within scenes.

Tuesday, April 12, 1988

Rehearsals continue. Kemp and the actors work on the show scene by scene. At the same time, cameras are moved into their designated positions. This gives the actors a sense of how to react to the cameras and how they will function during the actual performance. The day concludes with more specific fine tuning of scenes.

Wednesday, April 13, 1988—Production Day

Today represents the culmination of all the months of creation and preparation. The show will be filmed before a live audience.

Actually there will be two performances and two audiences. A common procedure for situation comedies is the recording of both the dress rehearsal and the performance show. This will allow Barry Kemp and the editors to choose moments from both for the final finished film.

The morning begins with more rehearsals for actors and cameras. The producer-director hopes to rehearse completely twice, before the dress rehearsal films at 4:00 P.M. Some minor technical problems, however, cause delays, and it is not possible to accomplish the two full rehearsals.

The dress rehearsal is delayed a half-hour to 4:30 P.M. There are 250 people in the bleachers, and this is the first time the actors are performing before anyone except stagehands and executives. The audience is responsive, and the cast rises to the occasion. Barry Kemp is pleased.

The evening performance show begins at 8:00 P.M. with another audience. Since this audience contains a number of friends of the actors, as well as agents and a large contingent of network people, there is higher anxiety.

The filming proceeds well but slowly, and there is one major mishap. As scripted, Craig T. Nelson is to enter his office from the room next door and confront his daughter. The script reads as shown in Figure 6.7. But in the performance show, the door is locked! Nelson futilely battles with it for a moment but then runs around to enter his office

```
                    HAYDEN (CONT'D)

        (SCREAMING)  You guys think you're ready

        to play football Saturday?!
HE SLAMS THE DOOR BEHIND HIM.  IN THE ROOM NEXT DOOR, WE HEAR
HIM RANTING.  KELLY LISTENS, ALMOST MESMERIZED.

                    HAYDEN (CONT'D - O.S.)

        (STILL SCREAMING)  You're not ready to

        play volleyball!  Twenty-three years

        I've been coaching and this is the worst

        team I've ever put on a field, and that

        includes a freshman intramural team in

        Chattanooga!  I'm embarrassed!  I am

        absolutely embarrassed!  If you're not

        going to practice any harder than that

        then let's not practice at all!  Hell, I

        don't need the practice.  I know what

        I'm doing!  But if you don't have any

        more pride than you showed out there

        today, then fine!  Let's just go out

        there Saturday and see how humiliated we

        can be!  You're dismissed!  You don't

        want to be here anyway so get out!
THE DOOR FLIES OPEN AGAIN AND HAYDEN STORMS BACK INTO THE
OFFICE, SLAMMING THE DOOR BEHIND HIM WITH ENORMOUS FORCE.  HE
TAKES A DEEP BREATH AND A PAUSE AND LOOKS AT KELLY, WHO IS
LOOKING BACK WITH A MIXTURE OF FASCINATION AND A SLIGHT BIT OF
FEAR.

                    HAYDEN (CONT'D)

        (TOTALLY CALM)  So, what do you think?

        Did you decide?
```

Figure 6.7   Excerpt from *Coach* final pilot script.

from the hallway door. The audience howls with laughter. It is a funny unplanned moment that works as if it were natural. It will be kept in the final film.

The show finishes around 11:00 P.M., and the audience goes home. Barry Kemp, the cast, and crew remain, however, for *pickups.* There were several minor actor flubs, or scenes in which actor and camera did not hit their mark correctly. These retakes will now be done without the pressure of an impatient audience.

The filming is completed at 1:00 A.M. Everyone is ecstatic. Barry Kemp feels this was the most complete experience he has ever had, guiding a project from idea to execution. He speculates that the dress rehearsal will provide 80 percent of the show. The evening performance will contribute another 15 percent, and the balance will come from pickups. He feels confident that he has everything needed for the editing process.

Thursday, April 14, 1988

The cast is gone. The crew is stowing things away. Barry Kemp relaxes. Meanwhile, Jay Kleckner is transferring the film to laser disc for the editing process. While the show was recorded on film, the rest of the production process will be on video. In the Laseredit™ system being utilized, all the film is transferred to laser discs, equivalent to those used for prerecorded movies for home use. The laser disc provides both a high-quality image and the ability to access any moment of any scene quickly and conveniently, much the way one can choose any selection of music on a conventional record or compact disc. The selected scenes are then ultimately rerecorded on a one-inch tape master, which becomes the final product.

For a situation comedy the postproduction process is relatively simple and takes place quickly. Universal executives are notified that they will see a rough cut of the completed show on Wednesday, April 20. ABC will see it either the following day or on Friday, April 22nd, depending on the studio executives' editing notes.

Friday, April 15, 1988

The main title sequence is filmed today. The concept has been changed. The UCLA Marching Band is gone, as is the football field. Instead, it has been decided to make the title intimate. The camera will pan slowly over the coach's cabin, examining his personal mementos and photos. The producer hopes that this, mixed with crowd sounds, band music, and a football announcer's voice in the distance will provide an audio-visual portrait of the man and the world in which he works.

Meanwhile, the editors are assembling the film and will continue to work through the weekend. Barry Kemp will check their progress and perhaps look at a rough assemblage.

Monday, April 18, 1988

On Sunday morning, Barry Kemp heard John Morris' theme music and loved it. He wants everyone involved in the project to hear it and has requested a temporary recording be made so that it can be added to the rough cut for the Wednesday screening for Universal executives.

Barry Kemp spends most of the day at the Laseredit™ studio working on the off-line cut of the show. At this point the show is five minutes too long.

Tuesday, April 19, 1988

Another day of editing. The show is still two minutes and fifteen seconds over, but producer-director Kemp has decided he will worry about cutting it to air time later. Right now he just wants to present the best show at whatever running time is needed.

Wednesday, April 20, 1988

Barry Kemp is pleased. This morning he saw the first cut of the main title sequence. It was the first time in his memory that he approved something with no notes whatsoever. Once more viewing the rough cut, Barry feels that, while long, the show is paced well. He screens the show for the Universal executives and listens to their notes, which are minimal. He plans to return to Laseredit™ to address them before the screening for ABC tomorrow.

Thursday, April 21, 1988

This morning Barry Kemp performs one of those small but important responsibilities of every producer. He must approve the spelling and placement of all the credits that will be superimposed over the picture.

The afternoon screening is held for ABC. It goes well. After the network screening, producer Kemp returns to Laseredit™ to address their notes.

The edited show must meet specific network credit policies for length of main titles, commercials, and ABC promos. The exact formula ABC required is shown in Figure 6.8.

Friday, April 22, 1988

The final polishing of the rough cut is completed, and *Coach* is "on-lined." This is the official and final assembly of the show.

CAPITAL CITIES/ABC, INC.
2040 Avenue of the Stars   Century City, California 90067   (213) 557-7777   **abc**

March 29, 1988

Mr. Sheldon Bull
UNIVERSAL TELEVISION
100 Universal City Plaza
Universal City, Ca   91608

Subject: COACH

Dear Mr. Bull:

Attached is a working format for the subject Pilot and a copy
of the ABC Credit Policy. Credits are to be approved by
Broadcast Standards and Practices and Program Administration
and should be submitted to Brett White and me as soon as possible.
Aside from the End Credit unit, credits may only be placed over
the Main Title and Act I.

If the show goes to series, you will be advised of series format
requirements.

In determining the length of the Main Title on the Pilot episode,
please be aware that on series programs, ABC requires an alternate
Main Title that runs :25 seconds shorter than the stet Main Title.
This alternate Main Title is to be furnished, one time only, with
the delivery of the first episode.

If this show is to be delivered in stereo, it is imperative you
notify me as soon as possible, and that the box the show is
delivered in be marked "stereo".

This Pilot is to be delivered per the attached format. Any revisions
or variations must first be cleared with Program Administration.
If it is impossible to deliver the show to time, please notify me
prior to delivery.

Sincerely,

Cathy Gouse
Program Administrator
CG/nw

xc: R. Eyanson, B. Kemp, K. Vogel - UNIVERSAL

     C. Bell, H. Miller, S. Nenno, J. Sharkey, B, White - ABC

Figure 6.8   Letter from ABC to Universal Television outlining pilot format for *Coach*.

```
COACH                                        program abc
A Universal Production
Pilot - Working Format                              format

  1.   Main Title
  2.   Commercial #1                                      1:00
  3.   Act I
  4.   ABC ID Bumper (Add'l Local ID Opportunity)          :03
  5.   Commercial #2                                      1:30
  6.   ABC Promo                                           :20
  7.   Act II
  8.   Title Art Work (v.o. "COACH
       will continue in a moment.")                        :05
  9.   Commercial #3                                      1:00
 10.   ABC Promo                                           :15
 11.   Tag
 12.   End Credits


                          TOTAL PROGRAM LENGTH        28:36


NOTES:

  1.   This Pilot must conform to this format.  Requests for
       revisions must be cleared with Program Administration.

  2.   The production company will deliver this episode with
       the Commercial, ABC ID Bumper and ABC Promo positions
       black slugged to time and with an additional :01 second
       of black between each numerical item, except between
       Items 4 and 5, there must be :02 seconds.

  3.   If Billboards are scheduled, Program Administration will
       advise.

  4.   Credits must comply with ABC Policy.




                                        CATHY GOUSE
                                        HANK MILLER
                                        ABC - HOLLYWOOD
                                        ISSUED: 3/29/88
```

Figure 6.8   *(continued)*

Monday, April 25, 1988

As Barry Kemp supervises, the music score is added to the on-line tape. A list of music cues is forwarded to the Universal music library. See Figure 6.9.

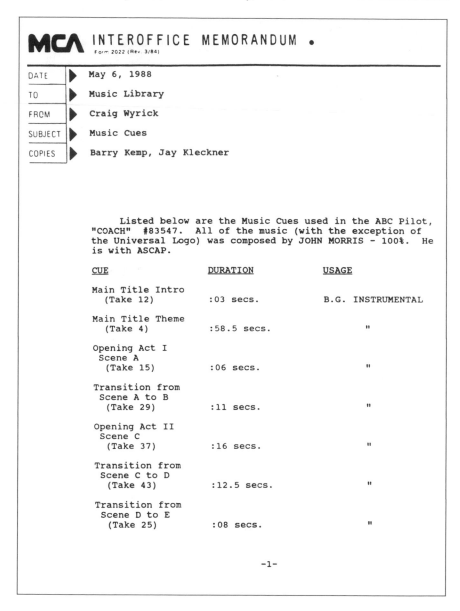

Figure 6.9   Interoffice memo from music library specifying music cues.

"COACH" MUSIC CUE'S - CONT'D

CUE	DURATION	USAGE
Underscore End of Act II, Scene E (Take 55)	:17.5 secs.	B.G. INSTRUMENTAL
End Credits Theme (Take 7)	:27 secs.	"
Universal Logo	:03 secs.	"

    "COACH" was delivered "best length" and will have to be re-edited and mixed before broadcast, therefore this is a TEMP. Cue Sheet. As of this date we DO NOT HAVE A scheduled Air Date.

-2-

Figure 6.9 *(continued)*

Tuesday, April 26, 1988

The sound-effects editors assemble the needed materials to add to the on-line tape the appropriate sounds effects, such as doorbells, phone rings, air-conditioner sounds.

Wednesday, April 27–Thursday, April 28, 1988

Barry Kemp supervises the "dubbing" of sound effects. The sound effects, music, and dialogue are combined in a "mixing" session at a dubbing stage. The show is finally completed.

Friday, April 29, 1988

The tape is delivered to ABC. Now Kemp and Universal await the reaction of the network senior management to *Coach*, and their decisions regarding the final disposition of the series. They will make the determination as to whether or not to proceed, and, if so, when *Coach* will premiere and where it will be placed on the ABC network primetime schedule.

At this point we interviewed Barry Kemp to assess his reaction to the pilot and to compare it with his initial vision of *Coach*. That discourse is presented in the following chapter.

7

Evaluation of the Production

THE PRODUCER'S ASSESSMENT

After spending months in development, casting, and production, the pilot for *Coach* was finally completed. Barry Kemp could now assess where the show met his initial expectations and where it fell short. To ascertain his personal and immediate reactions, the producer was interviewed before anyone else had seen the show—even before the network screened it. That conversation took place April 28, 1988.

As creator and producer, Barry Kemp seemed particularly pleased with the pilot. He thought it closely matched his initial vision.

> This is one of those very rare times when the show came out as close to my vision as anything I've ever been associated with. There's something really satisfying about *Coach* for me, because it wasn't easy. It wasn't easy conceptually. But it really came out looking and sounding and feeling like the show I wanted it to be.

He relied heavily on his production staff, and appreciated their expertise and trust. "It has helped a lot to have a core of people around me who I've worked with before. We understand each other. I understand their needs, they understand mine."

As for the cast members, the producer found them all realistic and credible in their roles.

> Craig Nelson . . . looks like what I thought Hayden would look like. [That's what] I love so much about this cast, from Shelley and Clare to Bill and Jerry. To me, no one looks like they've been cast in a television show. They're all actors, but they all look like real people.

The prolonged difficulty surrounding the casting for Coach Hayden Fox, and the apprehension during the extensive search for alternatives, took its toll. Barry Kemp expressed his anxiety about the initial casting of Craig T. Nelson as Coach. "Not knowing how comfortable [Craig Nelson] would be . . . how he was going to react to an audience. That was an unknown right up until the day we did it." But the producer's intuitive feeling about the actor paid off. He recounted this incident, which occurred the day of filming:

> [Nelson worked fine] with the live audience. He took one look at them and said to me, "Wow, what a rush." Then I knew that he'd be great. What it did, oddly enough, was focus him in a way that was just really interesting and surprising to watch.

The other major pressure on the producer was the prolonged business negotiations. He revealed the extraordinary tension this put him under:

> It's one of those parts of producing that wears you down, because it's one of the things that you don't expect to be a problem. . . . You sell the show and that's supposed to be the end of it. To find out that, after having gone through months of planning, with phone calls back and forth, and [intense work] on the show—to find out literally at the eleventh and a half hour that you may actually not be given any money to do it, or enough money to do it. . . . It just comes out of the blue and it just staggers you.

While he tried to ignore the ongoing business negotiations and to concentrate solely on the preproduction and rehearsal activities of *Coach*, it was literally impossible. He talked candidly about the extra stress it induced in the whole production, particularly the run through for the network—before the business deal was closed.

> We kid about the license fee, but nobody knew truly what that meant. I knew it was putting an extra weight and pressure on that show, and on the performances. . . . So, it created an unusual amount of anxiety. Fortunately, for me, I could defuse it [when I was] directing. I could focus on that. Otherwise, I would have just been dwelling on this [problem]. I would only allow myself to dwell on it when I walked away from the stage. I knew that we were sitting in a situa-

tion—to my knowledge—that no one had gone through before. No one had really gone through the situation of having a [television] show without a backer. We were really doing a backer's audition suddenly.

This was the first time Kemp had written, produced, and directed a pilot. He discussed the advantages of directing, particularly with respect to analyzing characters.

The great advantage that a writer has in directing his own work, for all that other people may perceive as disadvantages . . . is that he can tell an actor what a character is thinking at every moment—and why they're saying what they're saying.

This had special application in *Coach*, because Barry Kemp had taken extensive pains to create three-dimensional characters and he wanted to communicate that effectively to the actors. He discussed his script-interpretation approach and rehearsal techniques.

We have to take anything said on the page by a character as true, unless it's an obvious lie. By and large we are limited by what characters say about themselves and what others say about them. But in real life none of us say exactly what we think. It's all censored. It's filtered for various reasons. So, for example, in the scene with Hayden and Christine, we rehearsed it one time in which every single time the actors would say a line, I would tell them what the character was thinking—which was different from what the line read on the page. And we would ping-pong back and forth . . . for about twelve or fourteen lines.

What it did was get the actors thinking the way the characters thought. And when you can formulate the thought, then what comes out of your mouth is, in fact, a slightly different thing than what actually goes through your head. It suddenly creates a level of believability that I don't think you normally have, especially in a pilot situation.

Figure 7.1 provides a portion of the scene Barry Kemp referred to above. Hayden and Christine are having a romantic candlelight dinner. But Coach's mind is on something else. She has no idea what is bothering him. She may even think he wants to break up the relationship—until he mentions his daughter.

Note that the scene is virtually devoid of stage descriptions and character reactions. As Barry Kemp explained, the dialogue suggests the direction of the scene but leaves out the underlying emotional attitudes. In the rehearsal process, the cast uncovered each character's in-

```
            Revised 4/8/88                              33.
                                                       (D)


                          CHRISTINE
            ...things that really matter to us?
            (OFF HAYDEN'S SMIRK)  Well, if we're
            going to get to the business we both
            came for, I think we'd better clear up
            the other stuff first.
A BEAT.
                          HAYDEN
            (CONFESSING)  I was thinking about my
            daughter.
                          CHRISTINE
            (UNEASILY)  I thought you said you were
            thinking about the game.
                          HAYDEN
            I lied.  You still want to hear this?
                          CHRISTINE
            (SQUEAMISHLY)  This is really personal,
            isn't it?  Okay, go ahead.  Just go
            slow.  We're both new at this, remember.
                          HAYDEN
            (WITH A SIGH)  I was just wondering what
            kind of guy I am sometimes, that's all.
            I could've made Kelly stay this
            afternoon if I'd really wanted to, but
            the truth is there was a part of me that
            I wanted to be here tonight with you and
            not with her.
```

Figure 7.1   Excerpt from *Coach* final pilot script.

tentions and feelings. For example, Hayden is feeling guilty because this is the first night his daughter is in town. He feels he should be with her and is surprised by the power of his own paternal instincts. At the beginning of the scene, Christine sees him preoccupied and may think he has something terrible to tell her about their own relationship. She is

```
Revised 4/8/88                                    34.
                                                  (D)


                        CHRISTINE
          I'm having a hard time telling you that
          was a terrible thing.
                        HAYDEN
          It's not terrible, it's just selfish.
          My whole life I've told myself I was
          doing the noble thing by not being more
          a part of Kelly's life.  The truth is, I
          just didn't want to take the time.  I
          don't know why time scares me, but it
          does.  I wonder if I got into coaching
          because I really like it, or because
          four years is about all the time I'm
          capable of committing to any one human
          being.
                        CHRISTINE
          (PUSHING AWAY FROM THE TABLE)  O-kay,
          that's going deep enough.
                        HAYDEN
          (QUICKLY TAKING HER HAND)  I'm not
          talking about you.
     SHE STOPS.  HE LOOKS AT HER A MOMENT, HOLDING HER HAND.
```

Figure 7.1 *(continued)*

relieved to find out his preoccupation concerns his daughter and finds that an appealing character trait. She reinforces his decision to spend time with his daughter. As a result, they cannot consummate their romantic instincts. These attitudes form the comedy conflicts for the director and actors throughout the scene.

```
Revised 4/8/88                                    35.
                                                  (D)


                    HAYDEN (CONT'D)
        Can I say something really honest?
                      CHRISTINE
        (UNEASILY)  Yes.  If you really have to.
                      HAYDEN
        I wish I'd made Kelly stay today.  I
        know that's a lousy thing to say to you,
        but--
                      CHRISTINE
        Hayden, you don't have to be sorry for
        feeling something for your daughter.
        I'm not jealous.
                      HAYDEN
        No?
                      CHRISTINE
        No.  In fact...(SUDDENLY SURPRISED)...
        how's this for honest?  All those times
        I've told you I found you sexy?  Like
        when you're stalking the sidelines
        during a game, or when you're working in
        the den real intensely coming up with
        some brilliant new play?
                      HAYDEN
        Yeah?
```

Figure 7.1   *(continued)*

As both a producer and director of the project, Kemp was able to alter the traditional rehearsal procedure for *Coach.* By spreading the blocking over two days, he felt he improved the actors' concentration on characters.

```
                                                       36.
                                                       (D)


                       CHRISTINE
        You're not nearly as sexy as you are
        right now.
                        HAYDEN
        (SURPRISED)  Yeah?
                       CHRISTINE
        Yeah.  (A BEAT)  And now I have to leave
        you.
                        HAYDEN
        (CONFUSED)  Why??
                       CHRISTINE
        Because you have to call your daughter.
        The wrong person's hearing these things.
SHE RISES FOR HER COAT AND BAG.
                        HAYDEN
        (ALSO RISING)  But you don't have to
        leave.  You can wait.  I'll call my
        daughter while you're cleaning up the
        kitchen.  Or heck, I'll clean up the
        kitchen and you can just drink wine.
                       CHRISTINE
        (GATHERING UP HER THINGS; AMUSED)  Not
        tonight, Hayden.
                        HAYDEN
        But I don't think you realize how much
        better I feel now.
SMILING, SHE WALKS OVER TO HIM AND GIVES HIM A VERY LONG AND
TENDER KISS.
```

Figure 7.1 *(continued)*

By spreading the camera blocking over two days, at no point during the process did it ever become a technical process. We would camera block for half a day, dismiss the crew, and then go back and redo stuff again. So the last thing everybody was always left with, was

37.
(D)

CHRISTINE

I'll see you next time I'm in town.

SHE GRABS A SET OF HIS KEYS AND STARTS OUT.

HAYDEN

Christine, wait...

CHRISTINE

I'm taking your car. I'll park it
discreetly on the side street near the
hotel so no one will see it. You can
ride your bike in tomorrow.

HAYDEN

My bike?

CHRISTINE

It'll be good for you. I have a feeling
you're going to have a lot of pent up
energy to burn.

HAYDEN

Come on, don't do this to me...

CHRISTINE

(AS SHE HEADS OUT) Call your daughter,
Hayden.

HAYDEN

Christine!...

CHRISTINE

(AS SHE CROSSES THROUGH THE PORCH) And
clean your kitchen. (STOPPING AND
TURNING BACK) God, I want you.

Figure 7.1 *(continued)*

thinking about performance. We sort of let the technical stuff get cleaned up along the way, but we never let it become a show about hitting "marks."

In the past, Barry Kemp had often been frustrated during the filming of pilots by camera problems. As both the producer and director of *Coach* he took steps to ensure that this would not happen.

> We didn't have a cameraman miss a single shot. Ron Brown and I discussed it and went to a more high-powered battery for the cameras so they wouldn't run out during the show [a common problem]. We talked about where we wanted to load the film between scenes so we didn't run out of film during the scenes. Even though it meant wasting a little film occasionally—one thousand, two thousand feet of film—it's preferable to interrupting a scene and losing momentum.

Of course there were small problems in both performances. This is normal in the filming or taping of any show before an audience. The dual performances, however, gave the producer the opportunity to correct them.

> We made notes of that between shows. We know we don't have this moment, we know we don't have this phone call quite the way we want it. So, what we did was . . . pay particular attention to those places that we knew we missed in the afternoon to make sure we got them [in the evening].

There were two major departures from the norm, however. The first was a wardrobe mistake that occurred in the afternoon dress rehearsal with a minor character, a young man whom Coach Fox tries to recruit.

> Every single time we would rehearse it, [the actor] would be in short sleeves. It just didn't register with me that when he went off to do the scene in front of the audience that afternoon he went and put a sweater on. . . . Kerry [McCluggage] came up afterward and said, "I thought he was going to be in short sleeves." And I said, "I thought so too." I didn't pay any attention to [the fact] that he was in a sweater. So, we made a somewhat risky decision . . . to go ahead and shoot it that evening with him in short sleeves—which basically eliminates two of the three cameras we had in the afternoon.
>   Usually I don't go into a scene and purposely not match [the shots] with an afternoon show. But we did it there. [I felt] that scene was so consistent that [we were not] really going to lose a whole lot by doing anything differently in the evening.

Figure 7.2 provides the scene that was under discussion. Hayden in a lobby, waiting for Christine, notices a potential football recruit. The young man makes the wrong assumption about Hayden Fox's interest. When it was shot and edited, the scene showed the young man in short sleeves dealing with Hayden's inquisitiveness. The mixup of clothes in the performance was not noticeable on screen.

The second major unforeseen problem, as mentioned in the previous chapter, occurred in the last scene of the show. During the evening performance, the door from the ready room stuck. Craig T. Nelson was forced to improvise, racing around and bursting in from the main entrance. The spontaneity of that moment played unusually well. As Barry Kemp explains, he had to decide whether to keep the scene as it was filmed, or reshoot as it was written.

> It was a pure accident. Frankly, it played so well, we wanted to leave it in. But the camera [operators] were not sure whether they had picked it all up. So, we had to determine whether to go back and reshoot the scene the way we intended, or try to reconstruct what happened by accident and shoot pickups to make sure we were covered.
>
> The clock was ticking, and we had to make a decision. [Could] we risk not doing other pickups in order to spend an hour getting this pickup? [I thought] this was the climax of the show. I made the decision that . . . we [had to] reconstruct the scene, to make sure we had it.

Fortunately for the producer, the camera operators were quick enough to provide the needed film to keep the accident in the final film.

> Miraculously, we were able to reconstruct what happened by accident, using one of the pickup close-ups. In essence, we created a "shock" that the cameras had missed. . . . By being able to cut in the one pickup shot, we not only saved the scene, but we actually created an energy that we would not have had if we hadn't done the pickup.

In deciding whether to keep the original scene or the performance film with the altered incident, Barry Kemp had to assess whether the nature of Coach's character would be affected.

> While I wasn't concerned that we do something different, I wanted to make sure that we were not losing something that was important to the show. . . . [I didn't want to lose] a part of the manipulation of his character. [Would we] sacrifice that particular moment to show the desperation of his character? It was a trade-off, and we went

```
Revised 4/8/88                                    27.
                                                  (C)


HAYDEN CASUALLY CROSSES OVER TO THE WAITING AREA AND SITS
DOWN.  AS HE DOES, HE NOTICES THE ATHLETIC-LOOKING YOUNG MAN
NEARBY, LEAFING THROUGH A MAGAZINE.  HAYDEN PICKS UP A
MAGAZINE AND ALSO BEGINS LEAFING THROUGH IT, BUT THE YOUNG MAN
HAS HIS ATTENTION.  AFTER A MOMENT:

                        HAYDEN

          (CASUALLY)  Who do you play for?

                    YOUNG MAN

          (LOOKING UP)  Excuse me?

                        HAYDEN

          Football.  Who do you play football for?

                    YOUNG MAN

          Oh, I don't play football.

THE YOUNG MAN SMILES POLITELY AND RETURNS TO HIS MAGAZINE.

                        HAYDEN

          (LOOKING AROUND)  A big, husky guy like

          you?  You don't play football?

                    YOUNG MAN

          (SMILING)  No.

HE RETURNS AGAIN TO HIS MAGAZINE.

                        HAYDEN

          How come?
```

Figure 7.2 Excerpt from *Coach* final pilot script.

```
                                                             28.
                                                             (C)


                         YOUNG MAN

              (WITH A SHRUG)  I don't know.  Too busy

              running track, I guess.

    HAYDEN LOOKS AT THE YOUNG MAN, AMAZED.  THE YOUNG MAN
    CONTINUES TO LEAF THROUGH HIS MAGAZINE.

                         HAYDEN

              Track?  You're a track man?

                         YOUNG MAN

              Yeah.

                         HAYDEN

              What do you run?

                         YOUNG MAN

              Dashes.  Sixty and the hundred.

    HAYDEN GLANCES AROUND ANXIOUSLY.

                         HAYDEN

              What do you run the hundred in?

                         YOUNG MAN

              (SHRUGGING)  9.8 - 9.9.

                         HAYDEN

              (ALMOST SALIVATING)  Big, husky guy like

              you runs the hundred yard dash in under

              ten seconds?

                         YOUNG MAN

              (MODESTLY)  Yeah.

    HAYDEN LOOKS AROUND, UNABLE TO BELIEVE HIS GOOD FORTUNE, AND
    QUICKLY MOVES OVER CLOSE TO THE YOUNG MAN.  HE SITS DOWN
    BESIDE HIM.

                         HAYDEN

              Tell me, what size thighs do you have?
```

Figure 7.2 *(continued)*

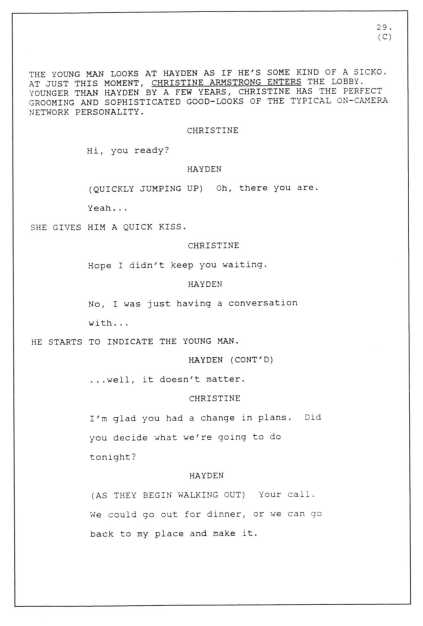

THE YOUNG MAN LOOKS AT HAYDEN AS IF HE'S SOME KIND OF A SICKO. AT JUST THIS MOMENT, <u>CHRISTINE ARMSTRONG ENTERS</u> THE LOBBY. YOUNGER THAN HAYDEN BY A FEW YEARS, CHRISTINE HAS THE PERFECT GROOMING AND SOPHISTICATED GOOD-LOOKS OF THE TYPICAL ON-CAMERA NETWORK PERSONALITY.

           CHRISTINE

Hi, you ready?

           HAYDEN

(QUICKLY JUMPING UP) Oh, there you are.

Yeah...

SHE GIVES HIM A QUICK KISS.

           CHRISTINE

Hope I didn't keep you waiting.

           HAYDEN

No, I was just having a conversation

with...

HE STARTS TO INDICATE THE YOUNG MAN.

           HAYDEN (CONT'D)

...well, it doesn't matter.

           CHRISTINE

I'm glad you had a change in plans. Did you decide what we're going to do tonight?

           HAYDEN

(AS THEY BEGIN WALKING OUT) Your call. We could go out for dinner, or we can go back to my place and make it.

Figure 7.2 *(continued)*

30.
(C)

                    CHRISTINE
        I think I'd like to go to your place and
        make it.
AS THEY PASS THE YOUNG MAN:
                    YOUNG MAN
        Lots o' luck, lady.
OFF BOTH HAYDEN AND CHRISTINE'S REACTIONS...

                                    <u>DISSOLVE TO</u>:

Figure 7.2   *(continued)*

back and forth a long time. We thought seriously about it, because the "be all" and "end all" was not to be funny—but to say something about those people. We ultimately decided that showing his desperation did just as much for the character as showing his manipulations. So we elected to go with [the altered incident].

In a smaller, less noticeable way, similar decisions were made throughout the postproduction process. Feeling that it would facilitate editing, Barry Kemp took the unusual step of inviting the film editor to the rehearsals.

We had our editor, John Neal, come in the first day of camera blocking to watch what we were doing, to see if he could find anything we were missing. So the editor had seen the show on the stage and had watched the camera coordinator. No one went into postproduction surprised by what they were seeing.

As mentioned in the previous chapter, Barry Kemp deliberately kept the script long, as a hedge against the Writer's Guild strike. The result in postproduction was an over-length show.

We did come in long. We came in longer than we normally do on a show. I don't remember ever doing a show that was almost six minutes long. Partly because of the writers' strike we kept cutting and cutting. But had there not been a strike, we would have been able to rewrite and cut more efficiently than we did. It really kept creating a big problem for us, because we weren't sure what we could legally do. So, we came in with a show that was longer than we anticipated. Also, to be honest with you, the audience response was greater than I had anticipated. I thought the audience would generally like the show. I didn't know they would vocally respond as much as they did.

Working with the editors, Barry Kemp slowly trimmed the length of the pilot. But it was still over acceptable broadcast time requirements when initially presented to the network.

We cut off the ends of scenes, because we knew we always let those go long anyway. We were able to pick up another thirty seconds there. We did some internal cuts in the scenes, line by line, that trimmed a little time. We took four different passes at the show and tried to snip away internally, rather than taking out hunks, trying to make trims an audience wouldn't notice. In fact, we have situations . . . where a response to a certain line was a response to a completely different line when we shot it. But you wouldn't know that looking at it now.

The show was finally delivered to the network, and the producer was satisfied with the results. Now he had to wait for their responses and reactions.

THE NETWORK'S EVALUATIONS AND RESPONSES

The finished version of the pilot was formally delivered to ABC on schedule. Like all the other pilots made in Spring 1988 it was turned over to the ABC research department for evaluation. *Coach* was tested on cable systems throughout the United States, and the results were reported back to ABC senior management and the program department.

The research concluded that, while the show was appealing, the character of Coach Hayden Fox was too negative. Specifically, researchers reported that test respondents disliked the fact that Coach Fox had not seen his daughter in many years and he seemed conniving and untruthful. They further cited that the strongest element in the show was the relationship between Coach Fox and his daughter, Kelly. The testing was not as favorable toward Christine. The research also stated that, while the show would appeal to men, they doubted many women would watch a show called *Coach* that featured such an unsavory character.

These rather negative test findings generated considerable debate among the network executives about the disposition of the series. The network program department found itself pitted against corporate management. Feeling that the pilot was well done and that, perhaps, the research was overstated in its concerns, and confident in the quality of work previously done by Barry Kemp, they argued for proceeding with *Coach.* The result of the debate was a compromise.

At the initiation of the whole project, as a show of faith in the producer, ABC had committed to 13 episodes for *Coach.* However, ABC always reserves the right to change its mind and simply pay a penalty for not proceeding. This sort of quasicommitment has become commonplace at all the networks in the past few years.

The compromise decision reached was to proceed with production of all 13 episodes of *Coach,* but not to premiere in the Fall. *Coach* would be held as a "backup" project. This would allow both sides to see more episodes and give Barry Kemp time to counteract the problems presented by research.

Like all series committed in 1988, production on *Coach* was delayed until the conclusion of the six-month Writer's Guild strike. Events then proceeded smoothly. At ABC's request, Coach Fox's character was softened somewhat, and the episode stories were redesigned to focus more on Coach's relationship with his daughter, Kelly. At one point the network suggested replacing Fox's girlfriend, Christine, but it was decided the initial unfavorable testing response to the character was more the result of her limited role in the pilot rather than the character herself.

The pilot was also re-edited to soften Coach Fox and to eliminate dialogue where he stated that he had not seen Kelly in years and did not think he could be a good father to her.

The Fall 1988 season for ABC and the other networks did not begin until late November. There were some indications in December that *Coach* would most likely premiere early in 1989, but no dates were set. In January 1989 there were several conversations between the ABC programmers, producer Barry Kemp, and Universal executives. Citing the research, the networkers had concluded that it might be better to premiere *Coach* with an episode entitled "Kelly and the Professor," rather than the pilot. In their view this funny episode would have stronger appeal to women and would demonstrate the series' focus on the relationship between Coach Fox and his daughter, rather than on football.

Barry Kemp and Universal argued that to premiere *Coach* without the pilot would be disastrous. To Kemp the whole essence of the character would be lost—he would simply become another bungling bachelor trying to be a good father. That was an old and familiar TV series concept, and it would make *Coach* seem like an old-fashioned show. Moreover, the pilot could not be played later in the series, since the attitudes and events would not logically fit. The pilot would have to be dealt with in one of three ways. First, it might be abandoned altogether, an expensive loss to ABC. Second, and more likely, it would become a "flashback" episode later in the series, as Coach and Kelly reminisced about meeting for the first time in 16 years. Third, if the series failed to get Nielsen ratings, the pilot would simply be aired at the end of the run. Its incongruity would not matter in that case.

Concerned, but willing to entertain arguments, ABC decided to test the "Kelly and the Professor" episode to see if their data could be instrumental in resolving the problem. The ABC executives also suggested that the title be changed. Again, research indicated that a show with the title *Coach* would not attract any women viewers, and this would be disastrous to the show's Nielsen ratings.

Upset and apprehensive about these events, Barry Kemp met with the Universal Studios executives. Two things were decided. First, to alter the perception that Coach Fox was an uncaring father, Barry would further re-edit the pilot with this problem in mind. At the same time, he would make changes in the dialogue that would indicate that Fox wanted to be a good father but was unfamiliar with the role. Second, both to help perceptions about Coach's girlfriend, Christine, and to quell test respondents' attitudes that Coach Fox lies and connives, Barry agreed to write a new opening for the show. This would replace the original "tease," where Coach Fox used sales tactics to convince a young man and his mother to come to Minnesota State. The new tease would feature the romance between Coach and Christine.

The ABC executives approved these changes, and they were implemented. When the revised pilot was viewed, they were pleased. They felt the testing problems had been neutralized, and that the whole show was more entertaining. The testing of "Kelly and the Professor" also continued, however.

Finally, in February, ABC formulated its program schedule for the balance of the 1988–1989 season. Barry Kemp and the Universal program executives were called into a meeting. The ABC executives complimented Barry Kemp on the consistent and fine quality of *Coach.* He was informed that the series would be scheduled on Wednesday nights at 9 P.M. beginning March 1, 1989. The producer was disappointed. There was intense speculation throughout Hollywood that ABC planned to move its new hit series *Roseanne* to 9 P.M. on Tuesday. The time period following *Roseanne* was coveted; the show would be handed a large audience. If the new show could hold most of that viewership, it would be declared a major success.

But the ABC executives were still concerned about the research and *Coach*'s perceived lack of appeal to women. Acknowledging its consistent quality, they decided to give it the more difficult time period. However, to assist in getting *Coach* sampled by an audience, they decided to premiere the show on Tuesday, February 28, 1989, following *Roseanne,* and then move it the next night to its regular time period.

The testing of the "Kelly and the Professor" episode was revealed. The results were considerably more positive than the original pilot, with stronger appeal to women. But, because the ABC cable testing procedure is very expensive, the revised pilot was not tested. The network programmers were convinced that *Coach* should premiere with the "Kelly and the Professor" episode. They further felt that the title had to be changed. They suggested "Fox," although they were very open to other thoughts.

Producer Barry Kemp and the Universal staff were upset. By not testing the revised pilot, the ABC executives were comparing apples and oranges. ABC, of course, has the right to schedule episodes of a series in any order it wishes. However, it usually does not want to engender the animosity of a producer or studio, and, therefore, hopes to reach a consensus.

The discussion was quite heated. Both sides wanted what they believed best for *Coach.* The ABC executives were concerned about the research findings, and particularly about the lack of female appeal in the pilot. With the large audience that *Roseanne* was expected to deliver to the premiere of *Coach,* an audience consisting mostly of women, they did not want an episode that would be unattractive to them. Barry Kemp and Universal felt that the show as a whole would draw women viewers and that the revised pilot more than addressed the problem. Without a test of the revised pilot, they felt it was improper to cite research on "Kelly and the Professor" as the rationale for the change. Moreover, the producer felt the whole concept of the series would be compromised if the pilot was not shown.

After lengthy consideration, a plan was proposed. Since the testing affirmed that "Kelly and the Professor" had female appeal, it was decided to play that episode on Tuesday night following *Roseanne*. It was to be advertised, however, as a "sneak preview" of the series, which would begin the following night. It was also decided to place a promotional piece in the show, which stated: "Tune in tomorrow to see how it all began." Then, on Wednesday night, the regular run of the series with the pilot would begin. All agreed that this was an acceptable alternative. The discussion regarding changing the title was dropped, and the meeting ended.

Coach premiered on February 28, 1989 inheriting a large audience from *Roseanne*. The greatest audience demographic were women between the ages of 25 and 54. It premiered the following night and again showed its greatest strength with women viewers.

Critical response to the show was mixed. Some reviewers criticized *Coach* as being the familiar mix of the bumbling bachelor trying to deal with a teenage daughter. A number of critics remarked about the "stupidity" of beginning the series without the pilot and then showing it the following night.

In the following months, *Coach* struggled to maintain an audience, although it performed in its time period almost as well as the major hit show *Wonder Years*. *Coach* averaged an 18 share, which placed it third in the time period. Its audience remained primarily women; its greatest liability was a small male audience.

The ABC programmers felt that a portion of the show's poor performance could be traced to its companion shows in the 9:00–10:00 P.M. hour: *Hooperman*, which was then replaced by the *Robert Guillaume Show*.

The Fall schedules are usually determined in May. As that time approached, ABC executives were divided into two opposing camps. ABC programmers strongly supported the renewal of *Coach*. They were aware of its difficult competitive position on the schedule and appreciated the quality of the series produced by Barry Kemp and his staff. The other camp opposed its renewal. These were executives in the research department, who reported poor test results, and other executives who did not like the show.

The resolution was a "standby" compromise. ABC decided to renew *Coach* for 13 additional episodes but did not assign it a time slot on the

Fall schedule. Once again *Coach* had been designated a standby to replace a failing show. It might air in midseason; it might not. Producer Barry Kemp was enormously frustrated by the network's actions.

In Spring 1989 there had been an executive shuffle within the ranks of ABC. Brandon Stoddard, who had initiated *Coach* on the recommendation of his vice-president of comedy development, Stu Bloomberg, had resigned. Stoddard's replacement was Robert Iger, former head of ABC Sports. Stu Bloomberg was elevated to a position in charge of all program development, including drama and comedy. Both Iger and Bloomberg looked favorably on *Coach* and promised that it would be given a time slot at the earliest opportunity.

Production of new episodes of *Coach* began in early August 1989 concurrent with production of ABC's other situation comedies premiering in the Fall. With the experience of the pilot and the first 13 episodes behind them, writing and production came easily and was problem free.

Robert Iger and Stu Bloomberg attended several of the filming sessions for the show and were pleased with what they saw. The completed episodes looked even better. Everyone agreed that *Coach* had found its identity. The actors were more comfortable, the scripts were better, and the whole show seemed funnier and more enjoyable.

At the beginning of the Fall season, one of ABC's highest hopes was a show called *Chicken Soup,* starring comedian Jackie Mason and popular performer Lynn Redgrave. It was produced by Carsey-Werner, the successful team responsible for NBC's greatest hit, *Cosby,* and for ABC's greatest hit, *Roseanne.*

But *Chicken Soup* was not performing well in the Nielsen ratings. Placed behind *Roseanne,* in the most coveted spot on the ABC schedule, it was weekly losing much of the enormous audience provided by its lead-in. Once the rival NBC show, *In the Heat of the Night,* began to out-rate *Chicken Soup,* the ABC executives knew they had to act.

Unannounced to Barry Kemp or the Universal executives, ABC management asked its research department to evaluate two new episodes of *Coach.* The conclusion, as reported in a memo, was:

> The new episodes of *COACH* appear to have significantly increased the program's appeal versus last season, especially among Women and frequent viewers of *ROSEANNE.*

See Figure 7.3 for the full report.

Thus, on November 21, 1989, almost two years after Barry Kemp presented the idea for the series to Stu Bloomberg and his assistants at ABC comedy development, *Coach* was placed on the network's Tuesday night schedule, in the coveted 9:30 P.M. time slot, immediately following *Roseanne,* where it performed significantly better than did its predeces-

Capital Cities/ABC Inc   (abc)

To: Those Listed Below

From: Gene Cooper

Date: November 1, 1989

Subject: COACH--Research Results

RESEARCH METHOD

In order to gauge the potential appeal of COACH in general as well as in the Tuesday 9:30 time period, we conducted interviews with a total of 150 viewers of ROSEANNE. The sample consisted of adults between 18 and 65 years of age (75 males and 75 females) who were interviewed on Monday, October 30, 1989, in five markets: Baltimore, Chicago, Detroit, Houston and San Antonio. Given the limited sample size, results should be considered directional rather than definitive or projectable.

BEFORE VIEWING
Prior to being shown two new COACH episodes, respondents we e asked whether they had seen COACH when it aired last Spring and Su n ar and, if so, how would they rate COACH on a five-point "Excellent-to-Poor" scale.

AFTER VIEWING
After viewing the two new episodes, all respondents were asked to rate COACH using the "Excellent-to-Prior" scale and asked how likely they would be to watch COACH again. Those who had seen COACH before this viewing compared it to COACH episodes seen in the Spring and Summer.

FINDINGS

BEFORE VIEWING
• Approximately two-thirds of the respondents saw COACH this past Spring and/or Summer. Self-reported viewing was equal among Men and Women.

• Among those who saw COACH previously, evaluation of the program was considerably below average among both Men and Women. Women had a somewhat greater "unfavorable" reaction.

	AVG. NEW 1/2 HOUR PROGRAM	SPRING/SUMMER COACH VIEWERS TOTAL	MEN	WOMEN
Favorable	43%	29%	30%	27%
Highly Favorable	17	2	2	2
Unfavorable	19	30	23	35

Figure 7.3   Memo from Capital Cities/ABC outlining research results for new episodes of *Coach*.

sor. In Spring 1990, expressing its pleasure, ABC ordered three additional episodes in order to have sufficient original shows to broadcast during the season. At long last, *Coach* established itself as a successful network television series.

- 2 -

AFTER VIEWING

A. Comparison to Last Season
- Over half the respondents who viewed the two new episodes considered it to be better than the episodes viewers recalled seeing previously. This was especially so among Women (61% "Better").

New Episodes Compared
To Ones Saw Before......

	Total	Men	Women
Better	56%	51%	61%
About the Same	40	45	35
Not as Good	4	4	4

- In all, virtually everyone (96%) agreed that the new episodes were as good as, or better than, last season's.

B. Evaluation of New Episodes
- Consequently, evaluation of the new episodes was significantly better than previously reported among both Men and Women.

Evaluation of New Episodes

	Total		Men		Women	
	Before Viewing	After Viewing	Before Viewing	After Viewing	Before Viewing	After Viewing
Favorable	29%	51%	30%	48%	27%	55%
Highly Favorable	2	10	2	8	2	12
Unfavorable	30	14	23	14	35	15

- Though "highly favorable" reaction is still somewhat below average (10% vs. 17% for category norm--New 1/2 Hour), "favorable" and "unfavorable" reaction is slightly better than average ("Favorable"--51% vs 43%; "Unfavorable"--14% vs. 19%).

Figure 7.3   *(continued)*

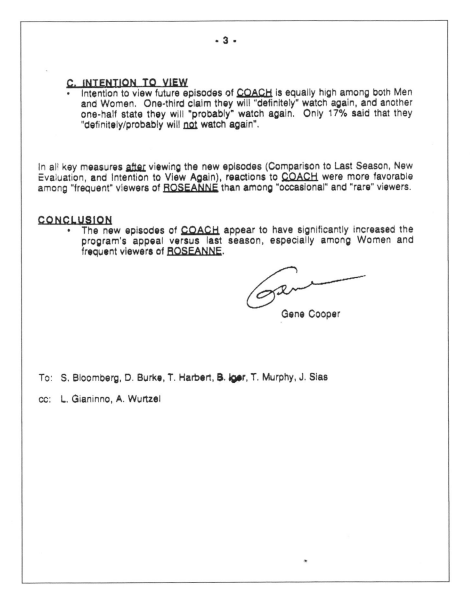

- 3 -

C. INTENTION TO VIEW
- Intention to view future episodes of COACH is equally high among both Men and Women. One-third claim they will "definitely" watch again, and another one-half state they will "probably" watch again. Only 17% said that they "definitely/probably will not watch again".

In all key measures after viewing the new episodes (Comparison to Last Season, New Evaluation, and Intention to View Again), reactions to COACH were more favorable among "frequent" viewers of ROSEANNE than among "occasional" and "rare" viewers.

CONCLUSION
- The new episodes of COACH appear to have significantly increased the program's appeal versus last season, especially among Women and frequent viewers of ROSEANNE.

Gene Cooper

To: S. Bloomberg, D. Burke, T. Harbert, B. Iger, T. Murphy, J. Sias

cc: L. Gianinno, A. Wurtzel

Figure 7.3 *(continued)*

A Case History of a Dramatic Series, *Law and Order*

8

The Development Process

THE CONCEPT FOR *LAW AND ORDER*

The pilot story for Law and Order *is told through the eyes of the two police officers assigned to the case and the two prosecuting attorneys who follow the case to its conclusion. The police officers are older detective-sergeant Max Greevey and younger detective Mike Logan. The prosecuting attorneys are assistant district attorney Ben Stone and his assistant district attorney Paul Robinette. Deliberately, there are no scenes without one of the principal characters present. The audience learns information only when it is revealed to the principal characters.*

In the pilot story, Greevey and Logan arrive on a crime scene, where a politically connected individual has been robbed and murdered. Tracking the perpetrators, they learn that the victim had been shot before the robbery. District attorneys Stone and Robinette are assigned to the case. Working with the prosecutors, they uncover a trail of coverup and police corruption at the highest levels. The four leading characters, working together, trap the mob leader responsible for the killing, along with his illicit political cohorts. The final scene features DA Stone delivering his opening remarks at the trial.

THE DEVELOPMENT OF *LAW AND ORDER*

A television pilot can be developed in any number of ways. This particular series was initiated in 1988 through a conversation between Barry Diller, president of the new Fox Television Network, and Sidney Sheinberg, president of MCA, the parent organization of Universal Studios. In that discussion, Diller recalled an old ABC show produced by Universal in 1963 called *Arrest and Trial*. During those early years, Diller was an executive at ABC and Sheinberg was head of Universal Television. The series *Arrest and Trial* was a 90-minute drama divided into two halves. The first followed police who battled a crime and busted the criminals. The second half focused on the lawyers who represented the criminals in trial. It was a short-lived series and was forgotten by most everyone—except TV trivia buffs and Barry Diller. In his new position, Diller thought a new one-hour version might be an intriguing series to establish the presence of the fledgling Fox network.

At Universal, Kerry McCluggage, president of Universal Television, had been discussing with producer Dick Wolf the idea of a one-hour show composed of two half-hour segments. In their early discussions, they were thinking of a medical drama, but police drama was also under consideration. Wolf had been one of the key writers on *Hill Street Blues* for MTM, wrote action features *(Masquerade),* and subsequently joined the Universal producer roster, where he wrote and executive produced the fourth year of *Miami Vice*.

Sid Sheinberg discussed Diller's idea with Kerry McCluggage who subsequently contacted Dick Wolf. Wolf was more than interested. A newly conceptualized version of the *Arrest and Trial* concept was very attractive to him.

Since everyone's memory—including Barry Diller's—was dim about the old show, a 16mm print of it was excised from the Universal film vaults, and it was transferred to half-inch videotape. In that form, it was screened for Dick Wolf and Universal executives.

To the producer and studio executives, viewing the 20-year-old dramatic series revealed a great deal about evolutionary changes in the medium. The original series was shot in black and white, and the production seemed painfully outmoded and slow paced—especially when compared to high-tech 1988. Two decades earlier, there were few color television sets and ABC did not even broadcast in color. The quality of broadcast transmission was relatively weak, television sets were not technologically complex, and sound quality was erratic. Given that production context, producers relied heavily on close-ups of the actors, spending little time on atmosphere or set decoration. Television truly consisted of "talking heads."

Even more revealing was the series' depiction of the U.S. criminal justice system. Produced in the "liberal" 1960s the first half of the episode focused on the efforts of the policemen, led by Ben Gazzara, who arrested the felon. The second half featured Chuck Conners, a defense attorney, proving the police were wrong. The criminal was misunderstood, and the felon's release was won. From the perspective of the late 1980s, where the criminal justice system was perceived as overburdened and ineffective, this seemed an exercise in judicial frustration.

Producer Dick Wolf was convinced that any new version of the concept must be more equitable in its depiction of police and the district attorneys. The Universal development executives wholeheartedly agreed.

CONCEPTUALIZATION: THE BEGINNING OF THE DEVELOPMENT PROCESS

Dick Wolf spent the following weeks developing the new show and its core of characters. It was agreed that the pilot should be 60 minutes in length, with equally divided stories between police and lawyers.

Deciding on the Length of the Pilot

As explained earlier, the decision to develop a one-hour pilot impacts significantly on potential revenues. A one-hour pilot simply will not have the same broad distribution appeal as a dramatic two-hour show. Still, Dick Wolf and Universal executives felt that a 60-minute version of *Law and Order* would be much closer to the creative vision of the show.

Wolf also felt that the uniqueness of the show's format would be appealing to network schedulers. In recent seasons, networks expressed interest in half-hour dramatic programming, but could not find suitable projects for airing. Networks formulate compatible programming in hour blocks, and need compatible programs for half-hour dramas. Dick Wolf analyzed the problem this way.

> The problem with doing half-hour dramas is "What do you do with the other half-hour?" You don't want to program a sitcom and drama in the same block, so you're forced to find a mate. And out of that grew the idea of doing a one-hour show which could be split in two— to give two discrete stories in the same hour.[1]

---

[1]Quotes in this chapter attributed to Dick Wolf are from personal communication in 1988.

The producer and the studio agreed that a one-hour pilot would be most consistent with the creative style of the series.

Deciding on the Atmosphere

As for the series atmosphere, Wolf decided that it should be docudrama in nature. The stories, while fictional, would appear as real and current as the daily news headlines. The cast of recurring characters could be large, but the show would focus on the two police detectives in the first half and the two district attorneys in the second half. The police and the DAs would appear in at least one scene of each other's sequences. Dick Wolf also wanted to minimize courtroom scenes, while focusing on behind-the-scenes activities of the attorneys.

The new project, titled *Law and Order,* was pitched to Barry Diller and the Fox Network program executives. The reaction was lukewarm. A few days later they called to "pass" on the project. In the intervening time, Barry Diller had decided that the Fox Network should focus only on half-hour projects, both comedy and drama. *Law and Order* did not fit that mandate.

The postmortem at Universal was traumatic. Dick Wolf felt that he had developed an unusually viable show, an attitude shared by Universal executives. It was decided to take the concept to CBS. That network's ratings were declining, and it was badly in need of new programs in all time periods. Given the realistic style desired by Dick Wolf, *Law and Order* could only be aired in late time periods, and CBS had those openings. NBC, on the other hand, was not likely to change its evening schedule. It was having success with its 10 P.M. programming, and would probably replace only the one show, *St. Elsewhere,* whose producers wanted to call it quits. The third alternative was ABC, but its programmers frequently voiced disdain for "cop shows," and were adamant in the belief that successful television featured characterization above storytelling. This "high-concept" story-based "cop show" would repel, rather than attract them.

The presentation of the idea at CBS to vice-president of drama development executive Pat Faulstich and his assistants went well. The approval to proceed to script was received the next day.

Wolf worked extensively on the script to convey the atmosphere, pacing, and story action. Upon receiving the first draft of the script, CBS immediately approved the project to proceed to film. Delighted with the progress, Dick Wolf commenced his preproduction activities.

DEVELOPMENT: THE PREPARATIONS
FOR ACTUAL PRODUCTION

Dick Wolf had always conceived the series as taking place in New York City. He strongly felt that the energy and ambience of the Big Apple were essential to complement the mood he wished to establish. But shooting a series in New York is difficult and expensive. Fortunately, Universal-TV had much recent experience. *The Equalizer* was in its third year, and the production team had learned how to shoot efficiently in the city. Jim McAdams, executive producer of *The Equalizer*, agreed to help the *Law and Order* production staff. He offered to share offices and key personnel and to assist in the production of the *Law and Order* pilot.

Dick Wolf contacted the New York City film commission to expedite clearances for location shooting in the city. While the commission was most helpful during the pilot preparation and production stages, Wolf realized he would need as much assurance as possible to convince Universal-TV he could manage the entire series production in New York. He wrote a letter to the mayor of New York to see if he could help in expediting production problems for the series. See Figure 8.1. The Mayor's Office responded positively and reinforced the producer's decision to shoot entirely on location in the city.

Location shooting, however, is costly. After analyzing the script's production needs, Dick Wolf utilized several techniques to arrive at a realistic working budget. (See Chapter 3 for the discussion of budget-control techniques.) Through tight production control, some union concessions, and the utilization of a National Association of Broadcast Employees and Technicians (NABET) crew in Manhattan (as opposed to the traditional International Alliance of Theatrical Stage Employees (IATSE) film union), Wolf compiled a budget acceptable to Universal executives. *Law and Order* was given the green light to proceed to film.

Needing a line producer to help, Dick Wolf wanted someone who could handle all the technical chores and work creatively with the staff and crew. He wrote a memo to Kerry McCluggage, head of Universal-TV, requesting that Joe Stern be hired in that capacity (a list of the producer's credits was attached). See Figure 8.2. The memo was written on *Miami Vice* stationery since *Law and Order* did not yet have its own letterhead or production office. Joe Stern was approved and hired as the line producer for the pilot.

Examining the Concept

We interviewed Dick Wolf in New York on the second day of pilot production. He was enthusiastic, talking about breaking new ground

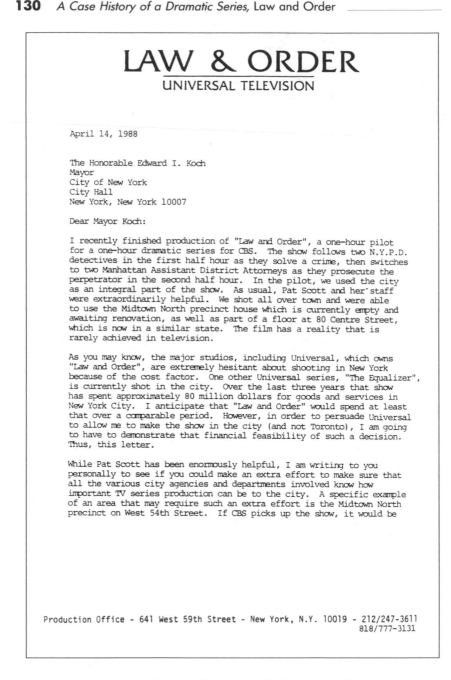

LAW & ORDER
UNIVERSAL TELEVISION

April 14, 1988

The Honorable Edward I. Koch
Mayor
City of New York
City Hall
New York, New York 10007

Dear Mayor Koch:

I recently finished production of "Law and Order", a one-hour pilot
for a one-hour dramatic series for CBS. The show follows two N.Y.P.D.
detectives in the first half hour as they solve a crime, then switches
to two Manhattan Assistant District Attorneys as they prosecute the
perpetrator in the second half hour. In the pilot, we used the city
as an integral part of the show. As usual, Pat Scott and her staff
were extraordinarily helpful. We shot all over town and were able
to use the Midtown North precinct house which is currently empty and
awaiting renovation, as well as part of a floor at 80 Centre Street,
which is now in a similar state. The film has a reality that is
rarely achieved in television.

As you may know, the major studios, including Universal, which owns
"Law and Order", are extremely hesitant about shooting in New York
because of the cost factor. One other Universal series, "The Equalizer",
is currently shot in the city. Over the last three years that show
has spent approximately 80 million dollars for goods and services in
New York City. I anticipate that "Law and Order" would spend at least
that over a comparable period. However, in order to persuade Universal
to allow me to make the show in the city (and not Toronto), I am going
to have to demonstrate that financial feasibility of such a decision.
Thus, this letter.

While Pat Scott has been enormously helpful, I am writing to you
personally to see if you could make an extra effort to make sure that
all the various city agencies and departments involved know how
important TV series production can be to the city. A specific example
of an area that may require such an extra effort is the Midtown North
precinct on West 54th Street. If CBS picks up the show, it would be

Production Office - 641 West 59th Street - New York, N.Y. 10019 - 212/247-3611
818/777-3131

Figure 8.1   Letter from Dick Wolf to Mayor Ed Koch regarding location shooting in New York.

-2-

very helpful to be able to shoot at least the first four or five
episodes in the precinct. This would require a short postponement
of the scheduled start of renovations. Clearly, a word from your
office would be extraordinarily helpful. Many people have high
hopes for "Law and Order" and feel that it may be an important
evolution of the hour genre. It's a show that should be kept in
New York City. I hope you'll be able to help me do that.

Sincerely,

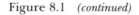

Dick Wolf
Executive Producer
"Law and Order"

DW/dt

cc: Pat Scott

Figure 8.1 *(continued)*

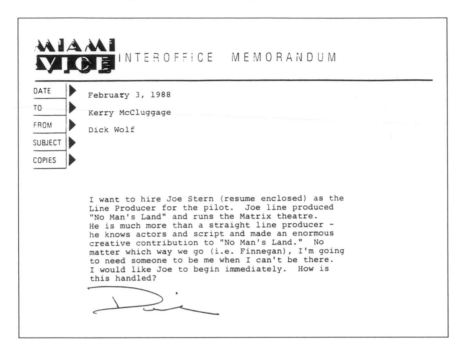

MIAMI VICE INTEROFFICE MEMORANDUM

DATE ▶	February 3, 1988
TO ▶	Kerry McCluggage
FROM ▶	Dick Wolf
SUBJECT ▶	
COPIES ▶	

I want to hire Joe Stern (resume enclosed) as the Line Producer for the pilot. Joe line produced "No Man's Land" and runs the Matrix theatre. He is much more than a straight line producer - he knows actors and script and made an enormous creative contribution to "No Man's Land." No matter which way we go (i.e. Finnegan), I'm going to need someone to be me when I can't be there. I would like Joe to begin immediately. How is this handled?

Figure 8.2   Interoffice memo from Dick Wolf requesting that Joe Stern be hired as line producer.

with the series. At the same time, he was mindful of the program's reality-based antecedents.

> Its ancestors are unquestionably *Dragnet, N.Y.P.D., Hill Street Blues,* the reality-based . . . historical cop shows that in their era have been the cutting edge of realism.

Wolf was eager to present television audiences with a fresh point of view about police investigation.

> This allows [us] to do away with a lot of conventions which, frankly, I think are clichéd. [Those conventions] have always bored me and annoyed me about cop shows. Every week they have to get in a car chase or shoot somebody. They have to be, essentially, comic-book visions of what crime fighters are, and present a glossed over image of how crime operates. . . . I've wanted to do a cop show for a long time where the principals never have to fire a gun.

Having worked on *Hill Street Blues,* Wolf was frustrated when that series ultimately gave way to television conventions.

I think *Hill Street* started out [innovatively]. . . . They [wanted to] present a cop show, a crime show, where a wash of it was closer to the truth than most of the programming on television. But they gave up on that too early.

For *Law and Order,* the producer was committed to a reality-based portrayal of the judicial system.

The aim of the series is to show how the criminal justice system works. . . . [It's not that] 90 percent of the shows won't go to trial, but a large part of the mix is going to be either successful or unsuccessful resolutions to cases—without going through a jury trial.

One of the delights of the *Law and Order* format, to Wolf, was the flexibility of its storytelling format.

The wonderful thing about the format is that it frees you up to do almost anything. For example, there may easily be a show where the prosecutors are in the first half. . . . They go to trial, and the case is thrown out on a technicality. They need new evidence to take it back to court, where they know they can get a conviction. And it is up to Greevey and Logan [the two cops] to come up with that piece of information. They're following a trail that's already well worn, looking for a new opening. There are also going to be cases that they lose.

Deciding on a Story-Driven Show

Dick Wolf was also excited about the opportunity to break many contemporary television conventions. Beyond its format, *Law and Order* was deliberately designed to exploit this opportunity. A key element was its emphasis of story over characterization: "It's totally story-driven, which has allowed us to do certain things that I've always [wanted to try]. I've objected to [the dominance of character-driven stories] in television shows."

During the era of *Arrest and Trial* (1960s), television was very much a story medium. While characters were naturally important, story was paramount. In contemporary series television, story/plot has become secondary to characterization. Network program researchers have convinced development executives that viewers tune in week after week to watch characters they like, not stories. Therefore, the network development process strongly focuses on the likes, lives, loves, and eccentricities of the leading characters. But Dick Wolf designed *Law and Order* as a show focusing on the story. Its leading characters are bound by the story, and characterization becomes subordinate.

> If the story is strong enough to drive the action—and certainly in the pilot it's an onion that has the layers peeled off—it gives you an opportunity to do a style of television that, initially probably, will be quite disconcerting. You're taking away a lot of the comfort factors that people have come to expect when they're watching a show. You [normally] get respites in between when cars drive up [or leads] walk into a building. *[Law and Order]* is going to be intensely story-driven and you're going to go from plot point to plot point.

With the networks facing escalating competition from cable, pay television, home video, and other venues, Wolf wanted to break the traditional network rules. He felt that *Law and Order* would seem fresh and fascinating against the flood of conventional character-oriented series. Moreover, while shifting the emphasis from characters to story, he was convinced that the characters would not be displaced or diminished. The viewer would not see the characters at home but would experience the characters' personalities, concerns, and desires against the foreground of work. The television audience would come to know these characters over the course of the television season, just as they've come to know colleagues in their everyday jobs.

> This is a job-oriented program. There is no question that, over the course of the entire season—because of a snatch of a phone call, an answer to a question that's asked off camera unseen—you will pick up enough bits and pieces about the four principals' lives. You will know as much about them as you do in a more freewheeling type of point-of-view show. I honestly believe that there is not going to be a lack of personality in these characters. But it is not the aim of the show to give them scenes during which they can expound on what wonderful, or troubled, or tortured, or altruistic people they are.

In that sense, Dick Wolf chose what writers call a "closed" story structure, as opposed to an "open" story for the show. In Hollywood jargon, a closed story is the classic mystery structure of the "whodunit" in books, plays, and motion pictures. The only information the viewer receives is information obtained by the principal characters.

In the open story, the viewer is provided with information that the principal characters do not have. In some instances, like *Columbo*, the audience quickly learns the identity of the murderer. The crux of the open mystery story is to see how one side triumphs over the other.

The closed style of *Law and Order* specifically complements the pilot's story-driven emphasis.

> There are going to be some conventional shots, but basically the audience only receives the information that the principals receive. In other words . . . one of the four principals is on screen 100 percent of the time in one way or another.

The first few pages of the pilot script written by Dick Wolf demonstrate the power of the story-driven premise. (See Figure 8.3.) The "teaser" (first few pages that will hook the viewer) sets up the action and the characters quickly. It's interesting that Wolf still felt compelled to delineate the nature and background of Detective Max Greevey and his partner Mike Logan as they are first introduced to the viewer. After the teaser, the script builds its relentless pursuit of the "bad guys," through the drive and professionalism of the four protagonists. (See Appendix B for the complete pilot script.)

The pilot script is reviewed by legal research staff at the studio to clear names and dialogue references, as well as location references. The memo in Figure 8.4 was sent to Dick Wolf concerning changes that might be necessary in the script. In this case, a reference to "Simonize Jackson" is considered derogatory and needs to be changed. On the second page of the memo, specific script pages and scenes are delineated for the producer to review and revise as necessary.

Style, Setting, and Visual Impact

Dick Wolf was intent on having the visual style and look of the show match the unconventional nature of the concept and script. To further reinforce the show's realism, he insisted on two things: filming in New York City, and abandoning the conventional procedure of shooting on sound stages. Shooting in New York made his work as producer more difficult, but he felt it was integral to the show.

> As I said when we first went to CBS, the bible of the show was the front page of the Daily News. . . . There is a story a day in New York. Most other cities have a story a week, and many of them have a story a month. That's [what I want to capture in production]—the magnitude of what happens [in New York] as a daily occurrence.

Shooting on location tends to invite a multitude of unforeseen production problems. But Dick Wolf felt that sound stages and sets would not be right for the reality he sought in *Law and Order*. "It's all 'practical.' I

LAW AND ORDER

EVERYBODY'S FAVORITE BAGMAN

TEASER

FADE IN

EXT. WAREHOUSE DISTRICT - NIGHT

Deserted streets. The intermittent high pitched whine of
garbage trucks compacting the day's industrial waste. The
background jabbering of a police radio is a continuous,
unemotional chronicler of the night.

                    POLICE RADIO (V.O.)
            ...340 West 26th...see the
            manager...man with a knife...all
            available units sector eight...Code
            3...shots fired...hit and run, Park
            and Astor, pedestrian down...

                                        CUT TO

INT. PATROL CAR - NIGHT

Their P.O.V. is through the windshield, we can hear, but
not see, the two patrol cops, as the car cruises the
industrial area.

                    POLICE RADIO
            Sector Four, nearest unit, domestic
            disturbance...540 West three
            one...3rd floor rear...

                    DRIVER
            I want the Coupe De Ville...I'm
            happy with the velour, not even
            leather...what do I end up with? A
            goddam Nipponese bug box...

The unit turns a corner into an alley bordering a series of
loading docks. Nosed into one of them is a Mercedes 560
SEL. As the headlights wash over the car, two black
seventeen year-olds, "Simonize" Jackson and Tremaine Lewis,
bolt from the Benz and head down the alley.

                    SHOTGUN COP (V.O.)
            Must've forgotten their keys...

His hand moves into frame and hits the lights and siren as
the V8 opens up and the patrol car leaps forward.

                                        CONTINUED

Figure 8.3   Excerpt from *Law and Order* final pilot script.

2

CONTINUED

Tremaine turns, sees the black and white hurtling down the alley and starts climbing the chain link fence that runs along one side. Simonize joins him as the cops fly past the Mercedes.

SHOTGUN COP'S POV:

Charles Halsey, an overweight fifty year-old, is sprawled half in and half out of the car, the entire front of his Vicuna coat blood stained.

                    SHOTGUN COP
          Hold it...we got a vic...

                                        CUT TO

EXT. ALLEY - NIGHT

The patrol car comes to a screeching halt. Tremaine and Simonize roll over the top of the chain link fence and drop into the courtyard of a deserted tenement. They pick themselves up and run into the gutted building. As the shotgun cop runs to Halsey the camera follows the driver as he takes off after the two perps, scaling the chain link fence, dropping into the courtyard and running to the door of the tenement. He stops, sticks his head into the hallway, comes back out and unholsters his gun. He wipes a thin film of sweat off his upper lip, and swallows off a sudden case of dry mouth. This is a cop's nightmare and the camera is right with him, showing us why -- the building is dark and ominous.

                                        CUT TO

INT. TENEMENT - NIGHT - CONTINUOUS

The driver takes a deep breath, listens to the thundering silence, races through the first floor and continues out to the street, the camera with him, step for step, as leather squeaks and handcuffs jingle.

EXT. TENEMENT - NIGHT - CONTINUOUS

The driver comes out of the tenement and checks out the bombed-out looking street. It's totally deserted. Breathing hard, he holsters his weapon and puts his fists on his hips, a portrait of total frustration, as he tries to get his breathing back under control.

                                        CUT TO

Figure 8.3 *(continued)*

3

INT. BODEGA - NIGHT

Detective Sergeant Max Greevey, 40's, is counting out four dollars and twenty-eight cents from a clumped up mass of small bills and change cupped in a ham sized paw. Three inches of cheap cigar are burning in the corner of his mouth. He's wearing a two hundred dollar suit and a tie a blind man wouldn't be seen in. What can't be seen is the mind, which on one level is a cornucopia of seemingly useless information, and on another is a veritable data base of Police information. He's been married to his high school sweetheart for twenty years and has three daughters, nineteen, fifteen and six, all of whom can wrap him around their little fingers. He's also an NBA fanatic, and a Knicks fan, an unfortunate combination that has cost him thousands in lost bets since the team's glory days of the early seventies. Greevey's been a cop for eighteen years and has seen everything twice, but he can't stand seeing the bad guys win. He squints at Jesus, the clerk, through a swirl of cigar smoke and shakes his head in disbelief.

>   GREEVEY
>   Since when's a ham sandwich two
>   seventy-five, Jesus?

>   JESUS
>   Since last Friday.

>   GREEVEY
>   Didn't know ptomaine had gone up...

The line goes right over Jesus' head.

>   JESUS
>   We don't use none of that...it's all
>   home made.

There's an impatient honk from outside. We follow him out the door.

>   CONTINUOUS

EXT. STREET - NIGHT

A green Plymouth Fury with no chrome's parked at the curb. Detective Mike Logan, early 30's, is a good looking Irishman with a temper to match. He's been Greevey's partner for the past two years. There's a mutual trust and respect, but it's a professional relationship - these guys don't spend any more time with each other than the job demands. They don't confide their secret fears to each other, they don't socialize, but they both know that the other would put his life on the line if the situation required it.

>   CONTINUED

Figure 8.3   *(continued)*

4

CONTINUED

Logan has a B.S. in Police Science, reads books, likes
Woody Allen's early comedies, has a Marine Corps screaming
eagle tattooed on his forearm, drinks Bushmills, and has a
mostly monogamous relationship with a uniformed
policewoman. He's never been married, but he has a five
year-old daughter that he supports and sees. He's putting
a bubble gum light on the roof of the unmarked car as
Greevey comes out of the bodega, pulls open the passenger
door and climbs in.

>   GREEVEY
> What?

>   LOGAN
> We got a 211...could turn into a
> homicide.

>   GREEVEY
> Vic conscious?

>   LOGAN
>   (shaking his head)
> Ambulance is on the way.

Greevey takes the lid off his coffee, sips and nods for
Logan to drive.

>   GREEVEY
> <u>Around</u> the potholes...suit's just
> back from the cleaner.

>   CUT TO

EXT. LOADING DOCK - NIGHT

Halsey, unconscious, is being lifted into the back of an
ambulance. Logan looks at the paramedic.

>   LOGAN
> Odds?

>   PARAMEDIC
> Fifty-fifty...but I'm an optimist.

Greevey looks down at the bloodless face.

>   GREEVEY
> I've seen this guy...
>   (calling uniform
>   over)
> Hey, Hochmeyer.

One of the uniforms leaves the Mercedes and crosses to the
ambulance.

>   CONTINUED

Figure 8.3   *(continued)*

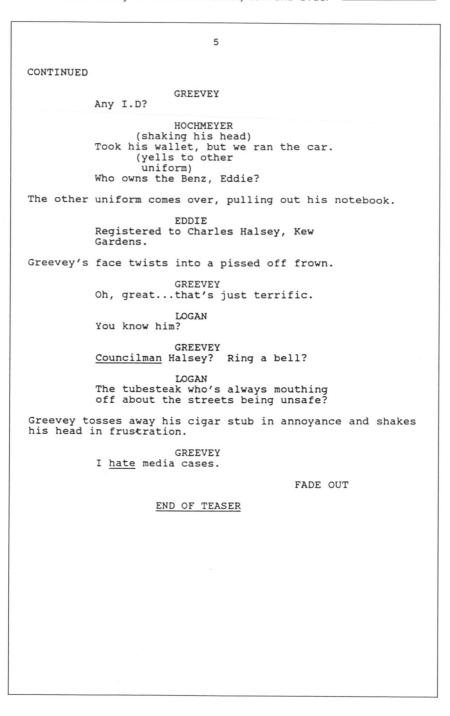

5

CONTINUED

                    GREEVEY
          Any I.D?

                    HOCHMEYER
               (shaking his head)
          Took his wallet, but we ran the car.
               (yells to other
                uniform)
          Who owns the Benz, Eddie?

The other uniform comes over, pulling out his notebook.

                    EDDIE
          Registered to Charles Halsey, Kew
          Gardens.

Greevey's face twists into a pissed off frown.

                    GREEVEY
          Oh, great...that's just terrific.

                    LOGAN
          You know him?

                    GREEVEY
          Councilman Halsey? Ring a bell?

                    LOGAN
          The tubesteak who's always mouthing
          off about the streets being unsafe?

Greevey tosses away his cigar stub in annoyance and shakes
his head in frustration.

                    GREEVEY
          I hate media cases.

                              FADE OUT

                    END OF TEASER

Figure 8.3   *(continued)*

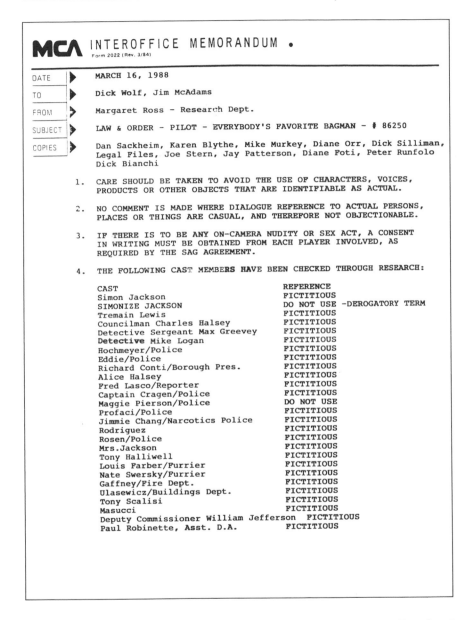

MCA INTEROFFICE MEMORANDUM •
Form 2022 (Rev. 3/84)

DATE ▶	MARCH 16, 1988
TO ▶	Dick Wolf, Jim McAdams
FROM ▶	Margaret Ross – Research Dept.
SUBJECT ▶	LAW & ORDER - PILOT - EVERYBODY'S FAVORITE BAGMAN - # 86250
COPIES ▶	Dan Sackheim, Karen Blythe, Mike Murkey, Diane Orr, Dick Silliman, Legal Files, Joe Stern, Jay Patterson, Diane Foti, Peter Runfolo Dick Bianchi

1. CARE SHOULD BE TAKEN TO AVOID THE USE OF CHARACTERS, VOICES, PRODUCTS OR OTHER OBJECTS THAT ARE IDENTIFIABLE AS ACTUAL.

2. NO COMMENT IS MADE WHERE DIALOGUE REFERENCE TO ACTUAL PERSONS, PLACES OR THINGS ARE CASUAL, AND THEREFORE NOT OBJECTIONABLE.

3. IF THERE IS TO BE ANY ON-CAMERA NUDITY OR SEX ACT, A CONSENT IN WRITING MUST BE OBTAINED FROM EACH PLAYER INVOLVED, AS REQUIRED BY THE SAG AGREEMENT.

4. THE FOLLOWING CAST MEMBERS HAVE BEEN CHECKED THROUGH RESEARCH:

CAST	REFERENCE	
Simon Jackson	FICTITIOUS	
SIMONIZE JACKSON	DO NOT USE	–DEROGATORY TERM
Tremain Lewis	FICTITIOUS	
Councilman Charles Halsey	FICTITIOUS	
Detective Sergeant Max Greevey	FICTITIOUS	
Detective Mike Logan	FICTITIOUS	
Hochmeyer/Police	FICTITIOUS	
Eddie/Police	FICTITIOUS	
Richard Conti/Borough Pres.	FICTITIOUS	
Alice Halsey	FICTITIOUS	
Fred Lasco/Reporter	FICTITIOUS	
Captain Cragen/Police	FICTITIOUS	
Maggie Pierson/Police	DO NOT USE	
Profaci/Police	FICTITIOUS	
Jimmie Chang/Narcotics Police	FICTITIOUS	
Rodriguez	FICTITIOUS	
Rosen/Police	FICTITIOUS	
Mrs.Jackson	FICTITIOUS	
Tony Halliwell	FICTITIOUS	
Louis Farber/Furrier	FICTITIOUS	
Nate Swersky/Furrier	FICTITIOUS	
Gaffney/Fire Dept.	FICTITIOUS	
Ulasewicz/Buildings Dept.	FICTITIOUS	
Tony Scalisi	FICTITIOUS	
Masucci	FICTITIOUS	
Deputy Commissioner William Jefferson	FICTITIOUS	
Paul Robinette, Asst. D.A.	FICTITIOUS	

Figure 8.4 Interoffice memo from research department regarding legal clearances.

```
CONTINUATION OF # 4                    3-16-88        #86250


CAST                                   REFERENCE
Ben Stone/D.A.                         FICTITIOUS
Edward Cosmatos                        FICTITIOUS
Sarah Nicksey/Pediatrician             FICTITIOUS
Judge Robards                          FICTITIOUS
Judge Kapstein                         FICTITIOUS
Judge Rosen                            FICTITIOUS
Judge Gonzales                         FICTITIOUS
Warren Wentzel/Lawyer                  FICTITIOUS
Eric Halsey                            FICTITIOUS
Alicia Heslin                          FICTITIOUS
Alfred Wentworth/D.A.                  FICTITIOUS
Judge Ichaso                           FICTITIOUS
Dr. Goldberg                           FICTITIOUS
John McCormack/Ass. U.S. Attorney      FICTITIOUS
Jackson                                FICTITIOUS
Judge Falk                             FICTITIOUS
Deputy Mayor Kostmeyer                 FICTITIOUS
Deputy Mayor VanDam                    FICTITIOUS
Vinny Capelleti                        FICTITIOUS


5.  THE FOLLOWING ITEMS HAVE BEEN CHECKED THROUGH RESEARCH:

P / SC                                 REFERENCE
1    1                                 340 West 26th St. - DO NOT
                                       USE _INSTEAD-1340 W. 26th.
1                                      Park & Astor - FICTITIOUS
1                                      540 W. 31th St.-DO NOT USE-
                                       INSTEAD - 1540 W. 31st
1                                      Nipponese Bug Box -  DO NOT USE
                                       A DEROGATORY TERM
8                                      Diamond Rolex-CASUAL REFERENCE
9                                      Nig-Kids - A DEROGATORY TERM
16                                     Air Jordan Basketball Shoe -
                                       AVOID IDENTIFICATION OF  BRAND
22                                     Meryl Streep -MAY BE CONSTRUED
                                       AS DEROGATORY
22                                     Whoopi Goldberg - MAY BE
                                       CONSTRUED AS DEROGATORY
23                                     Kornbluth Furs - FICTITIOUS
25                                     Karnak - CASUAL REFERENCE
26                                     Clarence Darrow - CASUAL REF.
29                                     Spuds Mackenzie - DO NOT USE
                                       BECAUSE OF COPYRIGHT
35                                     Lindy's Cafe - CASUAL REFERENCE
39                                     Carnegie Collections Com. -
                                       FICTITIOUS
40                                     Brademas - DO NOT USE
52                                     Alberto's Clam House -
                                       FICTITIOUS
56                                     Rotary Club Meeting -
                                       CASUAL REFERENCE

COMMUNITY HOSPITAL OF NEW YORK - FICTITIOUS
```

Figure 8.4   *(continued)*

hope it will continue to be all practical. I don't like sound stages. I don't like sets. I have never yet seen a set that is as good as a practical location if you can get it."

The producer took other unusual steps to heighten the perception

```
CONTINUATION OF # 5                          3-16-88

Provence Rest. - REAL - 38 Macdougal - 212-4757500

IF GOING TO BE USED LOCATION AGREEMENT MUST BE SIGNED.


P / SC                              REFERENCE
1                                   EXT. WAREHOUSE DISTRICT - NIGHT
2                                   EXT. ALLEY - NIGHT
2                                   EXT. TENEMENT - NIGHT
3                                   EXT. STREET - NIGHT
4                                   EXT. LOADING DOCK - NIGHT
9                                   EXT. HOSPITAL - NIGHT
16                                  EXT. TENEMENT #2 - DAY
17                                  EXT. ALLEY-DAY
19                                  EXT. LOADING DOCK
21                                  EXT. HIGH RENT SHOPPING AREA
28                                  EXT. APARTMENT BUILDING
48                                  EXT. PARK
56                                  EXT. ALBERTO'S CLAM HOUSE
```

Figure 8.4 *(continued)*

of reality. He wanted to use a hand-held camera, rather than a traditionally mounted camera on tripod, dolly, or crane. He also wanted to shoot large close-ups, to imprint a realistic style for viewers. He sought to break traditional conventions of television.

There is a very distinctive style that we're going for. Part of it is the hand-held camera, but part of it is a very immediate sense. In other words, large close-ups. People close to camera. People so close to camera that we [can] only have part of their heads in some of the closeups. . . . The camera becomes a participant in what's going on, but unobtrusively. [Viewers] shouldn't notice the camera work. What you should notice is that you are seeing things you don't normally get to see. Because you are usually stuck in that nice television "upframing"—you see two or three people from halfway up the stomach. You are used to certain percentages and proportions, which we have deliberately destroyed.

The production note that appears before the first page of the pilot script is shown in Figure 8.5. It clearly sets the style, setting, and visual impact Dick Wolf wanted.

The amount of footage shot with a hand-held camera was to be extensive, by design. "It's going to be decidedly different because of the enormous percentage of hand-held cameras. That's 90 percent of the show now."

With the decision to shoot practical locations, to use a hand-held

---

PRODUCTION NOTE

"Law and Order" represents a conscious shift away from many of the conventions of one hour dramatic series. Aside from the format change of following one case through the criminal justice system by telling two discrete stories with two separate sets of stars (Police and D.A.'s), there will be a visual difference which will help set the tone of the series. It is anticipated that the show will be shot on 16mm Panaflex and finished on tape, the aim being to achieve a cinema verite, semi-documentary look, replete with hand held camera and naturalistic lighting. In line with this look, almost all locations, with the exception of the requisite standing sets, will be practical. In addition, there will be an editorial style of "hard cutting". The series will avoid the use of transition shots of cars driving up, exterior establishing shots of buildings, people walking into rooms, etc. This style will also influence pace, which will, of necessity, be quick, as we will move from story point to story point. In addition, there will be a locked P.O.V. -- the audience will see or hear only what the cops or D.A.'s do. The fact that each half hour will essentially be telling the same type of story that might be seen in an entire hour of a typical cop show, necessitates a certain economy of style which will, in turn, become the series' stylistic signature.

Figure 8.5   Production note from beginning of *Law and Order* final pilot script.

camera, and to shoot in cinema verité style, it was an easy extension for Dick Wolf to decide to film *Law and Order* in 16mm film, rather than television's conventional 35mm format. "You're getting a slightly less rich negative on 16mm, which works to our advantage in terms of what we're doing. A normal process for delivery of a product to the network for air is . . . 35mm film." The procedure was unusual, especially for a large studio like Universal, where facilities are standardized on 35mm film. The studio had only one screening room with a 16mm projector, and there were no 16mm editing facilities on the lot. Dick Wolf solved the latter problem in a unique way.

> What we're doing is shooting on 16mm, editing on 35mm, blowing up. We're getting a 35mm black-and-white duplicate, which is actually what we're going to edit on, because it speeds up the process. That 35mm black-and-white dupe is then matched with the 16mm negative.

To further distinguish the visual appearance of *Law and Order,* Dick Wolf filmed test scenes in 16mm and then transferred them to videotape for special treatment. "We get a tape transfer of the 16mm answer print, which is a fresh print. We then take that tape transfer and we have an enormous number of options." The producer was intrigued by the ability to manipulate the filmed image electronically, once transferred to videotape and entered into an electronic editing system.

> You have to see to appreciate what the difference is in the look. But what happens, somehow, is that you don't have the warmth of film and you don't have the coldness of tape. You've got this weird amalgam, and . . . when I saw it, it's like Eureka! . . . Now, when you have this transfer that looks slightly different, you then get on the [system] and you can add grain, you can take color out.

Lowering the intensity of color saturation was an important side benefit of the process for him.

> We will probably also be taking out a lot of the color, because one of the things I want is a very desaturated look, more what the eye sees than what film sees. What we're used to looking at when you're sitting in front of a Technicolor movie screen, that's not reality.

As a producer, Dick Wolf understood that the visual look of the show projects a subliminal message to the viewer, which can either complement or conflict with the program content. The video technique was appealing, because it allowed him to control the visual appearance of every scene.

It takes an incredible degree of sophistication to achieve that look. And to anybody watching it, who appreciates what is going on, it's like "Wow, that's really unique looking." And it's not unique just to be unique. It's unique because it's creating the feeling that we're trying to establish. You're seeing something that you haven't seen before. I mean the visual style is saying "You've got to look at this differently." We're not presenting you with the normal information flow that you've been given for the past 30 years.

Sound would also become an important component. He chose to use natural sounds to further enhance the realism, not minding if a line or two of dialogue was lost to street noise—so long as the dialogue was not crucial to the storytelling.

For most of the film, Dick Wolf decided against a traditional music score. But music was important to him in establishing the feel of the program. He enlisted the work of Mike Post, who, among many Emmy-award-winning works, composed the theme for *Hill Street Blues.*

I think it's wonderful to be talking to Mike Post, whom I consider the absolutely premiere composer on television. . . . The great thing about the score or the theme that he gave us is that, like *Hill Street,* it's got those five notes that he can twist, turn, manipulate, make happy, sad, long, short, threatening, nonthreatening.

Casting

As conceived by Dick Wolf, *Law and Order* deals with characters in their working environment. Since the audience will only learn about the characters through their work, the casting process was more crucial than normal. The actors chosen for the four principal roles had to appear natural and believable in their parts, convey the professionalism of their professions, and show their characters' attitudes and personality through conversations taking place solely in their work environments.

For *Hill Street Blues* and *Miami Vice,* Dick Wolf spent considerable time with police detectives doing research for stories and learning police attitudes and behavior. It was this experience that led him to George Dzundza for the role of Detective Greevey in *Law and Order.* The actor virtually fit the character description, with an uncanny sense of working the street. He knew how to convey the dimensions of a realistic detective in the job.

We needed a very good actor because . . . detectives are [themselves] good actors. It's part of what they get paid to do. Secondly, we needed somebody who is willing to lay back and not play a television lead.

He has to understand what the demands and the parameters of the role are. And Dzundza, as soon as he was interested, had the part. Because the guy is just an extraordinary actor.

Wolf also liked the fact that George Dzundza was not the typical "pretty boy." It created more realism and authority for the role. "It goes against the stereotype of male lead casting for television. He had to be late forties, not in his thirties, he had to be believable as a guy who had been a New York street detective for a number of years."

Still, the producer realized that for the television marketplace, at least one of the four principal characters had to have "leading man" characteristics. (See Figure 8.6.) Early in the development process he decided it should be Greevey's police partner, Detective Logan. This is how he decided on newcomer Chris Noth for that role:

I didn't want a conventionally pretty looking guy. I did not want the guy who was the pinup guy for five years before this show started. But I needed somebody who was a leading man. And it wasn't that easy to find, because the ones who are leading men by that age are already leading men. And the ones who aren't, are usually not for a reason.

He found the unusual traits of Chris Noth to encompass leading-man looks with credibility in the role.

For the attorneys Stone and Robinette, the producer wanted Michael Moriarty, a well known and respected actor, and Richard Brooks, a relatively unknown black actor (see Figure 8.7). In his decision making, the principal defining criteria were intelligence and antistereotyping.

[I wanted] somebody who went against the cliché of what a prosecutor was supposed to be. Moriarty can be very tough, but what he exudes more than anything else is a mind that's working behind the face. And that's what I really wanted in this part. I didn't want a leading man. I didn't want somebody conventionally handsome. I didn't want somebody who had done a series before, had been a lead in a series.

He was equally specific in his reasons for choosing Richard Brooks:

I wanted a guy who was black, who would symbolize in a sense what is the good part of the criminal justice system—that you can be black, white, yellow. You can work in it; you can succeed in it. I just wanted somebody that would project a very positive black role model, as well as being smart.

Figure 8.6   First half of *Law and Order* final lead casting: George Dzundza (left) and Chris Noth.

Figure 8.7   Second half of *Law and Order* final lead casting: Michael Moriarty (left) and Richard Brooks.

Dick Wolf found exactly the character types he wanted and was satisfied with the credibility of his four leads. Still, the casting process is never a simple one. The actual process for casting *Law and Order* is detailed in the next chapter.

Despite a convoluted development in its earliest stages, *Law and Order* had a relatively easy birth at CBS. All parties were pleased with the progress of the pilot so far. Subsequent events, however, seriously jolted that optimism. Those events are chronicled in the following chapters.

9

The Production Process

Production of the pilot for *Law and Order* presented problems typical of those faced by any producer filming on location, distant from Hollywood sound stages. In this case, however, they were compounded by problems specifically related to the producer's stated production objectives. Dick Wolf sought a distinctive tone—in both the content of the show and in its visual impact. The consequences would have a significant impact throughout the production and postproduction process.

The following chronology highlights the activities of producer Dick Wolf, and examines the problems, choices, and decisions he had to make. The log begins a few days after CBS officially approved the pilot in mid-February 1988 and continues through production and postproduction activities.

Typically, the production schedule for a one-hour dramatic pilot requires 10–14 shooting days, with a realistic schedule of four weeks for the complexities of postproduction. *Law and Order* was scheduled to be filmed March 22–April 5, 1988, and the completed pilot was to be delivered to CBS on May 3, 1988.

As you will see, that date could not be realistically met, given the unfolding needs of production and postproduction.

THE PRODUCER'S DAILY ACTIVITIES

Friday, February 12, 1988

After evaluating a number of excellent choices for directors, Dick Wolf decides on John Patterson. They worked together on *Hill Street Blues* and have a long-established, complementary relationship. The producer sends a memo to Universal executives asking them to expedite the hiring of Patterson, and to follow up on the business deal for line producer Joe Stern. A co-producer, Dan Sackheim, is also hired.

Monday, February 29, 1988

Casting possibilities were initiated by Joan Sittenfield, head of casting for Universal Television. She suggested several actors for each role, and sent Dick Wolf a tape of Eric La Salle, whom she considered "a brilliant young black actor" for the role of Robinette. (See Figure 9.1.) Dick Wolf considers her suggestions and approves actors for "callbacks" and "mix and match." These are the actors now under serious consideration for each role. (See Figure 9.2.)

For the roles of Stone, Greevey, and Robinette, the executive producer is pursuing Michael Moriarty, George Dzundza, and Richard Brooks. For the role of Logan, he is still searching for the right actor. He has not yet committed to Richard Brooks as Robinette. He is thinking about an interesting departure in casting. Originally conceived as a male character, Wolf is now considering a black woman for the part. He will not make a final decision until he has seen Richard Brooks and a black actress read for the role. A highly recommended black actress, Penny Johnson, is flying to L.A. to read.

Today, Dick Wolf calls a meeting with director John Patterson and line producer Joe Stern, to discuss the visual look of the show. He wants to be sure everyone is clear about his intent before principal photography begins. In the first half of the show there will be more point-of-view shots. The camera will essentially follow the policemen (Logan and Greevey), seeing what they see. The second half will focus on the lawyers (Stone and Robinette). Since they already know the facts, the camera will be more of an omniscient observer.

Discussing postproduction, Dick Wolf and Joe Stern consider finishing the show on videotape. But neither of them has ever done that. They are apprehensive about jumping into something new and untried, especially with the May 2, 1988, delivery date to the network so close.

For theme music, a temporary sound track is commonly used, but Wolf wants to make sure that he delivers a completed show to CBS. He's

MCA INTEROFFICE MEMORANDUM .
Form 2022 (Rev. 10/84)

DATE	January 18, 1988
TO	Dick Wolf
FROM	Joan Sittenfield
SUBJECT	LAW AND ORDER
COPIES	Kerry McCluggage
	Dick Lindheim
	Charmaine Balian

As a follow-up to our conversations:

1. Sam Waterston <u>is</u> opening in a play on Broadway in Feburary for a minimum of 6 months.

2. Ray Sharkey is <u>very hot</u> and is being sent every script in town. He would be between $30,000 and $35,000 per episode. I definitely feel he could be a Stone because of the intensity and street intelligence he could bring to the role.

3. I am enclosing a tape of Eric La Salle, a brilliant young black actor I feel would be great for Robinette. Please return ASAP as I need it back quickly.

As we talked about the following are also real possibilities:

        Joe Morton
        Jim McDaniel
        Michael Beach
        Victor Love
        Courtney Vance (not quite as sure of his interest)

4. Scott Glenn is interested in doing a series. Could he be a way to go as Greevey?

5. Bill Sadler (Fontana from PRIVATE EYE) will be back in town on February 3. I think he would be an interesting Stone, as well.

Please call with your thoughts.

Joan

Figure 9.1   Interoffice memo from Joan Sittenfield, head of casting for Universal Television, to Dick Wolf regarding possible lead actors.

asked composer Mike Post to create a preliminary idea for the title sequence. Dick Wolf is very pleased with it.

Tuesday, March 1, 1988

A casting session is held in the Universal Tower. A test-option deal needs to be set for the key actors before they can participate in the mix and matches. The memo shown in Figure 9.3 reiterated the importance of setting a deal quickly, especially for actor George Dzundza.

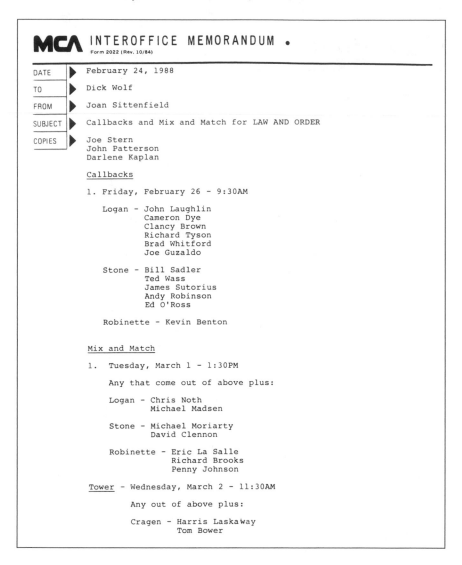

Figure 9.2   Interoffice memo from Joan Sittenfield, head of casting for Universal Television, to Dick Wolf regarding callback and mix-and-match sessions.

Wednesday, March 2, 1988

Line producer Joe Stern prepares to leave for New York to begin pre-production activities. Dick Wolf plans to fly to New York this weekend and will shuttle between coasts as needed.

In the meantime, there is casting to be concerned about. At this point, only one actor, George Dzundza, has been approved by the net-

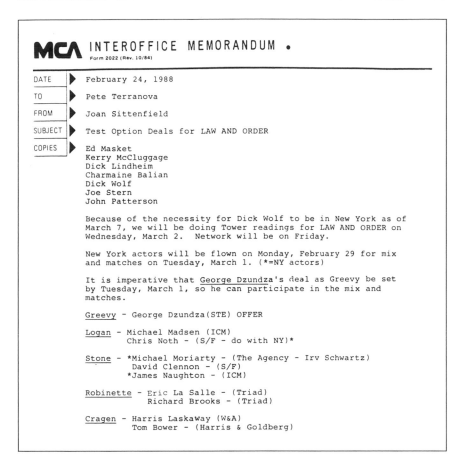

INTEROFFICE MEMORANDUM •

MCA
Form 2022 (Rev. 10/84)

DATE	February 24, 1988
TO	Pete Terranova
FROM	Joan Sittenfield
SUBJECT	Test Option Deals for LAW AND ORDER
COPIES	Ed Masket
	Kerry McCluggage
	Dick Lindheim
	Charmaine Balian
	Dick Wolf
	Joe Stern
	John Patterson

Because of the necessity for Dick Wolf to be in New York as of
March 7, we will be doing Tower readings for LAW AND ORDER on
Wednesday, March 2.   Network will be on Friday.

New York actors will be flown on Monday, February 29 for mix
and matches on Tuesday, March 1. (*=NY actors)

It is imperative that George Dzundza's deal as Greevy be set
by Tuesday, March 1, so he can participate in the mix and
matches.

Greevy - George Dzundza(STE) OFFER

Logan - Michael Madsen (ICM)
        Chris Noth - (S/F - do with NY)*

Stone - *Michael Moriarty - (The Agency - Irv Schwartz)
        David Clennon - (S/F)
        *James Naughton - (ICM)

Robinette - Eric La Salle - (Triad)
            Richard Brooks - (Triad)

Cragen - Harris Laskaway (W&A)
         Tom Bower - (Harris & Goldberg)

Figure 9.3   Memo requesting test-option deals for possible *Law and Order* cast.

work. But the contract between the actor and the studio has not been
finalized.

Today there is a casting session at CBS for other lead roles. Several
actors read before a combined group of key individuals from Universal
and CBS. For the part of Logan, the young policeman, they evaluate
John Laughlin, Michael Madsen, and Chris Noth. For the role of the
district attorney (Stone) they see James Naughton and Michael Moriarty.
For the part of Robinette, three actors are seen—Eric La Salle, Richard
Brooks, and Penny Johnson (reflecting the option of having a man or
a woman in the role).

After the readings, discussion centers on the role of Stone. Dick
Wolf likes Naughton, but prefers Michael Moriarty. So does Kim
LeMasters, the head of programming at CBS. There are some reser-
vations about Moriarty, however, because the actor began to improvise

at the end of the test scene. The network wants to be assured that he will stick to the script.

In discussing the role of Logan, the group feels that Michael Madsen has great sex appeal, but is a "counter puncher." They feel that with George Dzundza, the combination would not be good. Chris Noth seems a more compatible choice.

In the afternoon, Dick Wolf meets with Joan Sittenfield about the choice for a New York casting director. There are three possibilities, all of whom are talented. Dick Wolf's first choice is Bonnie Timmerman. He worked with her on *Miami Vice,* and he trusts her implicitly. She is busy, however, and would only be available to work on the series. Jim McAdams strongly recommends Lois Planco, who cast *The Equalizer.* She is available for both the pilot and the series. Joan Sittenfield recommends Lynn Kressel, a casting director under retainer at Universal for doing New York pilots. She is available but demands to work on the series as well as the pilot.

Problems such as this are common in the preparatory phase of any production. Dick Wolf, an experienced producer, calmly arbitrates. After delicate negotiations, he assigns Lynn Kressel to do the pilot and Bonnie Timmerman to cast the series.

At the end of the day, Mike Post calls Wolf to have him hear the latest version of the title theme. Dick thinks it is wonderful and asks for cassettes of it.

Thursday, March 3, 1988

The casting-personnel crisis has surfaced again. Lynn Kressel has decided that she will not cast the pilot if she cannot remain on the series. In compensation Dick Wolf promises her that she can be casting director for an *ABC Mystery Movie* segment he is developing. She accepts.

In New York Joe Stern and John Patterson meet with Jim McAdams, who has offered assistance in the production. He is heavily involved in producing *The Equalizer,* however.

In the afternoon, Dick Wolf plays the Mike Post theme music for the Universal executives, who are very pleased. The day concludes with a casting session at CBS. Two actors are presented as possibilities for the secondary role of Cragen—Harris Laskaway and Dann Florek. There was a problem concluding the contract with Laskaway, and at first it looked as if the session might have to be cancelled. Negotiations were finally concluded.

There is disagreement at the casting session. Dick Wolf expresses a preference for Florek. Jonathan Levin, director of drama development at CBS, has reservations because of the actor's performance in a CBS pilot the previous season. Kim LeMasters feels that the actor should not be judged on that one performance and defers to Dick Wolf. Florek is set.

Friday, March 4, 1988

Dick Wolf faces two major production decisions—whether to shoot on 16mm or 35mm film, and whether to edit the picture on film or videotape. The former decision will have a major and unexpected impact on the production.

Universal Studios has never shot a program on 16mm film, and all its facilities are geared to 35mm film production. Still, Dick Wolf is interested in shooting on 16mm film for two reasons: first, its grainier image quality will emphasize the docudrama look he desires; second, the show is to be filmed on practical locations, rather than on sound stages. The smaller 16mm cameras will facilitate production in this environment. Wolf recognizes the importance of this decision and continues to weigh the advantages and disadvantages of both. Today he seems to favor traditional 35mm shooting.

The second major decision, whether to postproduce the show on film or videotape, is also irreversible. Wolf is leaning toward editing on film. His reasoning is that, for the cinematic style envisioned, the editor must have a "good eye" for film. But if the editor works on videotape, he or she must also be familiar with the mechanics of that medium. Wolf thinks that in such a short period of time it will be difficult to find an editor with expertise in both areas. He is also worried about the inflexibility of the decision. While there are now frame-accurate videotape editing systems, which enable film editors to later conform the negative to the assembled videotape master, the process cannot be done quickly. There may not be enough time to deliver a finished film to the network, if the show is postproduced on videotape. It would have to be delivered to the network on videotape.

This impacts on Wolf's decision in another way. If transferred to tape, the network and potential advertisers for *Law and Order* will have to view the show on a video monitor. If it is finished on film, it can be both projected as film or transferred to tape for video viewing.

Monday, March 7, 1988

After arriving in New York over the weekend, Dick Wolf spends the morning looking at potential shooting locations in Harlem and Brooklyn before returning to the Manhattan offices the production company is sharing with *The Equalizer* staff.

He meets with director John Patterson, and director of photography Geoff Erb, who is working on *The Equalizer* series, but who will also work on *Law and Order.* John Patterson wants 80 percent of this production to be shot with hand-held cameras. He feels this will provide a more spontaneous look than tripod-mounted cameras. However, he does not want the final result to resemble jerky news footage.

At this point all agree that they would prefer to shoot on 35mm film. But unlike the use of a lightweight Steadicam, it will be physically tiresome for a film operator to hold a bulky 35mm camera on his shoulder for 10 days. Not many operators will be willing to try. They discuss an alternative—mounting the camera on a shopping cart, so that it would be fluid but not bumpy. Some camera tests are planned.

Tuesday, March 8, 1988

The studio has been trying to negotiate with agents for actor Roy Thinnes, whom Dick Wolf wants for the role of the district attorney's boss. Unfortunately, the agents are demanding far more than Universal is willing to pay for the performer. The studio will make a new offer.

Most of the producer's day is spent in scouting locations. At 5:30 P.M. a casting session begins. All are beginning to feel the pressure of impending production. The start date is just two weeks away. Only two locations have been set, and only five of the 55 major speaking roles have been cast.

Wednesday, March 9, 1988

Dick Wolf spends the morning looking at more possible locations. The afternoon is occupied by casting concerns.

He has extensive conversations with actors Michael Moriarty and George Dzundza. Both are known as highly intelligent, opinionated, and fastidious performers. As research for his role, Dzundza has been spending time riding along with police in his hometown, Chicago. He wants his performance to be as authentic as possible. Moriarty and Wolf plan to spend time together next week in the New York district attorney's office.

Meanwhile, the contractual conversations between Universal and Roy Thinnes' agent remain unresolved and stalemated. The only solution is to change Thinnes' part to an occasional guest star, instead of a regular character in the series. In that way, the studio can pay the actor more for each appearance, and still stay within the budget parameters.

The 16mm versus 35mm debate continues. Dick Wolf is attracted to the size, flexibility, and light weight of the 16mm equipment, but does not want to embark on shooting in one format and then have to switch to the other. It will be a critical decision, he realizes.

It is agreed that the exposed film will be processed in New York and then shipped to Los Angeles. This will allow John Patterson and Dick Wolf to see the dailies (the previous day's shooting) the following afternoon. The network and studio executives will have to endure a one-day delay. The editing and postproduction, however, will be performed at Universal Studios in Los Angeles.

At the end of the day, Wolf interviews potential costume designers. His first choice is not available, but he speculates costuming will not be as vital a factor in this production. Unlike Wolf's experience on *Miami Vice*, there will be no stylization of clothes. In fact, the actors may be encouraged to wear their own clothes.

Thursday, March 10, 1988

Kristi Zea, the costume designer, begins work today. Dick Wolf discusses costumes for the regular players and major supporting roles with her. He also has a meeting with production designer Richard Bianchi, and people who are responsible for stage props. They discuss the guns that should be carried, the objects that should be on desks of the district attorneys and the police officers, as well as the appearance of the stationery and police report forms.

The location manager has found a courthouse in Newark for courthouse scenes. For the police precinct they receive a lucky break—a station in midtown Manhattan has just closed for remodeling. The production company has received permission to use it for shooting, before the remodeling begins.

Friday, March 11, 1988

Michael Moriarty and Kristi Zea accompany Dick Wolf on a visit to the New York district attorney's office, where they tour the facilities. Over lunch they discuss how important wardrobe can be in establishing character.

Dick Wolf's afternoon is occupied by more casting sessions. In the evening, there are camera tests to determine the image quality of using a new high-speed film at night in Manhattan.

Monday, March 14, 1988

More photographic tests are scheduled today. In the hope of resolving the continuing debate about 35mm versus 16mm, there will be four test sequences: (1) 16mm under normal conditions, (2) 35mm under normal conditions, (3) 16mm using hand-held, (4) 35mm using hand-held.

In the morning, Dick Wolf meets with the production designer to discuss and approve decorating ideas for the interior sets. In the afternoon, casting once again is the prime concern. He spends the afternoon in casting sessions. It is becoming a real chore to cast the 50 or so speaking roles.

Tuesday, March 15, 1988

Casting continues. Meanwhile, George Dzundza and Chris Noth meet with real New York detectives for research on their roles.

Wednesday, March 16, 1988

Initially, Dick Wolf is not pleased with the camera test results. But he is experimenting. He orders the film transferred to videotape, where he can use electronics to alter the contrast, color balance, and apparent graininess of the image. He experiments with combinations until he finds a visual look he feels is pleasing and unlike anything seen before. He has a copy of the test tape rushed to Kerry McCluggage's office at Universal.

The remainder of Wolf's day is spent scouting locations and in casting sessions. He feels relieved that most of the major roles have been set.

Thursday, May 17, 1988

Dick Wolf's morning is occupied by a production meeting, with key crew members set for the *Law and Order* pilot. (See Figure 9.4.) In the production meeting, Wolf explains the pragmatic needs of the shoot and discusses issues raised by the different production area heads.

In the afternoon, there is a table reading for the principal actors and supporting players. The reading goes well. After the reading, Dick Wolf has lunch with Michael Moriarty. The producer feels that Moriarty's own personality is close to the role of Stone, and encourages him

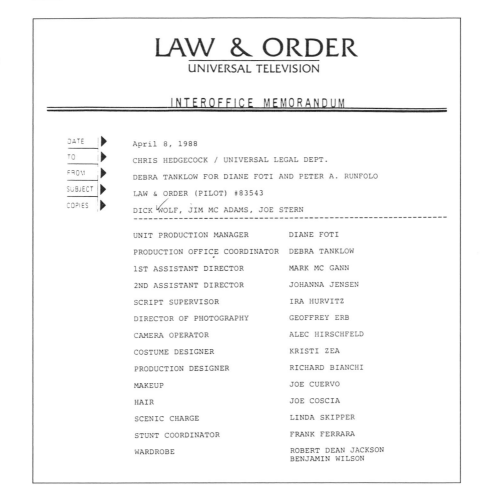

LAW & ORDER
UNIVERSAL TELEVISION

INTEROFFICE MEMORANDUM

DATE ▶ April 8, 1988

TO ▶ CHRIS HEDGECOCK / UNIVERSAL LEGAL DEPT.

FROM ▶ DEBRA TANKLOW FOR DIANE FOTI AND PETER A. RUNFOLO

SUBJECT ▶ LAW & ORDER (PILOT) #83543

COPIES ▶ DICK WOLF, JIM MC ADAMS, JOE STERN

UNIT PRODUCTION MANAGER	DIANE FOTI
PRODUCTION OFFICE COORDINATOR	DEBRA TANKLOW
1ST ASSISTANT DIRECTOR	MARK MC GANN
2ND ASSISTANT DIRECTOR	JOHANNA JENSEN
SCRIPT SUPERVISOR	IRA HURVITZ
DIRECTOR OF PHOTOGRAPHY	GEOFFREY ERB
CAMERA OPERATOR	ALEC HIRSCHFELD
COSTUME DESIGNER	KRISTI ZEA
PRODUCTION DESIGNER	RICHARD BIANCHI
MAKEUP	JOE CUERVO
HAIR	JOE COSCIA
SCENIC CHARGE	LINDA SKIPPER
STUNT COORDINATOR	FRANK FERRARA
WARDROBE	ROBERT DEAN JACKSON
	BENJAMIN WILSON

Figure 9.4 Memo to Universal's legal department specifying the production unit for the *Law and Order* pilot.

to play himself. Dinner is with George Dzundza, where they exchange thoughts about the character of Greevey, and how he should be portrayed.

In between, Wolf phones the Universal executives who have seen the video-altered film tests. They have reservations. While applauding the intent, they are concerned that the look is too unusual and will call attention to itself. Ideally, the effect should be almost subliminal. Wolf explains that he does not want to use the technique throughout the show, just in special places and during certain night sequences. It is agreed that they will only use the effect occasionally, and in a muted form.

Evaluating all the discussions and tests, Dick Wolf finally decides to shoot the pilot on 16mm film, a decision that he will come to regret; but no one could envision the problem it would create.

To facilitate editing, the 16mm negative will be blown up to a 35mm black-and-white work print. Therefore, all the editing will take place in Hollywood on 35mm film. When the editing is complete, the 16mm color work print will be spliced to produce a rough cut of the show for the network to see. Ultimately, the 16mm negative will be cut and an "answer print" of the show will be delivered.

All the locations are finalized today.

Friday, March 18, 1988

John Patterson spends the day touring all the locations with his crew chiefs, including the key grip, gaffer, and director of photography. Meanwhile, Dick Wolf has a meeting with Kristi Zea concerning final details of costume design. Then he meets with Jim McAdams about the budget.

Monday, March 21, 1988

This is the day before actual production begins. Activity is intense. There are last-minute changes in wardrobe and final casting for small parts. There are also continuing discussions about the budget—the projected shooting schedule is too long. For an extra $20,000, they will try to get an extra day's worth of shooting, since it has been learned that Good Friday is not a union holiday.

At the police precinct location, the actors rehearse with John Patterson. Playing the scenes in the actual location is a big help to them.

Tuesday, March 22, 1988—Production Day

Production begins uneventfully. Scenes are shot according to schedule.

Wednesday, March 23, 1988

Studio executive Richard Lindheim arrives from the West Coast and joins Dick Wolf and others for the screening of film from the first day of shooting. Everyone is very pleased.

Thursday, March 24, 1988

The executives on the West Coast and the CBS programmers screen the first day's dailies. Production is proceeding smoothly in New York.

Friday, March 25–Tuesday, April 5, 1988

Principal photography continues without major problems. There are a few scenes where reshooting would improve the performances, and it is ordered. There are also a few concerns about a scene being visually too dark. It will be reprinted to see if the processing lab can lighten it sufficiently to avoid reshooting.

Wednesday, April 6, 1988

This day is used for additional shooting that was not originally planned or budgeted. Since everyone is pleased with the production, Dick Wolf wants to reshoot a few short scenes in order to deliver the best pilot possible. Even though it puts the show further over budget, Universal grants the request. Everyone feels they have a "winner." The production company "wraps" principal photography at 1:00 A.M.

Thursday, April 7, 1988

John Patterson and Joe Stern return to Los Angeles to begin editing the show.

Friday, April 8, 1988

Although *Law and Order* is not finished, and CBS has not yet given the go-ahead for the series, Dick Wolf must address potential series production problems. While the filming in New York went well, the cost was considerably more than anticipated. Universal, therefore, is wary about shooting the series there, and wants Dick Wolf to consider Toronto. Because of the lower Canadian dollar, the smaller crew size in Canada, and lower salaries for crew workers, many television movies and several series have recently used Toronto for New York. The savings can be considerable.

Dick Wolf previously shot a feature in Toronto, and the experience was frustrating. It did not give him confidence in the production expertise in comparison with experience in New York and Los Angeles. He feels that trying to shoot *Law and Order* there would also be disastrous. He is angry that the studio business-affairs department was unable to get a larger episode budget from CBS. His best hope is that *The Equalizer* will be picked up for a fourth year. Having two series based in New York would be cost effective for Universal.

John Patterson has notified Dick Wolf that he will finish his director's cut on April 15. The Director's Guild contract with the Hollywood production studios insists that the director have first crack at editing the show. No one else can touch the film until the director is finished with his cut. Wolf is very concerned about the passing time, but must comply with the agreement. CBS is demanding that the finished film be delivered to them on May 2nd. It seems like an impossibly short time.

Monday, April 11, 1988

Dick Wolf returns to Los Angeles.

Tuesday, April 12–Thursday, April 14, 1988

While John Patterson works on editing the pilot, Dick Wolf concerns himself with the main title sequence. Additional assistant editors are added to the staff to try to speed up the editing process. The postproduction schedule that the producer and his editors were trying to achieve is shown in Figure 9.5.

Friday, April 15, 1988

John Patterson screens his cut of *Law and Order* to Dick Wolf and turns the film over to Wolf.

Tuesday, April 19, 1988

Dick Wolf has a version of the pilot with which he is satisfied. He takes a videotape of the black-and-white work print to Universal's Tower, where Kerry McCluggage, joined by other executives, watches it. The reactions, while positive, are mixed. They feel it moves so quickly that, at times, it is difficult to follow the story.

In the afternoon the Universal executives meet again with Wolf

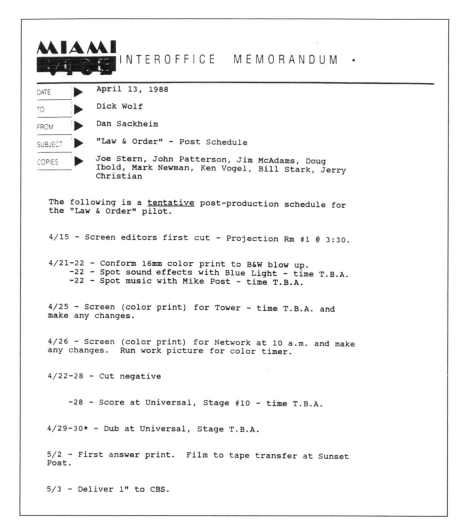

Figure 9.5   Memo outlining tentative postproduction schedule for *Law and Order*.

and screen the pilot anew. This time the tape is started and stopped, so that each scene can be discussed individually. The studio executives feel that the docudrama style, combined with the show's story orientation and density of technical language, makes it difficult for the uninitiated viewer to follow. They want to clarify locations and times and slow down the progress of the story, so that the viewer has time to absorb the information.

Dick Wolf feels the Tower wants him to add back elements, such as establishing shots and transition shots, that he specifically wanted to omit in creating this new style. After considerable discussion, it is decided to use a fade-out, followed by a fade-in, as the transition from scene to scene. While perhaps the oldest transitional technique in film, it will at least allow the viewer to know time has passed, and the location has changed. It will also be an effective breather for the viewer to absorb story information. For Dick Wolf the use of the fade-out/fade-in is an acceptable alternative. He does not want to use television's traditional "establishing shot" at the beginning of each scene.

For further clarification Wolf agrees to use a simple legend superimposed over the fade-in to each sequence, identifying the location, the date, and the time of the on-screen events. Figure 9.6 provides excerpts from Jim McAdams' notes to Dick Wolf, after seeing the first-cut screening. He points out specific scenes in the film that were initially confusing or needed clarification and offers suggestions for "tightening" the next edit.

Wednesday, April 20—Friday, April 22, 1988

Dick Wolf and the editors are absorbed in the changes agreed on with the Universal executives. At the same time, a test is ordered for making a 35mm print from the 16mm negative.

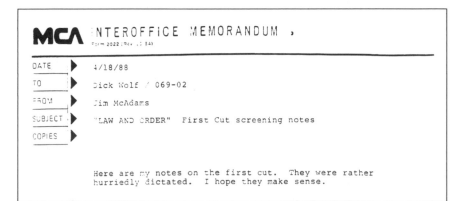

Figure 9.6   Executive Producer Jim McAdams' notes on the first-cut screening of *Law and Order.*

Monday, April 25, 1988

With the editorial changes complete, everyone wants to see the show in color and on a theater screen. A screening for the CBS program executives is scheduled for tomorrow.

```
McADAMS
First cut screening notes
"LAW AND ORDER"


REEL 1 - ACT 1

    It seems to me to be unnatural to cut into the car
as the two cops ride in silence. They turn a corner and
then are in the midst of a lively conversation. Seems
better to cut in first on the conversation about the "car
preference" and then let them ride in silence, listening
to police calls before spotting the two black suspects
and the victim.

    As I indicated to you after the screening, I don't feel
the the victim registers very well, which could have to do
with the black and white dupe. One could add a little to
the moving POV of the body stretched out of the car.

    I was a little confused and disoriented in the whole
area of the chase. It seemed to me we cut away from the
young cop going over the fence. We didn't bring the
young cop to the fence, we cut away from him going over
the fence to the other cop, and then back to the young
cop in what seems to be the beginning of the chase. I find
this whole area in need of smoothing out. I would let the
chase begin and then go back to the other cop going up to
the victim. I heard some discussion about the tail end of
the chase where the pursuing cop comes out. I was a little
thrown by it, even going back to view dailies. I don't know
what the specific answer is, but pass it along as a comment.

    I suggest a little head trim in the sandwich scene;
just start closer to dialogue.

    Again eavesdropping, I heard something about the be-
ginning of this scene, their arrival. I know you need a
bridge between their drive-off and their drive-in. Start-
ing with the light and panning to the victim seems kind of
a cliche to me. But, as I say, you do need the bridge.

    Is that the best take of the "I hate media cases." I
know there were quite a few. This one seems okay, but it
seemed to me that there was one that was better.

    The two-shot of Dzundza and Noth: I have a personal
thing about cutting too tight on movement. There is eye
```

Figure 9.6   *(continued)*

```
Page Two


movement when they look at Conti talking to press corps; he's
just moved his eyes around and his eyes are settling back and
we're very tight on that cut.

On the line, "Are you going to be able to catch these --" and
then there's that pause, I think you could sell the point you
wanted to make if there was a sharp look up from Dzundza and
Noth anticipating what he's about to say and then you go around
to Conti for "...these kids."

I know footage is a consideration, but have you considered ending
the scene after "short of one of them coming in and confessing"
rather than playing out the rest of that scene, which just goes
a little flat?

I think a little head trim on the ambulance, right before, Dzundza's
"That was smart."

Another eavesdrop, and I do agree, the scene outside between Noth
and Dzundza -- you mentioned, if possible, using the close-ups
from the original scene.  I'm sure you've done something about
that over the weekend.  It gets a little flacid and a little cute
at the end.

REEL 2


In the scene where they're in the cage area, there's an obvious
head trim on Dzundza's "He's good for nothing until he calms down."

Another trim right before the handshake:  I know he has to take a
little pause to think it over, but this is sort of an automatic
thing with them, so I don't know that we need that much deliber-
ation.

Query:  In the corridor outside the Jackson apartment, is there
another take of the little girl in which she says her line "You
the man?" a little faster?  Seemed to be kind of a delayed question,
and it slows up the timing there.

Interrogation scene:  A tiny thing:  I would do a head trim after
the black kid's line "You got that right."  I'd trim off Dzundza's
"Hmmm" and go right to "You know what we found?"

The scene with the truck driver:  as they're walking up to the
truck driver's truck to confront him, there's some dialogue about
joining the Actors' Studio, etc.  Is there a better performance
there?  It seems a little self-conscious.  The other alternative
would be to lay some different dialogue in.  I think where it
starts to go sour is "Yeah, you didn't know that?"  I'd have to
check the script if that's an ad lib or not, but the joke seems
to end with "...join the Actors' Studio."  The additional comment
```

Figure 9.6   *(continued)*

Major technical problems occur. There are few 16mm projectors at the studio. They are infrequently used and are not well maintained. Furthermore, since *Law and Order* is still a work in progress, the sound track is entirely separate from the picture. It exists on the industry's traditional 35mm magnetic film stock. To show the picture and sound

```
Page Three



from Noth steps on it.

On the approach to Maggie sitting in the car: this could be
tightened up a little bit.  Just a little pause before she
gets out of the car and all of that -- just general tightening.

In the first furrier scene, I would suggest you start with Dzundza's
line "So, is this coat Meryl Streep or Whoopi Goldberg?"  I don't
know -- it seems sort of here-we-are-explaining-fur-coats.  I think
the scene would play without it.

The scene with Swersky -- I suggest we trim Noth's smile before
he says, "Who's the gift for?"  Noth's smile seems more appropriate
to the line, "You gonna tell me what this is about?" and Dzundza
says, "No," rather than the line about what kind of car he drives.

Noth's line after "Karnack" line is pushing it.  A smile or a
smile from Dzundza, rather than that fullblown laugh would be
better if it exists.  To me, the laugh diminishes the joke.

REEL 3


D.A.'s office:  I had a little trouble with the woman talking
about the baby's head flopping.  It seems like the first exchange
between D.A. and lawyer works okay because we don't slow up for it,
but the second one seems like it's staged for our benefit.  It's
an easy drop if we want to make it, but again, it is my own reaction.

As Greevey and Logan approach Scalisi and his dog, and Noth holds
up his hand and says, "Anthony Scalisi," could we get in a short
pop there of Greevey's relaxed gun at his side?  They are dealing
with a known nit man and then suddenly the guns appear in a flash.
I think the gun at his side would indicate that it's a heavy sit-
uation and add tension.

END ACT 2
(Still in Reel 3)

I would trim the head from the judge at the beginning of Act 2:
"I'm loathe to withhold bail."  It's an automatic for him.  He
knows what Robinette is going to ask and he's already made up his
mind he isn't going to get it.  Again, I know footage is a consid-
eration, but I would end the scene with Robinette putting his
head down before the pan over to the defendant.  I certainly would
not go back to the judge.

Cosmatos and Robinette:  I would trim right on the elevator door
closing.

In the scene between Robinette and Stone in which we introduce
Stone:  First of all we're not quite sure who Stone is, but that
```

Figure 9.6   *(continued)*

together, the editors must first match the 16mm film with the 35mm sound track, and then the disparate projectors must be synchronized.

It does not work. The picture and sound track are constantly falling away from one another. And this is not the worst of it. As every splice in the 16mm work print goes through the projector, there is a visible jump in the image on the screen. The studio engineers feel the problem is twofold: splicing technique and antiquated equipment. Unlike 35mm film where a piece of transparent tape is used to "butt" splice the two ends of the film together, 16mm uses a "lap" splice, where the end of one piece of film is placed over the end of the other and they are cemented together. Thus, the film at each splice is slightly thicker.

Facing these problems, the consensus is to delay the network screening to Wednesday afternoon. Everyone is relieved that they had ordered a test of the 16mm to 35mm blow-up. This could be a solution if the projector problem is not solved.

Wolf and his staff are frustrated and worried. The problem must be solved. Three important actions are agreed upon. First, the producer asks to expedite the 16mm to 35mm test. It was supposed to be ready on Wednesday morning. It is vital to see it as soon as possible. Second, Charmaine Balian, vice-president of drama development, calls CBS to see if delivery to the network can be delayed from May 3. Every day and hour will help. Third, the studio engineers examine and test other 16mm projectors in other screening rooms.

Dick Wolf and the Universal executives also discuss what will be the best form in which to deliver *Law and Order* to CBS. With the synchronization problem it is deemed too risky to deliver a 16mm print with a 35mm sound track. A composite 16mm print with the sound track on the film can be made, but it will be costly and time consuming. A transfer to video is a viable option, but Wolf feels that having to see *Law and Order* only on a television set would be disadvantageous to the project. The most promising solution is the blow-up of 16mm to 35mm.

Tuesday, April 26, 1988

The principal actors arrive in Hollywood for ADR work, where they rework scenes that require replacement dialogue.

Universal decides to test the pilot in rough-cut form. Knowing that each network tests every pilot, studios frequently research the shows themselves, prior to delivering them. This gives the producer information that can be helpful in fine tuning the picture in the last stages of postproduction. It also provides the producer and the studio with a preview of what the network research report might say.

This evening, *Law and Order* is taken to Preview House on Sunset Boulevard in Los Angeles. An audience of 300 people is to watch the show on the theater screen and fill out questionnaires. A second group of 12 people is invited to participate in a discussion about the show, which is audiotaped for later analysis.

The projectionist at Preview House experiences problems similar to those at the studio. Most of the synchronization problems have been solved, but the screen image jumps at every splice. It is very disconcerting, although the audience tolerates it without comment.

The test results are encouraging. Test respondents enjoy the concept of the show enormously, and compare *Law and Order* in style to *L.A. Law* and *Hill Street Blues*. They rate the principal characters of Logan, Greevey, Robinette, and Stone positively, but some of the people in the discussion group state that they want to know more about the characters' personal lives.

The only significant criticisms are that the first half of the show seems to move a little too fast to follow and that there are no positive female roles in the picture. After the test, there is a postmortem by Dick Wolf and the Universal executives. They feel only minor additional editing is needed. All decide to make a videotape of the pilot for insurance if nothing more.

Wednesday, April 27, 1988

In the morning everyone convenes for the test of the 16mm film blown up to 35mm. It looks excellent, retaining a unique quality that is neither 16mm nor 35mm. Dick Wolf is enthusiastic, and decides to deliver *Law and Order* on 35mm film.

In the afternoon, there is a screening to allow the CBS network executives who have endorsed *Law and Order* from its inception to see it before final delivery. It also gives the drama-development executives the opportunity to suggest changes. This protocol is followed for every pilot at each network.

The 16mm film and 35mm sound tracks are tried again. The engineers have been working on the projector, and the sound synchronization problem has been solved. But the screen image still jumps irritatingly at most of the splices. Dick Wolf is miserable. The studio executives are frustrated. But the CBS executives are tolerant.

Pat Faulstich, the vice-president of drama development for CBS, is generally upbeat. He has some concerns about the density of information conveyed in the show and wants to make sure that all events are as clear and succinct as possible. He also ponders that the show may be too male-oriented; he hopes it will have some female appeal.

A videocassette of *Law and Order* will be given to Kim LeMasters, the head of programming at CBS, so that he can watch it tonight at his home.

Thursday, April 28, 1988

CBS has agreed to let the delivery date slide from May 3 to May 5. Dick Wolf continues final editing work. He learns that Kim LeMasters did not have a chance to see the pilot last night. He is scheduled to look at it this afternoon.

Friday, April 29, 1988

The process of dubbing begins. This involves mixing the dialogue with sound effects and music to produce the finished sound track.

Tuesday, May 3, 1988

Dick Wolf is not satisfied with the sound track. He feels it is the consequence of everyone on his staff being exhausted and too rushed. He demands that portions be redone.

This is a day filled with good and bad news. The good news comes from CBS' Pat Faulstich, who reports that Kim LeMasters finally saw and liked the show, although he will withhold final judgment until he sees it finished. Faulstich expects William Paley, long-term president of CBS, to recognize *Law and Order* as a descendant of shows with great longevity, *Naked City* and *Dragnet.* He also feels that Larry Tisch, the new owner of CBS, an intellectual, will probably like *Law and Order* as well.

The bad news is more ramifications from shooting in 16mm. While the blow-up to 35mm test of one scene worked fine, when whole sequences were processed, the 35mm images jumped at every splice, just as they did with 16mm projectors. Everyone is frustrated and confounded. Dick Wolf is filled with angst. The engineers and film laboratory experts are apologetic. They feel the problem lies with the optical printer, the machine used to project the 16mm image onto 35mm film stock. They can solve the problem in a couple of weeks.

But *Law and Order* must be delivered in two days! Wolf screams at the engineers—"This is Hollywood, the film capital of the world! You guys should be able to do anything!" The Universal technical production executives decide to bring in another lab and to attack the problem in two ways. First, the optical printing procedure will be redone at the Technicolor lab. At the same time, a procedure called "total immersion" will be tried at the MGM color labs. This technique uses direct contact to make a new 16mm print from the spliced 16mm version. The resulting 16mm film will contain no splices, and therefore should not "jump" in the projection gate.

In the meantime the Universal executives plead with CBS to push the delivery date of *Law and Order* from Thursday afternoon, May 5, to Friday morning, May 6. The CBS executive staff screening of *Law and Order* is now scheduled for Friday afternoon at 3 P.M.

Wednesday, May 4, 1988

With great trepidation Dick Wolf and the Universal executives screen a new test of the transfer to 35mm film. It works. The film plays smoothly. Everyone is relieved.

Thursday, May 5, 1988

Law and Order is delivered to CBS at 6 P.M.

Friday, May 6, 1988

The pilot is screened for CBS management at 3 P.M. The reaction seems favorable. Now Dick Wolf must wait until CBS announces its fall program decisions. This is scheduled to occur on Monday, May 23, 1988.

Immediately after the completion of the pilot, and before the CBS program announcements, we interviewed Dick Wolf. His thoughts and attitudes concerning the production, and the surprising future of *Law and Order*, are the subject of the next chapter.

Evaluation of the Production

THE PRODUCER'S ASSESSMENT

After filming was completed on the *Law and Order* pilot, we interviewed Dick Wolf to gain insight into the perceptions of a producer engaged in such a large and difficult production. This conversation took place on April 15, 1988, before the editors had even completed a first rough assemblage of the show, and well before any postproduction problems occurred.

At this time, Dick Wolf was pleased and confident about the results now being assembled by the film editors. He was especially satisfied with the quick pace of the show, an element for which he had strived.

> I feel relatively good now. I can't tell you we're seeing a full assembly, but we saw the first three acts assembled. . . . [The film sequences] moved so fast that nobody moved. I mean, this is not a show you can [even run out] to make microwave popcorn.

He was also gratified with the stylistic results. As described in Chapter 8, Wolf wanted *Law and Order* to represent the evolution of a new look in television programs. He had gone to great lengths to achieve that goal. He now thought the hand-held camera had provided a more subtle and pleasing look than he had originally thought it would.

> I would describe the show's style as being evolutionary. It is not going to rock people in terms of camera movements. . . . After the

first day of dailies they [suggested] jiggle the camera more, have it more in and out of focus. The entire show is hand-held. But Howard Hirschfield, the camera operator, is so good that we really only have a subliminal feeling that the camera is different. . . . It is evolutionary, but not as jarring visually as I'd initially anticipated with this much hand-holding. So, that was a surprise.

Wolf had fought an economic battle to film *Law and Order* in New York. While the shooting went one day over schedule, and consequently the show was over budget, he felt vindicated by the footage.

The other surprise was how important New York City was to the show. Again, that's something that reaches [viewers] in a way that you really can't document by looking at the film. In the opening scene, George [Dzundza] is in this bodega, and walks out across the street. Everybody knows that can only be New York City. There are no bodegas [like it] virtually anywhere else. It's that whole feeling of being in New York that does add something to the pilot.

A less pleasant surprise was the discovery that, when assembled, the running time of the show was going to be short of that required by the network for a one-hour broadcast. Wolf blamed the script supervisor, who is responsible for evaluating and reporting how the written pages will translate into screen time: "The first timing was 54 minutes. I said 'That's ridiculous.' The script supervisor said, 'It's a 60 page script.'" What the script supervisor apparently did not take into account was Wolf and director Patterson's desire for rapid pace and quick dialogue.

[The actors] are talking the way people really talk, at the pace they really talk. . . . And three days into production, the script supervisor, Ira, came up sort of white-faced and said, "I've just done a new timing." And I said, "What is it?" He said, "It's 45 minutes and 6 seconds—including titles and end credits."

That was rather startling to find out that we were short with a 60 page script, because I always figured *Hill Street Blues* scripts were 59 [minutes from a 60-page script]. But this moves faster than *Hill Street.* To keep up this pace the drafts are going to be 62 pages.

Wolf's solution was to add footage during production: "I don't think it's going to hurt us. It actually helps us. We did add a couple of driving shots in the city, which gives us some scope at a time when we need it."

As discussed previously, from the show's conception Dick Wolf knew that he was flying against television convention by making a show that was more story-dependent than character-dependent. While he felt he had accomplished this task, he also recognized the risk.

The characters are interesting, but one of the things that everyone was worried about creatively was whether they were likable enough for series characters. I hope I don't live to eat these words, but I don't think it's nearly as important for these guys to be likable as it is for them to be believable. Because what we discovered from the [film] assembly is that this is not a character-driven show. It is a story-driven show. We knew that. We talked about that from day one. But it's so much more a story-driven show than I even suspected.

He had no concerns, however, about the choice of actors for the leading roles, or their performances in the pilot.

Wolf was particularly pleased with George Dzundza as the character Greevey:

George exceeded anybody's expectation. . . . He looks like a cop. He acts like a cop. He talks like a cop. When they first researched the role, the [actors] were up in Harlem dealing with the cops. George was standing around the squad room taking notes. Two detectives came over and introduced themselves. One of them says, "Weren't you on the 'one-seven' about five years ago . . . ?" They thought he was a cop.

George Dzundza's interpretation of the role was so strong that it actually altered Wolf's original concept for the character.

This is not a show where you want to see the various colors of all the actors' personalities. George recognized this immediately. I mean, he is completely consistent from the first frame to the last in terms of that character. We came up with some [ideas about the character] at the beginning, then dropped what didn't work. It's fascinating. At one point the character's [dialogue] included the lines, "Goddamm it," and "For God's sake." George changed [the dialogue] to "For Pete's sake." I asked, "Why'd you do that?" He said, "I just had a feeling about this guy. How about we make him a member of the Holy Name Society and Knights of Columbus?" That is the type of personality shading that is very valuable.

Wolf was similarly enthusiastic in his evaluation of Michael Moriarty as Stone, the DA, although he had more of a problem obtaining the performance he desired from the actor.

Michael [Moriarty] ranges in the dailies from brilliant to bizarre—which we knew was potentially the case. I mean, it's lightning in a bottle when he is focused.

What I wanted [from his character] was absolute Brooks Brothers straight. Buttoned-down collar, but strong. I said to him, "Michael, in every scene if you just think of yourself as holding all the cards, that's the way to play the scene. Because you do hold all the cards. You represent the state of New York. . . . In your dealings with people you represent power, and that's what you should concentrate on at all times." And when he does that he is really terrific.

The two relative unknowns in the cast were Chris Noth as policeman Logan, and Richard Brooks as the DA Robinette. Dick Wolf felt their contributions to the project were highly commendable.

> Chris Noth did a very good job. He worked very, very hard. . . . And again, part of the process with Noth [was] telling him . . . "You're a cop. Most people are terrified of you. And the time it works best is when you use your likability to get information out of them. And that makes you more authoritative."
> Richard Brooks has definitely exceeded everybody's expectations. When we hired him, he did a terrific job in the readings, but nobody really knew what his potential was. He has . . . certainly exceeded my expectations.

Although Dick Wolf had affirmative assessments of his principal actors, there were artistic confrontations during production. Those conflicts necessitated reshooting two scenes. The producer acknowledged that the primary cause of those conflicts tied into the lack of rehearsal time in the tight production schedule.

> We got delayed because of the insecurity of actors in a new role, which you can't budget in. . . . They were understandably worried and protective about their characters. . . . This is something that I am going to remember in the future. The best money you can spend on a production is for a week of rehearsals with the actors.

In the case of *Law and Order* the production was held up several times by actors who wanted clarification of their roles from Wolf.

> It just is a fact. When you're starting from scratch, you're creating people that will have to live for potentially, hopefully, five years— as opposed to a movie, where it's over [immediately after filming]. The structuring of those characters is very important. But it should be done during rehearsal stages, not on the floor, when the "clock" is ticking.

The first scene that requires reshooting was a scene in which Greevey and Logan leave the hospital, after interviewing Mrs. Halsey (the wife of a politician found dead), and Mr. Conti (the borough president). (See

Figure 10.1.) Dick Wolf explained what happened during the shooting of that scene.

> Logan's [Chris Noth] personality surfaced to [such a] degree that Greevey [George Dzundza] became very defensive. He did not want to be lectured to by his partner. [This escalated] into an hour and a half discussion, with the crew sitting around picking their noses— and we never got it right. George Dzundza's performance was thrown off, because Noth was defensive as they were walking down the street. That made George madder, and then he went over the top. . . . It's the type of thing that actors feed on [internally], and then blow the entire scene. We knew we didn't have it, but it was one o'clock in the morning.

Watching the dailies, Wolf and the Universal executives were aware of the problems in the scene. The editors were instructed to assemble quickly the scene footage for evaluation. As the producer recalls: "When it was cut, it wasn't that bad. The problem was Noth's performance, not Dzundza's." But everyone agreed that it could be better. In a pilot where small things can make the difference between success and failure, Kerry McCluggage, president of Universal Television, decided to bear the cost of reshooting.

> We reshot it . . . at about the same time, one-thirty in the morning. But now I've taken George [Dzundza] aside, and I've said, "Look. We've got to get this. Just do it." And he said, "All right. All right." And he went out and he did it.

As a compromise, Wolf dropped a line of dialogue by Greevey that had disturbed actor Chris Noth: "I knew that if [the line] was in there we'd never get the thing out of Noth. So, we dropped the line, and now we've got the best of both worlds." They had to shoot a close-up of Noth in "limbo" (without visual reference points) so the new footage could be edited easily into the original footage.

The second scene reshot involved an interesting conflict between reality and perceived reality. In the scene, the suspect (Scalisi) is returning to his apartment after having taken his pitbull for a walk. Greevey draws his gun on the suspect and the pitbull. (See Figure 10.2.)

Actor George Dzundza felt very strongly that pulling a gun on the suspect was consistent with his character and the reality of cop behavior. However, Universal executives were worried that television audiences would consider the behavior a cliché.

Dick Wolf explained to the actor that the behavior seemed cliché for a cop show. But George Dzundza argued that the technical advisor approved the action as real.

7

CONTINUED

> CONTI (Cont'd)
> Our streets aren't safe for <u>anyone</u>.
> (beat; controlling
> himself)
> You can check with my office about
> Chuck's condition...we'll have
> regular updates...thank you, ladies
> and gentlemen.

The lights go off. A reporter, Fred Lasco, shouts a question.

> LASCO
> Mrs. Halsey - what do you think your
> husband was doing in that
> neighborhood late at night?

Before she can answer, Conti puts an arm around her shoulder and pushes through a pair of swinging doors into a doctor's lounge. The camera follows into --

> CONTINUOUS

INT. DOCTOR'S LOUNGE - NIGHT

Conti and Mrs. Halsey approach a surgeon in a sweat stained set of O.R. greens as Greevey and Logan enter the lounge behind them. Conti turns and shoots them an annoyed look as the surgeon pats Mrs. Halsey's arm.

> SURGEON
> Go home and get some sleep. He came
> through the surgery, which is half
> the battle...we'll call you
> immediately if there's any change.

As the doctor leaves, Conti moves toward Greevey and Logan.

> CONTI
> Who are you?

> LOGAN
> (flashing shield)
> I'm Detective Logan, this is
> Sergeant Greevey...

> CONTI
> You're the investigating officers?

> LOGAN
> Yes, sir.

> CONTI
> We heard it was two black kids.

> CONTINUED

Figure 10.1 Excerpt from *Law and Order* pilot script.

8

CONTINUED

> GREEVEY
> Two suspects were seen fleeing the
> scene.

> CONTI
> You have anything else?

> GREEVEY
> Not yet.

> LOGAN
> (to Mrs. Halsey)
> Could you give us a description of
> his personal items, ma'am?

> MRS. HALSEY
> (swallowing)
> He always carried a brown alligator
> wallet, a star sapphire ring, and a
> gold and diamond Rolex...he usually
> had about five hundred dollars in
> cash.

> LOGAN
> (writing notes)
> Diamonds around the outside or on
> the face?

> MRS. HALSEY
> Around the outside.

> GREEVEY
> Your husband have any enemies?

> CONTI
> Chuck Halsey is one of the most
> respected and liked men in this
> district.

> GREEVEY
> I'm sure he is...
> (looking at Mrs.
> Halsey)
> Ma'am?

> MRS. HALSEY
> What are you asking? I thought you
> knew who did it.

> LOGAN
> We know two black kids were there,
> but they didn't drive your husband
> to that location. You have any idea
> what he was doing way out there?

CONTINUED

Figure 10.1 *(continued)*

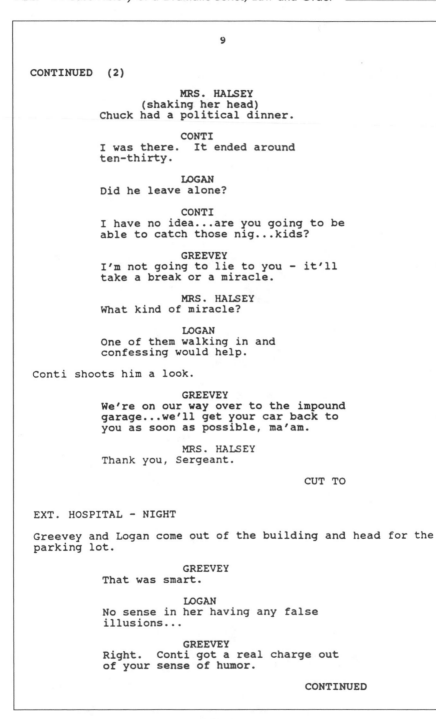

9

CONTINUED (2)

                    MRS. HALSEY
                 (shaking her head)
        Chuck had a political dinner.

                    CONTI
        I was there. It ended around
        ten-thirty.

                    LOGAN
        Did he leave alone?

                    CONTI
        I have no idea...are you going to be
        able to catch those nig...kids?

                    GREEVEY
        I'm not going to lie to you - it'll
        take a break or a miracle.

                    MRS. HALSEY
        What kind of miracle?

                    LOGAN
        One of them walking in and
        confessing would help.

Conti shoots him a look.

                    GREEVEY
        We're on our way over to the impound
        garage...we'll get your car back to
        you as soon as possible, ma'am.

                    MRS. HALSEY
        Thank you, Sergeant.

                                    CUT TO

EXT. HOSPITAL - NIGHT

Greevey and Logan come out of the building and head for the
parking lot.

                    GREEVEY
        That was smart.

                    LOGAN
        No sense in her having any false
        illusions...

                    GREEVEY
        Right. Conti got a real charge out
        of your sense of humor.

                                    CONTINUED

Figure 10.1 *(continued)*

10

CONTINUED

Logan stops and looks at Greevey, who stops and lifts an expectant eyebrow.

> GREEVEY
> Yeah?

> LOGAN
> You going to try and tell me that this plays right?

> GREEVEY
> Let's check the car.

> LOGAN
> What was he doing out there after a political dinner?

> GREEVEY
> (slowly;
>   deliberately)
> Let's check the car.

Logan's eyes narrow. He knows his partner.

> LOGAN
> Wait a minute, wait a minute...what have you got?

> GREEVEY
> Old rumors.

> LOGAN
> (getting pissed)
> That's great. When were you planning on telling me? What kind?

> GREEVEY
> Rumor was that he ran the pad in the Criminal Courts.

> LOGAN
> (can't believe it)
> He's a bagman!

> GREEVEY
> Was...if you believe the rumors.

> LOGAN
> This really frosts my cookies, Max. You mind telling me why you didn't tell me?

CONTINUED

Figure 10.1 *(continued)*

11

CONTINUED (2)

                    GREEVEY
                 (unrepentant)
         Because you're <u>already</u> leaping to
         conclusions, for God's sake...about
         the only <u>probable</u> conclusion we can
         draw is that the black kids took
         whatever they found.

Logan's as pissed at himself as he is at Greevey.   His
partner's absolutely right.

                    LOGAN
         Let's check the car.

                                        CUT TO

INT. IMPOUND GARAGE - NIGHT

A grease stained impound lot manager watches as Greevey
puts a key in the Mercedes' trunk.

                    MANAGER
         ...sixty bucks for a damn key,
         Sergeant. I coulda popped it for
         nothing.

                    GREEVEY
         Car belongs to a city councilman.

The manager's eyes widen.

                    MANAGER
         That real?

Greevey reaches into the trunk and comes out holding a lynx
coat.

                    GREEVEY
                 (to Logan)
         How much?

                    LOGAN
         Twenty-five and up.
                 (beat; deadpan)
         He must be crazy about his old lady.

                                        CUT TO

INT. CAPTAIN CRAGEN'S OFFICE - DAY

Cragen's in his early fifties and is looking at the Lynx
coat on his desk like it's a large turd.

                                        CONTINUED

Figure 10.1   *(continued)*

> The technical advisor said "If a cop thought it was dangerous [situation], he would go into the combat crouch with the gun out." . . . I said, "George, that may be true, but we are not doing reality here. The real reality—the television reality—is that people are going to see this and say, 'I've seen it ten thousand times before.' It's a visual cop show cliché."

The actor insisted that he could not grasp the proper internal motivation if he did not act in the proper manner. So, the scene was shot as written and adjusted in the editing process to make it play stronger. In the edited version, Dzundza reaches for his gun. Then the viewer sees a close-up of the policeman warning the suspect—if that pitbull moves, he's history. Edited that way, the scene created stronger dramatic tension and offered a better visual break.

The above circumstance illustrates the crucial role played by the creative producer as decision maker and mediator. Dick Wolf had to work with the actor to find a suitable middle ground, without compromising the final results. He also had to answer to the studio's concerns about the scene. In addition, he had to factor in the pragmatic costs of reshooting.

> I told George, everybody in the show wants to shoot it in New York. The only way we're going to be able to film in New York is if production operates at 98 percent efficiency—at all times. And this is not 98 percent efficiency. This is 2 percent efficiency.
>
> This is part of the ongoing battle we knew [would erupt] from the beginning. When we hired Dzundza and Moriarty, I said to Kim LeMasters [then head of programming for CBS] . . . "I want you to pay my psychiatrist's bill." I wasn't kidding. These are not easy people to deal with, because they're not dumb actors. I mean, the problem with George Dzundza is that he's too goddamm smart.

Despite Dick Wolf's efforts, production cost for the pilot of *Law and Order* did exceed the studio's projections. Wolf monitored the costs carefully and worked hard to minimize the overage. Analyzing the problem in hindsight, three reasons seem to emerge for the cost overruns. First, in the desire to produce a superior pilot—as close to Wolf's vision as possible—he and director Patterson demanded exacting performances from both cast and crew. This took time, and time in film production equates directly to cost. Second were the unanticipated events that occur with every new project. Finally, there was the reshooting, demanded by the studio executives and desired by the producer.

Although costs escalated, Dick Wolf was able to maintain tight control over the costs. He credited this to his support staff and the system they employed.

23

CONTINUED (2)

Logan mutters on expletive under his breath. Greevey gives him an I-told-you-so smile.

>   GREEVEY
>   I've sent a lot of guys away on
>   circumstantial evidence...anyway, I
>   think this is more than that.

>   ROBINETTE
>   What kind of more?

>   LOGAN
>   You know Halsey was a bagman?

>   ROBINETTE
>   Stone mentioned that.

>   GREEVEY
>   Then mention to Stone that Deputy
>   Commissioner Jefferson's been nosing
>   around...tell him I thought he'd
>   like to know...You're new...how long
>   have you been with Stone?

>   ROBINETTE
>   Eight months.

>   GREEVEY
>   (standing)
>   Must be a record...see you in court.

>   CUT TO

EXT. APARTMENT BUILDING - NIGHT

A doorman attended high rise. Greevey and Logan watch while the doorman uses the house phone.

>   DOORMAN
>   He must be out...no answer.
>   (looking over
>   their shoulders)
>   You guys just got lucky...here he
>   comes...

Greevey and Logan turn. Scalisi, a balding guy in his late thirties, is coming up the sidewalk with a bag of groceries in each arm.

>   LOGAN
>   Oh, no...

Scalisi is also walking a pit bull on a leash.

>   CONTINUED

Figure 10.2   Excerpt from *Law and Order* pilot script.

29

CONTINUED

               LOGAN
I <u>hate</u> pit bulls.

               GREEVEY
       (sotto)
He lets go of that leash, shoot the
dog first...

They split up on the sidewalk. When Scaslisi gets twenty
feet away, Logan yells out to him.

               LOGAN
Anthony Scalisi, I have a warrant
for your arrest...

The dog starts to growl.

               SCALISI
What's the charge?

               LOGAN
Assault with a deadly weapon and the
attempted murder of Charles Halsey.

Scalisi considers whether to make a play. Greevey steps
out of the shadows, his .38 out.

               GREEVEY
Spuds MacKenzie moves he's history.

Scalisi's eyes go from cop to cop, measuring, deciding,
while the dog's growls get louder. He comes to a decision
and raises his hand over his head.

               LOGAN
You have the right to remain
silent...

The dog growls even louder as we

                        FADE OUT

          <u>END OF ACT TWO</u>

Figure 10.2 *(continued)*

There was a constant watch on where the dollars were going, and that's where it was very valuable having *The Equalizer* people—Jim McAdams, Diane Foti, and Peter Runfolo, who could give me hourly figures. . . . To have that type of hour-by-hour update on what it's costing is enormously valuable. Then, we can really make intelligent decisions.

It was that close monitoring system that led Dick Wolf to extend production for an extra day, rather than simply shooting longer days, incurring overtime. He explained.

I made a decision . . . not to go into a 14 or 15 hour day on our last two days, because with New York work rules it became extremely expensive. Basically, the four hours of overtime that we would have had to use gave us a full extra day of shooting. They were triple time hours. So, it was a very close call [to find] the cheapest way to do it. [We analyzed what it would cost] to go into overtime, or cut the overtime and take an extra day. . . . The extra day was literally cheaper than trying to get it all done on schedule.

The combination of a large cast, a show filmed totally on the streets instead of on controllable sets, and a show produced at a distant location from the studio, contributed to make *Law and Order* the most difficult kind of production tackled in television. To successfully mount such an enterprise is considered a significant achievement in producing.

THE NETWORK'S EVALUATIONS AND RESPONSES

The finished version of the pilot was formally delivered to CBS on May 5, 1988. Reaction to the pilot was uniformly positive from all levels of the network programming staff. But when the Fall schedule for CBS was announced at the end of the month, *Law and Order* was not among the shows selected. This subsequent rejection was both shocking and perplexing to Dick Wolf and the Universal executives.

They subsequently learned that the principal cause of this action was due to research testing. In 1987, in a cost-saving measure, CBS disbanded its entire in-house testing operation (originally founded by Frank Stanton). The CBS executive staff made its program selections without the benefit of any research information. Whether the lack of research was a factor or not, the season for CBS was disastrous. It slid into third place.

In 1988 Larry Tisch, owner of CBS, ordered the resumption of program testing. The former in-house testing operation was reassembled outside the company and contracted to work for CBS. Other testing techniques, such as cable, were also initiated. It was reported that Tisch would not buy any program that did not test well, and *Law and Order* did not test well.

Not aware of Dick Wolf's deliberate emphasis on story and the slow evolution of characters, CBS research brought its conventional techniques to bear on *Law and Order*. They dutifully reported that the show was too male-oriented. More crucially, they stated that, while the story tested well and there was considerable interest in the concept, the characters did not come through strongly. Following the current television wisdom that a show without strong characters cannot succeed, they judged the pilot as having poor potential.

Several of the CBS programmers were as unhappy at the outcome as were Dick Wolf and Universal. Kim LeMasters, previewing his new shows to associates, was quoted as saying, "Now let me show you the best pilot we made, that we did not put on the air."

Each network negotiates to have two "bites" at a pilot, which means two opportunities to order it before the rights revert back to the producing entity. While *Law and Order* did not make the Fall schedule, there was still hope that CBS would order it as a midseason replacement show. Again, there were individuals within the organization who wanted it, but it was not to be. CBS's rights to *Law and Order* expired on December 31, 1988.

At the studio, Kerry McCluggage, Dick Wolf, and the Universal executive staff were not ready to forget *Law and Order*. They still believed passionately in it. Knowing that Dick Wolf was well respected at NBC for his work on *Hill Street Blues* and *Miami Vice*, the pilot was taken to Brandon Tartikoff, head of NBC. He screened it, along with network programming heads Warren Littlefield and Perry Simon. Overall, they liked the show and thought it had potential. Their only concerns were the lack of emphasis on characterization, and the male orientation of the story.

The pilot was tested by NBC research, using its cable testing technique. The results were similar to those obtained by CBS. While NBC uses research extensively, it is more flexible in its application. A meeting was held in Brandon Tartikoff's office with Dick Wolf and the Universal executives. The producer carefully explained his concept and philosophy regarding the show and presented a number of story ideas that would appeal strongly to women.

NBC executives were intrigued by the concept, supportive of Dick Wolf, but cautious due to the research findings and unusual format of *Law and Order*. They decided to invest enough money to hold the principal actors and to order six new scripts. It was their feeling that the additional scripts would provide the opportunity to see the unveiling and development of the continuing characters and permit Wolf to demonstrate stories that would have stronger female appeal.

Over the summer of 1989 Dick Wolf assembled a staff of writers who had successfully worked for NBC, including David Black and Michael Duggan *(Hill Street Blues)* and Robert Palm *(Crime Story).* The scripts were delivered to Brandon Tartikoff and his executive staff in the first week of October 1989.

The reaction from NBC executives was extremely positive. On November 30, 1989, over two years after the project began, NBC ordered 13 episodes of *Law and Order* for a slot on their fall 1990 schedule. On March 12, 1990, two years after the filming of the pilot, the cast was reassembled on the streets of New York and filming began for the series.

The series has been critically acclaimed and singled out for its unique dramatic impact and visual style, which were Dick Wolf's original creative focuses. The series also maintained excellent ratings for its time slot.

The original pilot, however, was temporarily an orphan. Having paid for its production, CBS retained possession of the pilot. In the summer of 1990 the two networks began negotiating for the pilot. Finally on August 31 NBC agreed on a price and obtained the pilot from CBS. Unfortunately, it was then too late for *TV Guide* deadlines. The pilot could not be used to launch the *Law and Order* series. Instead, the pilot aired at the end of October, achieving very strong ratings for its time slot.

Critical and Social Responsibilities of the Producer

Critical and Social Responsibilities of the Producer

Throughout this book we have looked at the practical and creative responsibilities of the television producer. Part One defined the tools and techniques of producing, while the case histories provided an in-depth analysis of the producing process in action. The case studies traced the choices made by Barry Kemp and Dick Wolf at every stage of production—and the ramifications those decisions had on their final productions.

Professional responsibility is tied largely to the successful completion of the project, no matter how complex it has been. One of the first goals of an effective television producer is to develop and create a show that will be appealing to buyers and viewers. The next step is to produce that show on schedule, under budget, and with solid production values.

As we've seen, those goals are accomplished against enormous odds. Producers have to stay on budget—even when the budget is highly classified (a pattern budget). They must negotiate through the divergent views of management—even when those views are inconsistent (networks versus studios). They rely heavily on the skills and expertise of everyone on the production, from writers, actors, and directors to key crew members. Given that context, it is astounding that so many television shows actually get produced.

Aside from the tangible completion of a project, however, the question of the producers' "responsibility" becomes a tenuous gauge to measure. Critical assessments are based on very different measures. In this chapter, we will look at "responsibility" from these specific viewpoints: *the management perspective, the social-scientific perspective,* and *the producer's perspective.*

Network and station management have pragmatic concerns about the role of the producer. Those concerns are tied largely to the ongoing needs of television programmers and historical trends in program formats (including comedy, drama, and reality-based programming).

Social scientists have a completely different perspective of the television producer, and the message of television programs. They view media in terms of social impacts, content analysis, and social effects (including the effects of violence).

Producers are the prime movers behind any television program, and they must deal with all practical, creative, and ethical issues surrounding the show. The fact that millions of viewers may see a program cannot be taken frivolously—especially in light of the producers' own battle for creative freedom and personal integrity.

THE MANAGEMENT PERSPECTIVE

Program executives at networks, cable and pay TV services, and independent stations are responsible for scheduling shows that fill their specific needs. Usually they want shows that appeal to the largest possible audiences, but in recent years that has become only one objective. They must also appeal to key demographic audiences. CBS targets its programming to an older and less urban audience. The Fox network focuses on young, urban viewers. The pay TV services tend to concentrate on male viewers. In this context, a producer is considered responsible if the show is delivered on time, on budget, and draws a significant number of the viewers desired.

Generally, quality is not an issue. The issue is ratings success, leading to financial rewards for the producer and distributor. Financial gains are possible from advertisers, domestic sales, and foreign distribution. This system minimizes elements of creativity, innovation, and programming quality. The issue of responsibility lies with the program buyer, whether that is the station or network programming executive, and it is tied to the pragmatics of acquiring competitive programs that appeal widely to prescribed audience targets.

Before the networks experienced the intense competition from cable, videocassettes, pay TV services, and strong independent stations, they simply sought the largest number of viewers. In those times broadcast executives used to operate on a philosophy expounded by then programming executive Paul Klein. His catchphrase LOP ("least objectionable programming"), while not the primary goal of networks, was acceptable, and that acceptance was made clear to series producers. As a consequence, the more banal the content, the more likely a show would offend no one and could, therefore, stay on the air for years.

Trends in Television Comedy

In the early days of television, inoffensive situation comedy prevailed, giving little opportunity for realistic dialogue or controversial themes. Producers were considered mavericks if they wanted to test new ground or create more realistic themes for their shows and characters. *I Love Lucy* showed Lucille Ball when she was pregnant, but the producers were not allowed to use the term "pregnant" on the air. *Ozzie and Harriet* had separate bedrooms, despite the fact that they were married and had kids. *I Dream of Jeannie* created a major incident when actress Barbara Eden's costume showed her navel on screen. (The producer, Sidney Sheldon, fought a long, hard battle with the networks over that one.)

Throughout the history of playwriting, comedy and satire paved the way for experimentation with controversial themes. From the periods of comic playwrights Aristophanes and Menander, through the time of Molière, contemporary trends and attitudes were reflected in the comic form.[1] Drama eventually incorporated those themes of relevance—after the audience was properly weaned.

In U.S. television, Norman Lear's *All in the Family* (1971) helped set the stage for more socially relevant comedy. At a time in which light fare like *The Beverly Hillbillies* reigned, *All in the Family* suddenly dealt with realistic issues—including bigotry, homosexuality, miscarriage, equal rights, menopause, and sexual impotence. Bob Wood, the CBS executive who approved the series, recalled its impact on reality-based comedy programming: "*All in the Family* really changed the face of television. . . . It got television up on its toes and things became sharper and better."[2]

Once audiences were provided with an opportunity to laugh at sensitive issues, the content of television shows were ripe for change. The predictable, slapstick situation comedy of the past gave way to "character" comedy, in which individual characters confronted the same problems faced by many of the viewers. The audience could identify with the characters caught in personal crises.

It was now the producer's responsibility to develop more "realistic"

---

[1]For a history of the situation comedy, and the comic tradition, see David Grote, *The End of Comedy: The Sitcom and the Comedic Tradition* (Hamden, Conn.: Shoestring Press, 1983).
[2]Horace Newcomb and Robert S. Alley, *The Producer's Medium* (New York: Oxford University Press, 1983), p. 176.

comedy fare. The producers who turned out *M*A*S*H**, *Taxi*, and *Cheers* became media heroes for their insights and willingness to challenge important issues, while at the same time maintaining ratings and turning a mighty profit for the shows in syndication. These shows became the backbone of the networks' primetime comedy schedules. From the standpoint of independent station managers, playing the syndication packages, they retained their strength in drawing local viewers and advertisers.

By the late 1980s, character comedy paved the way for contemporary comedy forms that reflected further changes in network programming standards—changes reflected within our own society. *The Cosby Show* dealt with typical family crises—but featured an upper-middle-class black family as the role model. *Dear John*, starring Judd Hirsch, focused on a divorced New York City teacher who joined a singles club to fight his loneliness. *Empty Nest*, created by Susan Harris *(The Golden Girls)*, featured Richard Mulligan as a widowed Florida pediatrician. *Roseanne*, played by comedienne Roseanne Barr, featured a heavy, sassy blue-collar mother, complete with wise-cracking husband and kids.

Themes of real life captured the interests of the audience and became an acceptable and "responsible" form of programming for the producer. It would not have been the case two decades before. Television executives were responding to the changing expectations of audiences who were exposed to more risqué programming on cable, pay television, home video, and syndication. Networks had to compete with the more freewheeling material, and audiences expected dialogue to be more realistic, themes more relevant, and jokes more poignant and hard-hitting.

Trends in Television Drama

The success of character comedy and comedy with realistic themes opened up new artistic freedom for producers of television drama—especially in the realm of television movies. For the first time in television history, producers and writers were permitted to explore forbidden themes— civil rights, police brutality, rape, child abuse, AIDS, and even the simple but sensitive theme of human dignity. In the early days, the networks took a nervous "wait and see" stance. Not only did an avalanche of objections not pour in but the ratings were competitive.

Examples of television movies and miniseries based on realistic themes are plentiful.[3] While network executives are, rightly, proud of

---

[3]For a detailed analysis of miniseries and television films, see Richard A. Blum and Richard D. Lindheim, *Primetime: Network Television Programming* (Boston: Focal Press, 1987), pp. 159–168.

many of them, and a number of them have had a profound impact on our laws, government, and society, the initial motives for airing them were not necessarily based solely on concern for social well-being. If themes tap into public consciousness, they can also be exploited to draw large audiences. Networks compete fiercely with other networks, stations, and cable TV programs for that promotional edge.

With the advent of more realistic, hard-hitting viewing alternatives, audiences expected more realism in episodic dramatic television series as well. The time was ripe for action shows like *Miami Vice, St. Elsewhere, Hill Street Blues,* and *L.A. Law.* The latter shows were examples of new, ensemble drama—each week, a show focused on different characters in the cast, with major plots and subplots interwoven.

Programming executives understood the shifting power of marketplace trends and viewer demographics. *Thirtysomething* featured a group of friends in their thirties who dealt realistically with problems of relationships, divorce, and work-related stress. It appealed to a new breed of audience, the middle-aged babyboomer, who had purchasing power for advertisers. Once that show passed the hurdle of acceptable network audience levels, other shows were developed for that same audience. *The Wonder Years* highlighted the childhood memories of growing up in the 1960s. But, more importantly, it highlighted the universal angst of high school relationships. *Almost Grown,* a romantic drama, highlighted the tempestuous relationship of a New Jersey couple from the 1960s to the late 1980s.

Reality Programming and Television Violence

Given the audience's demand for greater realism, program management faced a most complex problem—maintaining a balance between the need for action and the verboten line of violence. The networks behaved almost schizophrenically about this issue. While program executives wanted tense dramatic confrontations and graphic depictions of violent acts, the broadcast standards executives vigilantly exercised control over the language and scenes permitted. No clear rule prevailed, and, as a result, producers became as confused as the home viewer.

In earlier times, the department of broadcast standards and practices used to monitor every story, script, and rough-cut film for excessive use of violence, sex, and offensive dialogue. Along the way, sex and violence—completely separate elements—somehow became interwoven in the comments of network censors. Producers had to wade through a morass of rules and regulations that were exceedingly unclear. The issues were further muddied by the fact that social scientists and television critics differed on the question of articulation and impact of violence and sex.[4]

In 1988, with viewing levels dropping, realistic content demanded by primetime audiences, and competition from uncensored pay TV and videocassettes, the networks cut back on their broadcast standards and practices departments. They explained it as a matter of budget constraints. Ironically, there was hardly an uproar at the time about the cuts, and the issue of content control was thrown back into the arena of network programming management. The three networks insisted that the action would not reduce their commitment to "policing" the airwaves, but acknowledged that their standards were changing.[5] Producers saw more opportunities for realism, and network executives saw the need for more flexibility.

But, as often happens when tight controls are suddenly released, overreaction occurred. The most flagrant examples of this appeared on NBC in Spring 1989 with a Geraldo Rivera special on witchcraft and satanism, and with a miniseries, *Favorite Son*, which featured sexual acts, graphic violence, and partial nudity.

There was an immediate and outraged response from the television watchdog groups, which was followed by government inquiry and a condemnation by several advertisers. Sensing the public mood, the networks quickly clamped down and became more stringent than they had been for years.

After a cooling-off period, the networks proceeded again to liberalize program content, but with a more cautious attitude. Network executives generally agreed not to show "gratuitous" violence, although their definition of that shifted from time period to time period and from network to network. ABC has established "incident classification and analysis forms" to ascertain how closely incidents relate to the plot. CBS insists that shows reflect societal norms. NBC produces guidelines permitting violence only if it is "sensitively" portrayed and not gratuitous or excessive. According to Alan Gerson, NBC vice president of program standards and marketing, "We take a long, hard and careful look at violence. . . . We show the consequences rather than the physical impact. . . . Sometimes we don't get credit for the care we take."[6]

In a special report on violence in network television, *Variety* interviewed executives responsible for determining network policies and

---

[4]See, for example, "Crime, Violence, and the Mass Media" and "Sex and Sensationalism in the Mass Media," in Ray Eldon Hiebert and Carol Reuss, *Impact of Mass Media: Current Issues*, 2nd ed. (New York: Longman, 1988), pp. 123–160, 161–176.
[5]"Snipping the Censors," *Electronic Media* (October 24, 1988): 19.
[6]"How the Networks Set Standards for Portraying Violent Behavior," *Variety* (August 16–22, 1989): 44.

guidelines.[7] From their perspective, television does not impact or change behavior, but rather reflects and mimics behavior. The trade paper candidly points out that network executives use the nonimpact declaration as a defense against social critics, but it would surprise advertisers who spend billions of dollars to influence viewers' behavior.

After the cutbacks in broadcast standards, followed by its renewed vigor, it is understandable why producers became very concerned about the problems of censorship. Marshall Herskovitz *(Thirtysomething)*, Steven Bochco *(L.A. Law* and *Hooperman)*, and Bruce Paltrow *(Tattinger's* and *St. Elsewhere)* had numerous confrontations over these issues in relation to their shows, and they remain convinced that the battle will continue to permeate the industry.[8]

Perhaps the heart of the problem resides in the industry's dual perspective of "responsible" producing. Producers feel it is essential to maintain the integrity of their shows by featuring more realistic situations and content. Network executives view that freedom nervously, especially when it creates problems with advertisers. While they recognize that sex and violence are part of the program spectrum, program executives also realize that reality-based programming can be exploitive. All this is complicated by the realization that these elements are a prime resource for competitive ratings.

Reality Programming and "Tabloid TV"

With the advent of exploitive and controversial programming in syndication and cable TV, the boundaries of acceptable "taste" became increasingly blurred. Independent station managers around the country found that low-budget, exploitive programs drew viewers. In some cases, they actually outperformed network shows in the Nielsen ratings. Informally designated "tabloid TV" or "trash TV," programs like *The Morton Downey Jr. Show, Geraldo, America's Most Wanted, Unsolved Mysteries,* and *Crimes of Passion* appealed to a viewer's baser instincts.

Interestingly, producers of these kinds of shows defended their own style as being public-affairs oriented, while they berated others as being "trash TV."[9] In fact, during the 1989 television season, Fox-TV's *America's Most Wanted* was directly responsible for the capture and arrest of several infamous criminals. The series re-created crimes, profiled the offender, and asked the public to call a toll-free phone number if they

---

[7]Ibid.
[8]Ibid.
[9]" 'Trash TV'? It's What the Others Do," *Electronic Media* (November 28, 1988): 16.

had pertinent information. With each capture, the ratings spiraled and the show gained more respectability as a legitimate public-affairs offering.

The trend toward "tabloid TV" was so ethically problematic that *Electronic Media* surveyed producers, network executives, station managers, syndicators, cable programmers, and broadcast scholars for their reactions.[10] These were some of the main conclusions:

- Programs that shock people date back to ground-breaking shows like *Joe Pyne* and *All in the Family.*
- Intense competition between networks, independent stations, and cable TV led to an atmosphere of desperation, where programmers broke barriers to attract viewers.
- TV was responding to changing public tastes, reflective of the times. These shows were a legitimate "alternative" form of public-affairs programming.
- Ultimately, by their decision to view, and, consequently, by the high Nielsen ratings, the public decides what is acceptable and what is not.

Anguishing over the ethics of producing and programming for this genre, Ted Harbert, vice president of primetime for ABC Entertainment, mused:

> This programming trend suggests some potentially disturbing things about our society. . . . People suddenly seem apathetic about standard cop shows. Now they want to see the real thing instead, from Geraldo getting a chair thrown at him to the reenactment of grisly crimes. . . . But we live in a competitive world. You can't take away the fact that people are watching these programs and that they are relatively easy and inexpensive to produce. . . . Personally, these are not the kinds of shows I would like to see us do as series.[11]

In the same survey, NBC president Robert Wright noted that "tabloid TV" proved that audiences had a wider appetite for "bolder" shows. Although he considered the trend a fad, he felt NBC needed to stay on top of those trends: "It is not in our past, present, or future to ignore the issues, shows, and concepts that appear to have strong audience appeal."[12]

CBS was trying to stay out of the foray. Although third in the ratings race, Howard Stringer, president of CBS broadcast group, did not want to resort to exploitive programming to win back audiences: "If we are to regain our Tiffany luster, we certainly are not going to do it

---

[10]"Industry Split Over 'Trash TV': Is Genre Honest Controversy or Low Brow Sensationalism?" *Electronic Media* (November 28, 1988): 1, 16.

[11]Ibid., p. 16.

[12]Ibid.

by stooping to trashy TV."[13] He expressed concern that a long-term effect of the proliferation of this type of programming might be a Congressional watchdog role, or legislation by the Federal Communications Commission.

In August 1989 the U.S. House of Representatives voted to give the television industry three years to adopt voluntary guidelines for depicting violence. This came on the heels of a Senate bill that urged the industry to examine its portrayal of sexuality and drug use. The issue of censorship versus artistic freedom was vigorously debated, but broadcasters knew they would face rigorous Congressional directives if they did not curb violent programming.

Industry reaction to the prospect of self-imposed guidelines for violence was decidedly mixed. Broadcast and cable networks generally opposed the idea, asserting that the current mechanism provided adequate checks and balances. Reflecting the views of the networks and cable executives, Jamie Kellner, president of Fox Broadcasting Company, had this to say:

> [There is] a very fine line between what gets on the air and what does not. You try to be as responsible as you can, but let creative people have an outlet to demonstrate ideas. I doubt these kind of things can be legislated or handled in a code. You need responsible executives looking at these issues at each stage of program development, from concept to broadcast.[14]

While some producers concurred with that view, others supported the call for more vigilance in programming content. David Levy, a highly established producer-writer, and head of the Caucus for Producers, Writers, and Directors expressed that point of view: "The problem is . . . one segment of the entertainment industry breaks through [with excessive violence, sex, or abusive language] and competitors feel they have to match that with their own titillating action or excessive violence."[15]

THE SOCIAL-SCIENTIFIC PERSPECTIVE

A totally different perspective of television production comes from social scientists who have always debated the meaning and impact of shows produced for the mass media.[16]

---

[13]Ibid.
[14]"Mixed Reactions to Violence Standards Plan," *Broadcasting* (August 7, 1989): 33.
[15]Ibid., pp. 32–33.
[16]See for example Arthur Asa Berger, *Media U.S.A.: Process and Effect* (New York: Longman, 1988); Clifford G. Christians, Kim B. Rotzoll, and Mark Fackler, *Media Ethics: Cases and Moral Reasoning*, 2nd ed. (New York: Longman, 1988); Hiebert and Reuss, *Impact of Mass Media*; Horace Newcomb, ed., *Television: The Critical View*, 4th ed. (New York: Oxford University Press, 1987).

In this context, producers are considered responsible for the form, content, and social values expressed in messages to the public. Social scientists ask, Does the show reflect contemporary values? Does it provide clear or confusing social messages? What ethical dilemmas and resolutions are posed by the show? What impact does the content have on the viewing audience?

There is no single perspective common to all communication scientists, social critics, and cultural analysts. Some "content analysts" closely examine shows to measure how reality is reflected or distorted. They identify and document social and behavioral patterns presented in television programs.[17]

Some scholars perceive the producer's product as an aesthetic form that informs and influences the mass audience.[18] Some argue that the television producer creates "ritual masks" of contemporary society, conveying the essence of our culture through the program content created.[19]

Consequently, a television program is examined as a source for analyzing cultural symbols, media ethics, and the impact of media on the public. The importance of that point of view has been articulated by two scholars of television, Horace Newcomb and Paul Hirsch: "Television presents us with our most prevalent concerns, our deepest dilemmas, our most traditional views, those which are repressive and reactionary, as well as those which are subversive and emancipated."[20]

The field of cultural analysis has grown in recent years, with arguments for hidden messages and their influence on the public. Television is viewed, along with film, music, and video, as a "pop culture" art form. Yet despite extensive research reports and publications, surprisingly little agreement has been reached on the actual impact of television messages on the lives of our citizens.[21]

One study, sponsored by the U.S. Department of Education, reviewed virtually all previous research on the effects of television on children's learning, and concluded—contrary to popular belief—that television has no perceived negative effects.[22]

---

[17]For example of content analyses, see Mary Cassata and Thomas Skill, *Live on Daytime Television: Tuning in American Serial Drama* (Norwood, N.J.: Ablex, 1983); Bradley S. Greenberg, *Life on Television: Content Analysis of U.S. TV Drama* (Norwood, N.J.: Ablex, 1980).
[18]See, for example, Herbert Zettl, "The Hidden Message: Some Aspects of Television Aesthetics," in Berger, *Media U.S.A.*, pp. 207–224.
[19]Newcomb and Alley, *The Producer's Medium*, p. 44.
[20]Horace Newcomb and Paul Hirsch, "Television as a Cultural Forum: Implications for Research," *Quarterly Review of Film Studies* (Summer, 1983): 44.
[21]For a diversity of views, see Hiebert and Reuss, *Impact of Mass Media;* Joshua Meyrowitz, *No Sense of Place: The Impact of Electronic Media on Social Behavior* (New York: Oxford University Press, 1985); Newcomb, *Television.*
[22]Daniel Anderson and Patricia A. Collins, *The Impact on Children's Education: Television's Influence on Cognitive Development*, Working Paper No. 2 (University of Massachusetts, Amherst, Psychology). Office of Educational Research & Improvement, U.S. Department of Education, Washington, D.C. Report No. OR 88-507; ERIC ED 295-271 (April 1988).

Social scientists have argued for years over the interpretation of violence and its impact on television viewers. There is no doubt about the prevalence of violence and crime on television, but there is considerable debate about its effect. Throughout the 1970s, when television violence was of particular concern to social scientists, George Gerbner, then dean of the Annenberg School of Communications at the University of Pennsylvania, regularly tracked violent trends in U.S. television. He and his colleagues counted incidents of violence on television, as well as trends in program content. Those reports were published regularly in the *Journal of Communication*.[23]

Other studies chronicled social stereotypes and trends found in program content. One of the more venerable was Ben Stein's documentation of negative images of business and businessmen in network television.[24]

Producers tend to think that studies of violence and social criticism misrepresent their work. The late Richard Levinson and his partner, William Link, had this reaction to Gerbner's research and Ben Stein's studies:

> If you believe George Gerbner . . . and others, there's a reinforcement of racist, elitist, anti-feminist, and anti-age, a reinforcement of totally establishment values as opposed to more radical and theoretically humane attitudes. Television eschews those and deals primarily with establishment values. And if television does reinforce establishment values in any given country it may be damaging to the fringe areas of humanity.
>
> In Ben Stein's book . . . he discusses Columbo [a character created by Levinson and Link] going against the very rich people, but that was not intentional on our part. That was for purposes of drama and juxtaposition and contrast. . . . The Stein book has some interesting half-truths in it. . . . But there are too many exceptions.[25]

Norman Lear argues that the producer's primary responsibility is to entertain audiences. He thinks it is impossible to reinforce any social stereotypes in the process:

> I find myself in disagreement with a lot of the research I read. . . . Sometimes, we're accused of—through Archie *[All in the Family]*— enforcing bigotry, and sometimes given credit for having diffused a lot of prejudice and bigotry. I don't think either is true. . . . I don't believe at all that [a television program] reinforces anything in

[23]For example, George Gerbner et al. "Violence Profile: Trends in Network Television Drama and Viewer Conceptions of Reality," *Journal of Communication*, No. 7 (1976).
[24]Ben Stein, *The View from Sunset Boulevard* (New York: Basic Books, 1979).
[25]Newcomb and Alley, *The Producer's Medium*, p. 151.

society. . . . I would be a horse's ass if I thought that one little situation comedy would accomplish something that the entire Judeo-Christian ethic hasn't managed in two thousand years.[26]

Throughout the 1980s and early 1990s, research on television violence generally retains the incident-counting design popularized by George Gerbner. Studies count the number of antisocial messages and incidents within a show. It is up to other social scientists to interpret the data.

One recent example is a study commissioned by *Variety*, identifying the 25 most violent and crime-filled programs during one week of prime-time (the week of March 27, 1989).[27] In that study, these programs accounted for 81.2 percent of all incidences of crime and violence on network television: *Beverly Hills Cop* (movie), *A Man Called Hawk*, *B.L. Stryker*, *Hillside Strangler* (movie), *In the Heat of the Night*, *Wildcats* (movie), *The Equalizer*, *Stroker Ace* (movie), *Murder She Wrote*, *MacGyver*, *Hunter*, *Hard Times on Planet Earth*, *The Wonder Years*, *Unsolved Mysteries*, *The Morning After* (movie), *20/20* (news magazine), *Thirtysomething*, *Academy Awards* (film clips), *Matlock*, *The Shaggy Dog* (movie), *Midnight Caller*, *Moonlighting*, *Tour of Duty*, *West 57th* (news magazine), and *48 Hours* (news magazine).

The film *Beverly Hills Cop* accounted for the most instances of crime and violence, and some of the action shows predictably followed the pattern. However, some surprises materialized—including the appearance of *The Wonder Years*. The particular episode studied had 11 separate incidents of violence, including shoving, beating, and fistfights. The lead character, a winsome preadolescent, tried to stand up for his girlfriend and faced the fury of a school bully. Some would interpret the show's violence count as intrinsically damaging, but psychologist Dr. Lawrence Balter of New York University interpreted it as providing a healthy catharsis for adults who themselves were bullied.[28]

THE PRODUCER'S PERSPECTIVE

The impact of television content on society is a fundamental concern of communication scientists and sociologists. Producers, however, are preoccupied with the quality of their production and with satisfying the needs of the network. As sociologist Muriel Cantor noted, producers perceive the network as their primary audience.[29] As we've seen, they

[26]Ibid., p. 193.
[27]"The 25 Shows with the Most Crime and Violence," *Variety* (August 16–22, 1989): 39.
[28]"Beating, Shoving, and Slugging in 'Wonder Years,'" *Variety* (August 16–22, 1989): 45.
[29]Muriel G. Cantor, *The Hollywood TV Producer: His Work and His Audience*, rev. ed. (New Brunswick, N.J.: Transaction Books, 1988).

also perceive themselves as creative storytellers—not social advocates or station managers.

Reconciling these divergent points of view is a difficult task, but it is not impossible. We can attempt a resolution through the producer's perspective. It is the producer, ultimately, who turns out programs that will be viewed by millions of people.

In the collaborative environment of television, a producer tries to maintain his or her singular vision. Both Barry Kemp and Dick Wolf had specific ideas about the concepts for their shows, but reality dictated compromise. Throughout development and production, they faced mediation with studio executives, casting personnel, art directors, actors, directors, agents, production crew, editors, and—of course—the buyers of their product, network management. Still the basic tone was set for each of their shows.

Given the extraordinary number of people, issues, and detail a producer must contend with, daily production problems gain priority attention. As Barry Kemp and Dick Wolf demonstrated in their daily production activities, certain decisions make or break the program, and they are not always immediately ascertainable. Easily identifiable issues of casting, script, and overall production quality are paramount but not all encompassing. Other factors, like submerged rocks in a bay, can rip the bottom out of the producer's ship.

With the producer preoccupied with these factors, questions of social value are simply not likely to be relevant—unless those questions impinge directly on the show. For example, Barry Kemp wanted humorously to deal with the angst of a football coach going through a midlife crisis in the Midwest. Dick Wolf wanted to present a crime show that would be told in raw, realistic tones. Those decisions had a lasting effect on the production value of each show. There was no context for predicting social impacts or potential incidents of violence.

Producers are creative individuals who take pride in their work. As in any competitive field, some think more clearly about their mission and impact than others. A producer who strives for high quality in his or her show will likely retain that sense of integrity throughout the development and production process. A producer who gives in to lesser standards may end up at the lower end of the artistic spectrum.

While writers commonly have a definite social point of view to their material, and often are very well aware of the "message" they wish to communicate, the converse is the normal situation for most producers. As has been extensively explored in this text, producers are generally more preoccupied with the production process itself than with the consequences of the end product.

The late Richard Levinson and his partner, Bill Link, would be amused by the diverse sociological interpretations of the character they created, Columbo. They drew the character from literary antecedents and felt the "open-mystery" plotting would provide an unusual and entertaining method of telling stories. They had no pretensions of anything more than that.

The astute producer knows, however, that, beyond its entertainment value, television content, both implied and incidental, can have an effect. Frequently, negative impacts are publicized (such as instances of real criminals replicating behaviors shown on fictional TV crime dramas). But the impact of television can also be healthy and enduring. It is difficult today to imagine any community without paramedics and trauma centers. What is forgotten is that these life-saving functions were derived from a model in a television show called *Emergency*. That series was created in the early 1970s to fill a desperate programming need by NBC. *All in the Family* had just emerged as a gigantic television hit. It was *The Cosby Show* of its era. *All in the Family* was programmed at 8:00 P.M. Saturday, and CBS dominated the Nielsens, following it with *Bob Newhart* and *Mary Tyler Moore*, among other shows. To try for some ratings respectability, then head of NBC programming Herb Schlosser turned to the research department. He wanted to find any vulnerability to *All in the Family*. Research reported that the only possible audience that might be lured to an alternative program was children, especially young boys.

After brainstorming, the NBC programmers came to the realization that most boys liked fire engines. Schlosser turned to Jack Webb, who had created *Dragnet* and *Adam-12* for NBC. Would he be able quickly to create a show about fire trucks? Webb and his associate, Bob Cinader, explored the possibilities. Having close connections to the Los Angeles Police Department they learned of a new, experimental rescue program shepherded by the fire department. The program was fighting for funding and existed at one fire station in Carson, an industrial suburb of Los Angeles. Cinader and Webb saw it simply as the solution to Schlosser's programming problem. It became, of course, much more.

Emergency premiered on January 22, 1972. Never a big hit, it functioned perfectly for NBC by attracting the only audience not committed to *All in the Family* in those pre-VCR days. The series ran for five years, and by the end of that time paramedics had become a common word and emergency service programs and trauma wards had spread throughout the United States.

Television does have positive impacts, from innovative children's shows like *Sesame Street* to television movies that forge public debate and help shape public attitudes. It is that function which producers need to keep in mind. Their shows do affect public attitudes.

With the globalization of television and the consequent distribution of U.S. TV programs around the world, it is imperative that producers become more aware of this impact. Today, children in Asia and Europe may be as familiar with *Miami Vice* and *The Wonder Years* as are children in Omaha or Seattle. From personal experience these authors have met individuals abroad who fear to come to the United States because of the violence portrayed on television. After watching *Wise Guy, The Equalizer, Miami Vice, Crime Story,* and other shows, they fear that they will face physical danger in the United States.

And the reverse stereotyping occurs for Americans. While created by the unintentional efforts of producers, Americans are often given stereotyped and distorted images of other nationalities. The long-term consequences of this situation should be comtemplated by the responsible television producer.

Television producers may not think of themselves as political harbingers of the Bill of Rights, but inevitably they get caught up in those same issues. Artistic freedom and the right to free speech are vital to our democracy. They are also vital to any public entertainment forum. Producers are creative artists who are ultimately responsible for the final vision on screen. As true of any creative artist, they bristle at the thought of censorship. Some may overcompensate by challenging and testing the boundaries of acceptable programming. In the process, they may provoke network management or social critics. However, the battle is not for television to be the oasis of questionable programming but rather for the right to create a range of programming choices for audiences. It is ultimately up to the audience to select the programs that will survive.

A talented, creative producer can make the emotions of television viewers soar. Through carefully crafted drama or comedy, a television producer can provide us with profound opportunities to enjoy and appreciate the universality of the human condition. It is, perhaps, that vision—crafted in entertainment—that contributes most significantly to our society.

Annotated and Selected Bibliography

BOOKS

Bach, Stephen. *Final Cut* (Bergenfield, N.J.: New American Library, 1987). A detailed description of the development, production, and extraordinary budgetary problems encountered by producers of the United Artists film, *Heaven's Gate.*

Barnouw, Erik. *Tube of Plenty: The Evolution of American Television*, rev. ed. (New York: Oxford University Press, 1982). A comprehensive and thorough history of television, this book is a condensation of Barnouw's earlier three-volume classic, *History of Broadcasting in the United States.*

Berger, Arthur Asa. *Media U.S.A.: Process and Effect* (New York: Longman, 1988). A compilation of essays organized by content and theme. Two sections specifically examine television and film. Themes covered include ethics, sociopolitical aspects of media, textual analysis, aesthetics, sexuality, visual images, audiences, genres and formats, media makers, and heroes and heroines.

Blum, Richard A. *Working Actors: The Craft of Television, Film, and Stage Performance* (Boston: Focal Press, 1989). Candid interviews with successful actors about the pragmatics of acting in television and film, including discussions about casting, working in primetime series, miniseries, and soaps.

———. *Television Writing: From Concept to Contract* (Boston: Focal Press, 1984). An examination of the development process for new series and television scripts, with sample stories and scripts.

Blum, Richard A., and Richard D. Lindheim. *Primetime: Network Television Programming* (Boston: Focal Press, 1987). A detailed account of the roles and responsibilities of producers and management in the development, production, and scheduling of network shows.

Broughton, Irv. *Producers on Producing: The Making of Film and Television* (Jefferson, N.C.: McFarland, 1986). Interviews with producers, writers, and program executives.

Brown, Les. *Encyclopedia of Television* (New York: Zoetrope, 1982). Analysis of network programming, including information on content, staff, and economics by *The New York Times'* television critic. This is a revision of Brown's *New York Times Encyclopedia of Television.*

Cantor, Muriel G. *The Hollywood TV Producer: His Work and His Audience,* rev. ed. (New Brunswick, N.J.: Transaction Books, 1988). Updated introduction places this classic sociological study in perspective. The original study (1971) examined the workplace of producers and concluded that the most important audience for the producer is the network for whom projects are delivered.

Cassata, Mary, and Thomas Skill. *Live on Daytime Television: Tuning in American Serial Drama* (Norwood, N.J.: Ablex, 1983). Content analysis of the soap-opera genre, including analysis of social issues and character interactions.

Chambers, Everett. *Producing TV Movies* (New York: Prentice-Hall, 1986). Discussion by a major producer of the development process and production problems faced in made-for-television projects.

Christians, Clifford G., Kim B. Rotzoll, and Mark Fackler, *Media Ethics: Cases and Moral Reasoning,* 2nd ed. (New York: Longman, 1988). Ethical foundations and perspectives on news, advertising, and entertainment.

Eliot, Marc. *Televisions: One Season in American Television* (New York: St. Martin's Press, 1983). A look at the 1981–1982 television season by a producer and critic.

Fiske, John. *Television Culture* (London: Methuen, 1987). An analysis of television as an agent of popular culture and a commodity. Uses textual analysis to examine meaning for television audiences.

Gianakos, Larry James. *Television Drama Series Programming: A Comprehensive Chronicle, 1982–1984* (Metuchen, N.J.: Scarecrow Press, 1988). An encyclopedia of programs produced on the major networks, including cast and broadcast date. Earlier volumes encompass television programs from 1947 on.

Gitlin, Todd. *Inside Primetime* (New York: Pantheon Books, 1983). A behind-the-scenes look at programming, based on interviews with producers, executives, and agents.

Greenberg, Bradley S. *Life on Television: Content Analysis of U.S. TV Drama* (Norwood, N.J.: Ablex, 1980). Content analysis of dramatic programming on primetime television.

Grote, David. *The End of Comedy: The Sitcom and the Comedic Tradition* (Hamden, Conn.: Shoestring Press, 1983). Scholarly survey of the history of comedy, from its origins to the sitcom form on television.

Head, Sydney W., and Christopher Sterling. *Broadcasting in America: A Survey of Electronic Media,* 5th ed. (Boston: Houghton Mifflin, 1987). Coverage of broadcasting technology, economics, regulation, history, social effects, and programming.

Hiebert, Ray Eldon, and Carol Reuss. *Impact of Mass Media: Current Issues,* 2nd ed. (New York: Longman, 1988). Essays organized by theme, including impact of mass media, freedom versus responsibility, ethics, pressure groups, crime and violence, sex and sensationalism, politics, minorities, media and culture, new technology.

Levinson, Richard, and William Link. *Stay Tuned: An Inside Look at the Making of Prime Time Television* (New York: St. Martin's Press, 1981). An account of the development and production challenges faced in preparing quality shows for the networks by two of the most prolific writer-producers in television.

Meyrowitz, Joshua. *No Sense of Place: The Impact of Electronic Media on Social Behavior* (New York: Oxford University Press, 1985). A theory that television shapes our culture by revealing different roles and blurring the distinctions played by age, gender, and authority.

Newcomb, Horace, ed. *Television: The Critical View,* 4th ed. (New York, Oxford University Press, 1987). An anthology of critical essays that encompasses wide-ranging points of view on television as a cultural forum. Some are contradictory but show the diverse viewpoints among social critics of television.

Newcomb, Horace, and Robert S. Alley. *The Producer's Medium* (New York: Oxford University Press, 1983). Informative interviews with eight successful television producers.

Postman, Neil. *Amusing Ourselves to Death: Public Discourse in the Age of Show Business* (New York: The Viking Press, 1986). A provocative look at the critical and cultural impact of television.

Shaffer, William Drew, and Richard Wheelwright. *Creating Original Programming for Cable TV* (Washington, D.C.: National Federation of Local Cable Programmers, 1983). A guide for producing shows for local origination on cable television.

Shales, Tom. *On the Air* (New York: Summit Books, 1982). Perceptions about the medium by an award-winning television critic.

Shanks, Bob. *The Primal Screen: How to Write, Sell, and Produce Movies for Television* (New York: Fawcett Columbine, 1986). An informal explanation of the process of developing and producing motion pictures for television by a producer and former network executive.

Sklar, Robert. *Prime Time America: Life on and Behind the Television Screen* (New York: Oxford University Press, 1980). A critical assessment of television as a popular art form.

Stein, Ben. *The View from Sunset Boulevard* (New York: Basic Books, 1979). Documentation of negative business stereotypes portrayed in network television.

Verna, Tony. *Live TV: An Inside Look at Directing and Producing* (Boston: Focal Press, 1987). Interviews with directors and some producers of news, sports, and talk shows and special events programming.

Zettl, Herbert. *Television Production Handbook,* 4th ed. (San Francisco: Wadsworth, 1984). Coverage of all technical aspects of production, from camera and lighting to digital production equipment and postproduction.

ARTICLES AND REPORTS

Anderson, Daniel, and Patricia A. Collins. *The Impact on Children's Education: Television's Influence on Cognitive Development,* Working Paper No. 2 (University of Massachusetts, Amherst, Psychology). Office of Educational Research & Improvement, U.S. Department of Education, Washington, D.C. Report No. OR 88-507; ERIC ED 295-271 (April 1988).

"Beating, Shoving, and Slugging in 'Wonder Years,' " *Variety* (August 16–22, 1989): 45.

"Carsey-Werner: The Little Programming Engine That Could," *Broadcasting* (July 18, 1988): 60–61.

Gerbner, George, et al., "Violence Profile: Trends in Network Television Drama and Viewer Conceptions of Reality," *Journal of Communication*, No. 7 (1976). Updates available from Annenberg School of Communication, University of Pennsylvania, Philadelphia, Pennsylvania.

"How the Networks Set Standards for Portraying Violent Behavior," *Variety* (August 16–22, 1989): 44.

"Industry Split Over 'Trash TV': Is Genre Honest Controversy or Low Brow Sensationalism?" *Electronic Media* (November 28, 1988): 1, 16.

"Mixed Reactions to Violence Standards Plan," *Broadcasting* (August 7, 1989): 32–33.

Newcomb, Horace, and Paul Hirsch, "Television as a Cultural Forum: Implications for Research," *Quarterly Review of Film Studies* (Summer, 1983): 40–50.

"Snipping the Censors," *Electronic Media* (October 24, 1988): 19.

"Steven Bochco: Dialogue on Film," *American Film* (July/August, 1988): 16.

" 'Trash TV'? It's What the Others Do," *Electronic Media* (November 28, 1988): 16.

"The 25 Shows with the Most Crime and Violence," *Variety* (August 16–22, 1989): 39.

INDUSTRY PERIODICALS

Advertising Age
220 E. 42nd St.
New York, NY 10017

Adweek
ASM Communications, Inc.
820 2nd Ave.
New York, NY 10017

Backstage
1411 Broadway
New York, NY 10036

Broadcasting
1735 DeSales St., N.W.
Washington, D.C. 20036

Cablevision
2500 Curtis St.
Denver, CO 80205

Channels
Box 2001
Mahopac, NY 10541

Current
Box 53358
Washington, D.C. 20009

Daily Variety
1400 N. Cahuenga Blvd.
Hollywood, CA 90028

Electronic Media
Crain Communications, Inc.
740 Rush St.
Chicago, IL 60611

Emmy
Academy of Television Arts &
    Sciences
4605 Lankershim Blvd.
North Hollywood, CA 91602

The Hollywood Reporter
6715 Sunset Blvd.
Hollywood, CA 90028

*Journal of Broadcasting & Electronic
    Media*
Broadcast Education Association
1771 N St., N.W.
Washington, D.C. 20036

Journal of Communication
Annenberg School of
    Communication
Box 13358
3620 Walnut St.
Philadelphia, PA 19104

Journal of Popular Film and Television
Heldref Publications
4000 Albermarle St., N.W.
Washington, D.C. 20016

Media Report to Women
3306 Ross Place, N.W.
Washington, D.C. 20008

Multichannel News
633 Third Ave.
New York, NY 10022

Ross Reports
Television Index, Inc.
150 Fifth Ave.
New York, NY 10011

Show Business News
1301 Broadway
New York, NY 10036

Television Quarterly
National Academy of Television
    Arts & Sciences
110 W. 57th St.
New York, NY 10019

Television/Radio Age
1270 Avenue of the Americas
New York, NY 10010

Variety
154 W. 46th St.
New York, NY 10036

*View: The Magazine of Television
    Programming*
150 E. 58th St.
New York, NY 10155

INDUSTRY DIRECTORIES

Acquisitions & Development Directory
Omni Artists Management Group,
    Inc.
12021 Wilshire Blvd., Suite 459
Los Angeles, CA 90025-1021

Broadcasting Yearbook
1735 DeSales St., N.W.
Washington, D.C. 20036

Cable File
Tisch Communications
2500 Curtis St.
Denver, CO 80217

Cable TV Program Data Book
Kagan and Associates
26386 Carmel Rancho Lane
Carmel, CA 93923

Pacific Coast Directory
6331 Hollywood Blvd.
Hollywood, CA 90028

*The Producer's Masterguide:
The International Production Manual
    for Motion Picture, Television,
    Commercials, Cable, Videotape
    Industries*

Billboard Publications, Inc.
611 Broadway
New York, NY 10012-2608

Television Factbook
1836 Jefferson Place, N.W.
Washington, D.C. 20036

APPENDIX A
Pilot Script: *Coach*

"COACH"
Pilot

Written by
Barry Kemp

FINAL DRAFT
April 7, 1988

<u>COACH</u>

"Pilot"

<u>CHARACTERS</u>

```
HAYDEN FOX .......................CRAIG T. NELSON
LUTHER VAN DAM ...................JERRY VAN DYKE
CHRISTINE ARMSTRONG .............SHELLEY FABARES
KELLY FOX ........................CLARE CAREY
DAUBER DYBINSKI .................BILL FAGERBAKKE
YOUNG MAN ........................GARY KASPER
SECRETARY ........................PAT CRAWFORD BROWN
CLERK ...........................BILL SHICK
ELOISE DUPREE ...................GRETA BROWN
A MAN ...........................
LIVINGSTON DUPREE ...............
```

<u>SETS</u>

<u>TEASER</u>

INT. LIVING ROOM – NIGHT

<u>ACT ONE</u>

INT. COACH'S OFFICE – DAY

INT. HAYDEN'S CABIN – ONE WEEK LATER – LATE AFTERNOON

<u>ACT TWO</u>

INT. HOTEL LOBBY – THAT NIGHT

INT. HAYDEN'S CABIN – LATER THAT NIGHT

INT. COACH'S OFFICE – THE FOLLOWING AFTERNOON

```
                    "COACH"

                    Teaser

                                        (HAYDEN,
                                         ELOISE,
                                         LIVINGSTON,
                                         DAUBER)


FADE IN:

INT. LIVING ROOM - NIGHT

THE TINY AND VERY MODEST HOME OF ELOISE DUPREE AND
HER 17 YEAR OLD SON, LIVINGSTON. BOTH OF THEM ARE
SEATED ATTENTIVELY ON THE SOFA, LISTENING TO THE
VETERAN HEAD FOOTBALL COACH OF MINNESOTA STATE
UNIVERSITY, HAYDEN FOX. SEATED NEXT TO HAYDEN IS
HIS 25 YEAR OLD ASSISTANT, MIKE "DAUBER" DYBINSKI.
HAYDEN IS PRESENTLY IN THE MIDDLE OF A RECRUITING
SESSION. IT'S SOMETHING HE'S DONE A THOUSAND TIMES
IN HIS LIFE, AND SOMETHING HE CAN BE DANGEROUSLY
GOOD AT.

                    HAYDEN
          Mrs. Dupree, when a mother gives me
          her son - and that's what you'll be
          doing if Livingston comes to play
          football for Minnesota State - I
          consider that an act of faith. And
          that's not something I take
          lightly. I think "Dauber" here can
          attest to that. (INDICATING
          DYBINSKI) I've always called him
          Dauber because the way he's built
          always reminded me of a mud dauber.
          (HE SMILES AFFECTIONATELY AT
          DYBINSKI) At any rate, a few years
          back when I was recruiting this
          young man to play for the Screaming
          Eagles, his mother was very ill. In
          fact, she was more than just ill.
          She was dying. Her last wish for
          her boy was for him to graduate
          from college. And she knew she

                    MORE
```

                    HAYDEN (CONT'D)
          wasn't going to be around to
          guarantee that.

DYBINSKI LOOKS APPROPRIATELY MISTY-EYED. THIS
SPEECH OF COACH'S ALWAYS GETS TO HIM.

                    HAYDEN (CONT'D)
          On the final day of high school
          recruiting that year, I went to see
          Dauber's mother in the hospital.
          And right there, in front of her,
          and the doctors, and God, and all
          those machines, I promised her I'd
          see to it he did just that.
          (EMOTIONALLY) That was seven years
          ago. And even though Dauber's
          mother never lived to see that
          graduation, I never forgot the
          promise I made. And next year, or
          maybe the year after, when Dauber
          finally has enough credits, he's
          going to graduate.

EVERYONE IS NOW EMOTIONALLY SUCKED INTO THE TALE
COACH IS WEAVING.

                    HAYDEN (CONT'D)
          And I don't mind telling you when
          that day comes, there's going to be
          a lump in this guy's throat. (HE
          INDICATES HIMSELF) And I'll tell
          you something else. I think America
          is going to have itself a helluva
          gym instructor.

COACH LOOKS AT DYBINSKI AND AFFECTIONATELY TUSSLES
HIS HAIR. MRS. DUPREE LOOKS AT COACH. HOW COULD A
MOTHER NOT LOVE THIS MAN?

                    MRS. DUPREE
          (REVERENTLY) Where do we sign, Mr.
          Fox?

HAYDEN LOOKS AT MRS. DUPREE AND SLIDES A NATIONAL
LETTER OF INTENT TOWARD HER. IT'S A MOMENT OF
ENORMOUS IMPORT FOR HER AND HER SON. FOR HAYDEN,
IT'S ALSO A BIG MOMENT, FOR BENEATH HIS SOMBER AND
SAINT-LIKE EXTERIOR, A COMPETITIVE HEART IS BEATING

IN ANTICIPATION, WONDERING IF LIVINGSTON IS THE
KIND OF FINE YOUNG MAN CAPABLE OF SOMEDAY KNOCKING
AN OHIO STATE BUCKEYE ON HIS BUTT.

SFX: A WHISTLE BLOWS (POST)

FADE OUT.

END OF TEASER

ACT ONE

SCENE A

(HAYDEN,
LUTHER,
DAUBER)

FADE IN:

INT. COACH'S OFFICE - DAY

LOCATED IN THE BASEMENT OF THE FIELDHOUSE, THE
OFFICE IS A COLLECTING BIN FOR EVERY POSSIBLE ITEM
YOU CAN MAKE TO PROMOTE MINNESOTA STATE FOOTBALL,
INCLUDING COFFEE MUGS, GLASSWARE, LAMPS, WASTE
BASKETS, BLANKETS, CALENDARS, KEY RINGS, SEAT
CUSHIONS, CAPS, SWEATSHIRTS, BUMPER STICKERS,
LITTLE STUFFED SCREAMING EAGLE MASCOTS, ETC. ALSO
PROMINENT ARE A BLACKBOARD, A WEIGHT SCALE, A
POSTER OF THE UPCOMING SEASON'S SCHEDULE, AND A
LARGE WALL-HANGING PROCLAIMING: "THIS IS MINNESOTA
STATE FOOTBALL!" AT THE MOMENT, HAYDEN IS SITTING
BEHIND HIS DESK, FEET UP, ENDURING AN INTERVIEW ON
THE PHONE.

                HAYDEN
      (INTO PHONE) Well, East Texas is a
      physical team -- well-coached. They
      had some tough luck last year
      winning only two and losing nine
      but a break here or there and they
      could just as easily have been nine
      and two.

LUTHER VAN DAM SUDDENLY ENTERS. IN HIS MID '50'S,
MARRIED ONLY TO FOOTBALL, AND WITH A WALK THAT
LOOKS AS IF HE'S BEEN BLOCKED IN THE KNEES ONE TOO
MANY TIMES, LUTHER IS A MAN LIVING FOREVER UNDER
THE BELIEF THE SKY IS FALLING, AND IT'S ABOUT TO
LAND ON HIM.

                LUTHER
      Well, you can kiss the next four
      years goodbye.

> HAYDEN
> (INTO PHONE) Listen, can we do this
> another time? Something's come up
> . . . Thanks. Its always a pleasure
> to talk to the press.

HAYDEN HANGS UP THE PHONE.

> LUTHER
> Guess where Tommy Jordan just
> announced he's going to school?

> HAYDEN
> (TAKING A GUESS) Miami?

> LUTHER
> Do you believe that? Best high
> school quarterback in the country
> and he's going to Miami. And you
> <u>know</u> the only reason he's going is
> the weather. A kid goes down there
> and sees all that sunshine and
> those beaches and they fix him up
> with some girl in a bikini and he's
> as good as signed. Then we try to
> compete with that by bringing him
> up here to the tundra and taking
> him ice fishing with a girl in a
> parka. I'm telling you, Hayden,
> we're never going to win here.

HAYDEN LOOKS AT LUTHER AS <u>DAUBER ENTERS</u> CARRYING A
LARGE STACK OF ENVELOPES.

> DAUBER
> Excuse me, Coach, mail just came.

> HAYDEN
> Put it on the desk.

> DAUBER
> It's all divided. (INDICATING THE
> STACKS) Ticket requests, speaking
> requests, questions from alumni.
> (INDICATING A SINGLE ENVELOPE) And
> one marked "personal." I didn't
> open it because I thought it might
> be, you know. . .

                    HAYDEN
Personal?

                    DAUBER
Yeah.

                    HAYDEN
(TO LUTHER) Sharp as a tack, isn't
he?
(OPENING THE ENVELOPE) I'm going to
miss you when you graduate,
Dybinski.

                    DAUBER
This could be the year, Coach.

                    HAYDEN
(READING THE LETTER) Let's hope so.
(REALIZING) Hey, this is from
Kelly.

                    DAUBER
Your daughter Kelly?

                    HAYDEN
No, Gene Kelly. (READING THE
LETTER)
She's going to be a freshman in
college this year. I told her to
write me when she knew where she
was going.

                    DAUBER
You ought to have her come here.

                    HAYDEN
(STILL READING) That'd thrill her
mother.

                    LUTHER
(FONDLY) Doesn't seem possible
Kelly's old enough to go to
college. First time I ever saw her
was the day Beth brought her into
the locker room at half time of
that Louisville game. She couldn't
have been more than a few weeks
old. God, we played lousy that day.

HAYDEN, WHO HAS CONTINUED READING THE LETTER, NOW
SUDDENLY RISES.

> DAUBER
> What's the matter?

> HAYDEN
> (STUNNED) Kelly wants to come to
> school here.

> LUTHER
> You're kidding.

> HAYDEN
> No. She's already been accepted.
> She just wants to know before she
> comes how I feel about it.

> LUTHER
> How <u>do</u> you feel about it?

> HAYDEN
> I haven't been a father to Kelly
> since Beth and I split up. That's
> been sixteen years. I can't
> suddenly be responsible again. I
> wasn't all that responsible before.

> DAUBER
> Coach, I doubt if she wants you to
> be responsible.

> HAYDEN
> She wants something from me.
> Otherwise, why is she coming?

> LUTHER
> What does she say in the letter?

> HAYDEN
> (MOCKINGLY) Some cockamamie thing
> about us having a terrific dance
> and music department.

> DAUBER
> (INNOCENTLY) Maybe we do.

> HAYDEN
> So do a lot of other schools. She
> could go anywhere. She's obviously
> coming here because <u>I'm</u> here.

```
                    LUTHER
          He's right. Otherwise, she could go
          to Miami.

                    DAUBER
          So what are you going to tell her?

                    HAYDEN
          (A BEAT) I don't know.

                    LUTHER
          You don't think she'd want to live
          with you, do you?

HAYDEN SHOOTS A LOOK AT LUTHER. HE HADN'T THOUGHT
OF THIS.

                    DAUBER
          Actually, I think all freshmen
          girls have to live at the market.

                    HAYDEN
          The what??

                    DAUBER
          Shaeffer Hall. It's called "the
          market" because it's a tradition
          each year for all the jocks to go
          over there and check out the fresh
          . . .

DAUBER STOPS HIMSELF, REALIZING WHAT HE'S ABOUT TO
SAY.

                    DAUBER (CONT'D)
          . . . faces.

                    HAYDEN
          Oh, great. See, this is what I'm
          talking about. I don't want to be
          responsible for this. I don't even
          want to know about this.

                    DAUBER
          So what are you going to tell her?

HAYDEN SCOWLS.

                    HAYDEN
          She's my daughter. I have to tell
          her the truth. (SADLY) And the

                         MORE
```

                    HAYDEN (CONT'D)
          truth is, if she's coming here for
          an education, fine. But if she's
          coming expecting to find a father,
          she might as well go someplace
          else. (A BEAT) Would you guys
          excuse me? I've got to make a phone
          call.

                    DAUBER
          Sure.

THEY BOTH WAIT FOR HAYDEN TO GO.

                    HAYDEN
          I meant you guys leave.

                    DAUBER AND LUTHER
          Oh.

HAYDEN HEADS BOTH OF THEM OUT. AS HE DOES, LUTHER
TAKES HIM ASIDE.

                    LUTHER
          Listen, I know that's not going to
          be an easy conversation. I just
          want you to know . . . well, I
          don't know what I want you to know.
          That I know that, I guess.

                    HAYDEN
          (CONFUSED) Thanks.

HAYDEN TAKES A DEEP BREATH; THEN VERY DELIBERATELY
DIALS A LONG DISTANCE NUMBER.

                    HAYDEN (CONT'D)
          (INTO PHONE) Hello, Kelly? . . .
          Oh, Beth. Boy, you two sound more
          alike everyday. It's Hayden, how
          are you? . . . Oh? What's wrong?
          . . . Yeah, well, that's why I'm
          calling. I just got it a few
          minutes ago . . . Well, I was
          surprised, obviously. And thrilled,
          of course . . . Beth, I don't know
          as I'd call it a "tragic"
          decision . . .

AS HE TALKS, HAYDEN NERVOUSLY PICKS UP A FOOTBALL
AND TOSSES IT IN THE AIR.

                    HAYDEN (CONT'D)
          No, I realize being a parent was
          never my long suit, but I've
          changed since then . . . Look, is
          Kelly there? Maybe I should talk to
          her about this . . . Oh. Well, when
          she gets back would you tell her I
          called and let her know I-I
          couldn't be more pleased about her
          coming . . . No, I really am. I'm
          looking forward to getting to be
          the father I've never been . . .
          Honestly, I couldn't be more
          excited . . . You be sure and tell
          her that, okay? . . . I will. You,
          too . . . Goodbye.

HAYDEN SMILES AND HANGS UP.

                    HAYDEN (CONT'D)
          (TO HIMSELF) There, that wasn't so
          hard. The <u>truth</u> would've been hard.

                        <u>DISSOLVE TO:</u>

SCENE B

(HAYDEN, LUTHER)
KELLY, A MAN)

INT. HAYDEN'S CABIN - ONE WEEK LATER - LATE
AFTERNOON

A ROUGH-HEWN HOME ON THE WATERFRONT OF ONE OF
MINNESOTA'S SMALL LAKES. IT'S A VERY MASCULINE
ENVIRONMENT, WITH A LARGE STONE FIREPLACE
DOMINATING THE UPSTAGE WALL OF THE LIVING ROOM,
FLANKED ON EITHER SIDE BY LARGE WINDOWS LOOKING OUT
OVER THE LAKE VIEW. A SMALL DEN IS STAGE RIGHT WITH
A WINDOW THAT LOOKS OUT TO THE FRONT SCREENED-IN
PORCH. IT IS THROUGH THIS PORCH THAT PEOPLE PASS TO
GET TO THE FRONT DOOR. THE OPEN KITCHEN IS STAGE
LEFT, ALL KNOTTY PINE AND ACTUALLY VERY COZY. THE
HOME IS FURNISHED WARMLY IN ODDS AND ENDS, BUT
NOTHING IS "DECORATED." A LARGE MOUNTED FISH
INDICATES ONE OF HAYDEN'S OTHER PASSIONS. EXCEPT
FOR A FEW THINGS IN THE DEN, THERE ARE VERY FEW
REMNANTS OF HAYDEN'S LIFE AS A COACH. RATHER, THIS
PLACE IS AN ESCAPE FROM THE PRESSURES OF THE JOB.
AT THE MOMENT, HAYDEN IS IN THE KITCHEN DOING
DISHES. OFF-STAGE, WE CAN HEAR THE SOUND OF AN
ELECTRIC SWEEPER RUNNING (LIVE). IN A MOMENT, IT
SHUTS OFF. IN ANOTHER MOMENT, LUTHER ENTERS FROM
THE DOOR LEADING TO THE BEDROOMS, CARRYING THE
SWEEPER.

> LUTHER
> I think I just broke your vacuum.

> HAYDEN
> Don't worry about it.

> LUTHER
> I think it sucked up a comb.

> HAYDEN
> It's okay, Luther.

> LUTHER
> I'll put it back on the porch.

LUTHER CARRIES THE SWEEPER TO THE PORCH.

                    HAYDEN
          (CALLING) How do you think the
          place looks?

                    LUTHER
          (RE-ENTERING) I thought it looked
          okay before we spent six hours
          cleaning it.

                    HAYDEN
          I just want to make a good
          impression.

                    LUTHER
          You're going to make such a good
          impression she's going to end up
          wanting to stay here, you wait and
          see.

                    HAYDEN
          That's out of the question. This is
          going to be enough of an adjustment
          without complicating matters by
          living together.

SFX: OUTSIDE, A CAR HORN HONKS.

                    HAYDEN (CONT'D)
          Is that her?

                    LUTHER
          (LOOKING OUT THE WINDOW) White
          Mustang?

                    HAYDEN
          (RIPPING OFF HIS APRON; EXCITEDLY)
          That's her. I bought her that car
          for her sixteenth birthday. Guess
          she must have liked it, huh?

HAYDEN QUICKLY MOVES TO THE WINDOW AND LOOKS OUT.
HIS WHOLE EXPRESSION CHANGES AS SOON AS HE SEES
HER.

                    HAYDEN (CONT'D)
          Oh, Luther, would you look at that?
          (A BEAT) My God, I can't believe
          she's that grown up.

LUTHER
You don't need me here. I'll just
slip out the back way.

HAYDEN
No, I want you to meet her.

LUTHER
Well, good, because there isn't any
back way, I just realized.

THROUGH THE SCREEN PORCH WE SEE KELLY CROSS TO THE
FRONT DOOR. HAYDEN SMILES AS HE OPENS THE DOOR. SHE
STOPS AS THEY STAND THERE FOR A MOMENT, JUST
LOOKING AT EACH OTHER.

HAYDEN
Well, well, well, look who's here.

KELLY
(SOMEWHAT SHYLY) Hello, Dad.

HAYDEN
Hello, sweetheart.

THERE IS AN AWKWARD MOMENT BEFORE HAYDEN REACHES
OUT AND THEY SORT OF HAVE A HUG.

HAYDEN (CONT'D)
Welcome to Minnesota. (REMEMBERING)
This is a good friend of mine,
Luther Van Dam. This is my
daughter, Kelly.

LUTHER
Actually, I met you once before at
a game at Louisville. You don't
remember. You were about . . .
(INDICATING HER SIZE) . . . ten
weeks old.

KELLY
(SMILING) No, I don't remember.

LUTHER
Well, listen, you two have things
to talk about. Nice to meet you,
Kelly. Hope I see you again real
. . . somewhere. (TO HAYDEN) See
you at practice tomorrow.

LUTHER EXITS OUT THE BACK. THERE IS A BEAT. LUTHER
RE-ENTERS AND EXITS OUT THE FRONT.

                    HAYDEN
          Thanks, Luther. (EXPLAINING) I
          asked Luther to come and kind of
          help me get the place in order.
          With the season starting things are
          sort of in a mess.

                    KELLY
          It looks fine. (LOOKING AROUND) I
          like it.

                    HAYDEN
          Do you? It's pretty secluded. Of
          course, that's on purpose. I really
          need to have a place to get away
          from everybody.

A MAN SUDDENLY APPEARS AT HAYDEN'S WINDOW.

                    A MAN
          (CALLING) Hey, Coach, how's it
          goin'?

HAYDEN SMILES AND WAVES AND CLOSES THE DOOR.

                    HAYDEN
          Of course, they pretty much find
          you no matter where you are. (AN
          AWKWARD BEAT) You look wonderful,
          by the way. You must have left a
          few broken hearts behind in Ohio.

                    KELLY
          (KINDLY) Just Mom's.

                    HAYDEN
          (REALIZING) Yeah, right. (ANOTHER
          BEAT) Well, so, where are you going
          to be staying? Here, I hope.

                    KELLY
          (CAUGHT OFF GUARD) Here?

                    HAYDEN
          There's plenty of room.

> KELLY
> Actually, I wasn't sure that'd be
> such a good idea. This is going to
> be enough of an adjustment without
> complicating matters by living
> together.

> HAYDEN
> Well, golly, I hadn't thought about
> that but maybe you're right.

> KELLY
> To tell you the truth, I wasn't all
> that sure you'd really want me
> here.

> HAYDEN
> Wouldn't want you here? Didn't your
> mother tell you how excited I was
> you were coming?

> KELLY
> Yeah. She also told me you
> sometimes say whatever you think
> people want to hear. I just didn't
> want to come out and mess up your
> life.

A BEAT.

> HAYDEN
> (GENUINELY) Kelly, I may not always
> have shown it, but the happiest day
> I've ever had in my life was the
> day you came into it.

SHE LOOKS UP AT HIM AND SMILES, SOMEWHAT
EMBARRASSED.

> KELLY
> And now I'm back.

HE FORCES AN AWKWARD SMILE.

> HAYDEN
> Right.

SFX: THE PHONE RINGS.

HAYDEN (CONT'D)
That's probably a reporter. Sorry.
(ANSWERING THE PHONE) Coach here
. . . (CAUGHT OFF GUARD)
Christine . . .

HE SHOOTS A NERVOUS LOOK TOWARD KELLY.

HAYDEN (CONT'D)
What a surprise. Where are you
calling from? . . . (NERVOUSLY) No
kidding, that close, huh? (HE CUPS
THE PHONE) Christine's a
sportscaster in Minneapolis. We're
. . . friends.

KELLY NODS. AS HE TALKS, KELLY BEGINS TO ROAM ABOUT
THE HOUSE LOOKING AT VARIOUS MEMENTOES OF HER
FATHER'S LIFE, INCLUDING PHOTOGRAPHS. AS SHE DOES,
SHE GRADUALLY BEGINS TO REALIZE HOW MUCH OF HIS
LIFE THERE IS, AND WHAT A LITTLE PART OF IT SHE
APPARENTLY IS.

HAYDEN (CONT'D)
(INTO PHONE) What? . . . Oh, I was
just talking to my daughter . . .
Yeah, she just got into town a
little while ago . . . Uh, four
years. She's going to be going to
school here . . . (HE SMILES
NERVOUSLY AT KELLY) . . . Gee, I'd
love to, but it's her first night
and all. You understand . . . But
we'll take a raincheck, okay? . . .
Yeah, if anything changes . . .
You, too . . . G'bye.

HE HANGS UP AND SMILES.

KELLY
(SELF-CONSCIOUSLY) Dad, if you want
to go out tonight you should go. I
don't expect you to change your
whole life just because I'm here.

HAYDEN
Changing my life is no big deal.
(OFF HER LOOK) I mean, I wasn't
expecting to do anything anyway.

> KELLY
> Do you and Christine see each other
> a lot?

> HAYDEN
> You know, whenever schedules
> permit.

> KELLY
> Well, tonight they permit so I
> really think you should go out and
> I should go back to the dorm.

> HAYDEN
> But I was counting on being with
> you.

> KELLY
> But now you want to be with
> Christine, and I understand that.
> I'll see you tomorrow.

> HAYDEN
> Kelly, wait . . .

> KELLY
> I'm not going to be an intruder.

> HAYDEN
> (TRYING TO STOP HER) You're not.

> KELLY
> Well, I feel like it tonight, so
> please let me go. I'll call you
> tomorrow. We'll catch up then.

SHE GIVES HIM A VERY QUICK KISS ON THE CHEEK AND
HURRIEDLY HEADS OUT THE DOOR, ACROSS THE PORCH AND
DOWN THE STEPS.

> HAYDEN
> Kelly, please, I want you to
> stay . . .

THERE IS A BEAT AS HAYDEN WATCHES HER GO.

> HAYDEN (CONT'D)
> (CALLING OUT) Okay, but tomorrow
> for sure, huh?

SFX: (O.S.) A CAR DOOR OPENS AND SHUTS (POST).

SFX: IN ANOTHER SECOND, THE ENGINE STARTS (POST).

AS HAYDEN CLOSES THE DOOR, KNOWING HE'S BLOWN THEIR
FIRST NIGHT TOGETHER, WE . . .

FADE OUT.

END OF ACT ONE

ACT TWO

SCENE C

                                      (HAYDEN,
                                      CHRISTINE,
                                      YOUNG MAN,
                                      CLERK)

FADE IN:

INT. HOTEL LOBBY - THAT NIGHT

SFX: FIRE IN FIREPLACE

THE VERY SMALL LOBBY OF A TINY DOWNTOWN HOTEL,
CONSISTING PRIMARILY OF A RESERVATION DESK, A
MAGAZINE STAND, AND A SMALL SEATING AREA. THE ONLY
PEOPLE PRESENT ARE A CLERK AND A VERY ATHLETIC-
LOOKING YOUNG MAN SITTING IN THE WAITING AREA.
HAYDEN ENTERS, DRESSED IN SLACKS AND A SWEATER, AND
APPROACHES THE RESERVATION COUNTER.

                    HAYDEN
          Excuse me, would you call Christine
          Armstrong's room and tell her
          Hayden Fox is here?

                    CLERK
          (BRIGHTLY) Sure, Coach.

HAYDEN CASUALLY CROSSES OVER TO THE WAITING AREA
AND SITS DOWN. AS HE DOES, HE NOTICES THE ATHLETIC-
LOOKING YOUNG MAN NEARBY, LEAFING THROUGH A
MAGAZINE. HAYDEN PICKS UP A MAGAZINE AND ALSO
BEGINS LEAFING THROUGH IT, BUT THE YOUNG MAN HAS
HIS ATTENTION. AFTER A MOMENT:

                    HAYDEN
          (CASUALLY) Who do you play for?

                    YOUNG MAN
          (LOOKING UP) Excuse me?

                    HAYDEN
          Football. Who do you play football
          for?

                    YOUNG MAN
          Oh, I don't play football.

THE YOUNG MAN SMILES POLITELY AND RETURNS TO HIS
MAGAZINE.

                    HAYDEN
          (LOOKING AROUND) A big, husky guy
          like you? You don't play football?

                    YOUNG MAN
          (SMILING) No.

HE RETURNS AGAIN TO HIS MAGAZINE.

                    HAYDEN
          How come?

                    YOUNG MAN
          (WITH A SHRUG) I don't know. Too
          busy running track, I guess.

HAYDEN LOOKS AT THE YOUNG MAN, AMAZED. THE YOUNG
MAN CONTINUES TO LEAF THROUGH HIS MAGAZINE.

                    HAYDEN
          Track? You're a track man?

                    YOUNG MAN
          Yeah.

                    HAYDEN
          What do you run?

                    YOUNG MAN
          Dashes. Sixty and the hundred.

HAYDEN GLANCES AROUND ANXIOUSLY.

                    HAYDEN
          What do you run the hundred in?

                    YOUNG MAN
          (SHRUGGING) 9.8 - 9.9.

                    HAYDEN
          (ALMOST SALIVATING) Big, husky guy
          like you runs the hundred yard dash
          in under ten seconds?

                    YOUNG MAN
          (MODESTLY) Yeah.

HAYDEN LOOKS AROUND, UNABLE TO BELIEVE HIS GOOD
FORTUNE, AND QUICKLY MOVES OVER CLOSE TO THE YOUNG
MAN. HE SITS DOWN BESIDE HIM.

                    HAYDEN
          Tell me, what size thighs do you
          have?

THE YOUNG MAN LOOKS AT HAYDEN AS IF HE'S SOME KIND
OF A SICKO. AT JUST THIS MOMENT, <u>CHRISTINE
ARMSTRONG ENTERS</u> THE LOBBY. YOUNGER THAN HAYDEN BY
A FEW YEARS, CHRISTINE HAS THE PERFECT GROOMING AND
SOPHISTICATED GOOD-LOOKS OF THE TYPICAL ON-CAMERA
NETWORK PERSONALITY.

                    CHRISTINE
          Hi, you ready?

                    HAYDEN
          (QUICKLY JUMPING UP) Oh, there you
          are. Yeah . . .

SHE GIVES HIM A QUICK KISS.

                    CHRISTINE
          Hope I didn't keep you waiting.

                    HAYDEN
          No, I was just having a
          conversation with . . .

HE STARTS TO INDICATE THE YOUNG MAN.

                    HAYDEN (CONT'D)
          . . . well, it doesn't matter.

                    CHRISTINE
          I'm glad you had a change in plans.
          Did you decide what we're going to
          do tonight?

                    HAYDEN
          (AS THEY BEGIN WALKING OUT) Your
          call. We could go out for dinner,
          or we can go back to my place and
          make it.

                    CHRISTINE
          I think I'd like to go to your
          place and make it.

AS THEY PASS THE YOUNG MAN:

                    YOUNG MAN
          Lots o' luck, lady.

OFF BOTH HAYDEN AND CHRISTINE'S REACTIONS . . .

                                        <u>DISSOLVE TO:</u>

<u>SCENE D</u>

(HAYDEN, CHRISTINE)

<u>INT. HAYDEN'S CABIN - LATER THAT NIGHT</u>

<u>SFX: FIRE IN FIREPLACE</u>

HAYDEN AND CHRISTINE SIT AT THE CANDLE LIT TABLE,
HAVING DINNER AND A BOTTLE OF RED WINE. BEHIND
THEM, THE REMNANTS OF A FIRE CRACKLES IN THE
FIREPLACE. EVERYTHING THEY USED TO MAKE DINNER IS
STILL SITTING OUT IN THE KITCHEN, BUT IT DOESN'T
LOOK SO BAD IN THE ROMANTIC GLOW OF FIRELIGHT.
HOWEVER, IT'S OBVIOUS BY HAYDEN'S DEMEANOR THAT HE
IS NOT REALLY INTO THE ROMANCE OF THE EVENING,
ALTHOUGH THAT'S NOT ANY FAULT OF CHRISTINE'S. SHE'S
MAKING AN EFFORT.

                    CHRISTINE
          (INDICATING HIS PLATE) Didn't you
          like it or were you just not
          hungry?

                    HAYDEN
          (REALIZING) No, it was good. I was
          . . . just trying not to get too
          full, that's all.

                    CHRISTINE
          Somehow I don't feel like I have
          your full attention tonight.

                    HAYDEN
          (SHRUGGING THIS OFF) It's the game
          Saturday. I'm always this way
          before the season starts, you know
          that.

                    CHRISTINE
          You want to talk about it?

                    HAYDEN
          What, about our rule? I thought we
          decided we have so little time
          together we wouldn't waste it
          discussing . . .

                              CHRISTINE
                     . . . things that really matter to
                     us? (OFF HAYDEN'S SMIRK) Well, if
                     we're going to get to the business
                     we both came for, I think we'd
                     better clear up the other stuff
                     first.

A BEAT.

                              HAYDEN
                     (CONFESSING) I was thinking about
                     my daughter.

                              CHRISTINE
                     (UNEASILY) I thought you said you
                     were thinking about the game.

                              HAYDEN
                     I lied. You still want to hear
                     this?

                              CHRISTINE
                     (SQUEAMISHLY) This is really
                     personal, isn't it? Okay, go ahead.
                     Just go slow. We're both new at
                     this, remember.

                              HAYDEN
                     (WITH A SIGH) I was just wondering
                     what kind of guy I am sometimes,
                     that's all. I could've made Kelly
                     stay this afternoon if I'd really
                     wanted to, but the truth is there
                     was a part of me that I wanted to
                     be here tonight with you and not
                     with her.

                              CHRISTINE
                     I'm having a hard time telling you
                     that was a terrible thing.

                              HAYDEN
                     It's not terrible, it's just
                     selfish. My whole life I've told
                     myself I was doing the noble thing
                     by not being more a part of Kelly's
                     life. The truth is, I just didn't

                              MORE

```
                    HAYDEN (CONT'D)
          want to take the time. I don't know
          why time scares me, but it does. I
          wonder if I got into coaching
          because I really like it, or
          because four years is about all the
          time I'm capable of committing to
          any one human being.

                    CHRISTINE
          (PUSHING AWAY FROM THE TABLE)
          O-kay, that's going deep enough.

                    HAYDEN
          (QUICKLY TAKING HER HAND) I'm not
          talking about you.

SHE STOPS. HE LOOKS AT HER A MOMENT, HOLDING HER
HAND.

                    HAYDEN (CONT'D)
          Can I say something really honest?

                    CHRISTINE
          (UNEASILY) Yes. If you really have
          to.

                    HAYDEN
          I wish I'd made Kelly stay today. I
          know that's a lousy thing to say to
          you, but--

                    CHRISTINE
          Hayden, you don't have to be sorry
          for feeling something for your
          daughter. I'm not jealous.

                    HAYDEN
          No?

                    CHRISTINE
          No. In fact . . . (SUDDENLY
          SURPRISED) . . . how's this for
          honest? All those times I've told
          you I found you sexy? Like when
          you're stalking the sidelines
          during a game, or when you're
          working in the den real intensely
          coming up with some brilliant new
          play?
```

                    HAYDEN
          Yeah?

                    CHRISTINE
          You're not nearly as sexy as you
          are right now.

                    HAYDEN
          (SURPRISED) Yeah?

                    CHRISTINE
          Yeah. (A BEAT) And now I have to
          leave you.

                    HAYDEN
          (CONFUSED) Why??

                    CHRISTINE
          Because you have to call your
          daughter. The wrong person's
          hearing these things.

SHE RISES FOR HER COAT AND BAG.

                    HAYDEN
          (ALSO RISING) But you don't have to
          leave. You can wait. I'll call my
          daughter while you're cleaning up
          the kitchen. Or heck, I'll clean up
          the kitchen and you can just drink
          wine.

                    CHRISTINE
          (GATHERING UP HER THINGS; AMUSED)
          Not tonight, Hayden.

                    HAYDEN
          But I don't think you realize how
          much better I feel now.

SMILING, SHE WALKS OVER TO HIM AND GIVES HIM A VERY
LONG AND TENDER KISS.

                    CHRISTINE
          I'll see you next time I'm in town.

SHE GRABS A SET OF HIS KEYS AND STARTS OUT.

                    HAYDEN
          Christine, wait . . .

                    CHRISTINE
          I'm taking your car. I'll park it
          discreetly on the side street near
          the hotel so no one will see it.
          You can ride your bike in tomorrow.

                    HAYDEN
          My bike?

                    CHRISTINE
          It'll be good for you. I have a
          feeling you're going to have a lot
          of pent up energy to burn.

                    HAYDEN
          Come on, don't do this to me . . .

                    CHRISTINE
          (AS SHE HEADS OUT) Call your
          daughter, Hayden.

                    HAYDEN
          Christine! . . .

                    CHRISTINE
          (AS SHE CROSSES THROUGH THE PORCH)
          And clean your kitchen. (STOPPING
          AND TURNING BACK) God, I want you.

     SHE TURNS AND EXITS FROM THE PORCH. HAYDEN IS LEFT
     ALONE.

                    HAYDEN
          (TO HIMSELF) This isn't fair . . .

     AS HE CLOSES THE DOOR, WE . . .

                                        DISSOLVE TO:

SCENE E

(HAYDEN, KELLY,
LUTHER,
SECRETARY)

INT. COACH'S OFFICE – THE FOLLOWING AFTERNOON

THE OFFICE IS EMPTY AS THE HALLWAY DOOR OPENS AND
KELLY IS LED IN BY A <u>SECRETARY</u> FROM THE ATHLETIC
DEPARTMENT.

> SECRETARY
>
> Practice just let out so you can
> wait here. He should be in any
> minute.

> KELLY
>
> Thank you.

> SECRETARY
>
> There's a pop machine around the
> corner if you're thirsty.

> KELLY
>
> I'm fine, thanks.

THE SECRETARY EXITS. KELLY TAKES A MOMENT TO LOOK
AROUND THE OFFICE, SEEING YET ANOTHER PART OF HER
FATHER'S LIFE THAT SHE'S NEVER REALLY BEEN PART OF.
SUDDENLY, SHE HEARS HAYDEN'S VOICE APPROACHING, AND
IT'S LOUD.

> HAYDEN (O.S.)
>
> (ANGRILY APPROACHING) Is that what
> they call effort? <u>I</u> didn't see any
> effort out there! Tell them I want
> to see 'em in the study room in two
> minutes! No showers! Two minutes!

HE <u>BURSTS THROUGH THE DOOR</u> HEADING STRAIGHT FOR HIS
DESK.

> HAYDEN (CONT'D)
>
> (TO HIMSELF) That's the most
> pathetic excuse for a practice I've
> <u>ever</u> seen . . .

HAYDEN SLAMS HIS CLIPBOARD DOWN ON HIS DESK AND
TURNS, SUDDENLY SEEING KELLY.

```
                    KELLY
(SELF-CONSCIOUSLY) Hi.

                    HAYDEN
(CAUGHT OFF GUARD) Kelly. I didn't
know you were here.

                    KELLY
I just came. I called ahead to find
out when practice was over.

                    HAYDEN
(ALSO SELF-CONSCIOUS) Just ended.

                    KELLY
So I heard.

                    HAYDEN
I was hoping to see you earlier
today. Did your roommate tell you I
called last night?

                    KELLY
Yeah, I didn't get back 'til late.

                    HAYDEN
I thought we could have lunch or
something. Probably won't be a lot
of time once classes start
tomorrow.

                    KELLY
I don't think I'm going to be going
to classes tomorrow.

                    HAYDEN
(CONCERNED) What do you mean?

                    KELLY
I realized last night when I
thought about it that I wasn't
being honest about any of this.

                    HAYDEN
(DISCOURAGED) Great. The one trait
you got from me.

                    KELLY
(SMILING) I've been trying to tell
myself all along that I was coming

                    MORE
```

                    KELLY (CONT'D)
          here to study my dance and my music
          and that it was just kind of a neat
          coincidence that you happened to be
          here, too. But that's a lie. I did
          come here because of you. And I
          think I was expecting something
          from you that I had no right to
          expect.

                    HAYDEN
          You mean that I'd be a father and
          be interested in you and think more
          about you than I thought about
          myself?
          (SARCASTICALLY) Yeah, that's a lot
          to ask.

KELLY LOOKS EMBARRASSED. THERE IS A BEAT.

                    HAYDEN (CONT'D)
          Kelly, I don't want you to leave.
          And I'm not saying that because I
          think it's what you want to hear.
          I'm saying it because it's what I
          want. That's selfish, I know, but
          that's the kind of guy I am.

SHE FIGHTS A SMILE.

                    HAYDEN (CONT'D)
          Look, I know I have no right to ask
          any of this, but will you give me a
          chance?

SHE LOOKS AT HIM, TORN BETWEEN WANTING TO SAY YES
AND WONDERING IF IT'S REALLY THE RIGHT THING TO DO.
THE DOOR BEHIND HAYDEN'S DESK OPENS AND LUTHER
POKES HIS HEAD IN.

                    LUTHER
          Hayden . . . (SPYING KELLY) . . .
          oh, sorry, I thought you were alone
          in here. Hi Kelly. (TO HAYDEN) The
          team's in here waiting.

                    HAYDEN
          One second.

LUTHER DUCKS BACK OUT.

> HAYDEN (CONT'D)
> (TO KELLY) Don't make a decision
> yet. Take another second and think
> about it. (INDICATING THE OTHER
> ROOM) I've got to go do this but
> I'll be right back.

HE BACKS OFF TURNS TO THE DOOR; THEN TAKING A DEEP
BREATH, HE SUDDENLY HURLS THE DOOR OPEN WITH
TERRIFIC FORCE.

> HAYDEN (CONT'D)
> (SCREAMING) You guys think you're
> ready to play football Saturday?!

HE SLAMS THE DOOR BEHIND HIM. IN THE ROOM NEXT
DOOR, WE HEAR HIM RANTING. KELLY LISTENS, ALMOST
MESMERIZED.

> HAYDEN (CONT'D — O.S.)
> (STILL SCREAMING) You're not ready
> to play volleyball! Twenty-three
> years I've been coaching and this
> is the worst team I've ever put on
> a field, and that includes a
> freshman intramural team in
> Chattanooga! I'm embarrassed! I am
> absolutely embarrassed! If you're
> not going to practice any harder
> than that then let's not practice
> at all! Hell, I don't need the
> practice. I know what I'm doing!
> But if you don't have any more
> pride than you showed out there
> today, then fine! Let's just go out
> there Saturday and see how
> humiliated we can be! You're
> dismissed! You don't want to be
> here anyway so get out!

THE DOOR FLIES OPEN AGAIN AND HAYDEN STORMS BACK
INTO THE OFFICE, SLAMMING THE DOOR BEHIND HIM WITH
ENORMOUS FORCE. HE TAKES A DEEP BREATH AND A PAUSE
AND LOOKS AT KELLY, WHO IS LOOKING BACK WITH A
MIXTURE OF FASCINATION AND A SLIGHT BIT OF FEAR.

> HAYDEN (CONT'D)
> (TOTALLY CALM) So, what do you
> think? Did you decide?

> KELLY
> (COMPLETELY DUMBFOUNDED) That was
> all for effect? (SHE INDICATES THE
> OTHER ROOM) How does anybody know
> when you're really serious?? How am
> I supposed to know?

A BEAT.

> HAYDEN
> I'm serious about wanting you to
> stay. And I'm serious about wanting
> to change. I'm not saying I can,
> but I'm serious about wanting to.

> KELLY
> (CAUTIOUSLY) If I stay, I stay at
> the dorm.

> HAYDEN
> I'm not going to have a daughter of
> mine staying at "the market."

> KELLY
> Then I'm not staying.

> HAYDEN
> Okay, stay at the dorm. God, I'm
> terrible at this. (OFF HER SMILE)
> But I will get better. You'll see.
> A man can change, Kelly. Even a
> son-of-a-bitch like me.

HAYDEN TAKES KELLY AND HOLDS HER CLOSE TO HIM, ONLY
THIS TIME IT'S NOT A "SORT OF" HUG, IT'S A REAL ONE
— THE KIND PARENTS AND CHILDREN HAVE WHEN THEY FIT
TOGETHER RIGHT. BEHIND THEM, THE DOOR TO THE
MEETING ROOM OPENS AND DAUBER STICKS HIS HEAD IN.

> HAYDEN (CONT'D)
> (IRRITATED) I'm having a hug here,
> Daub, you want to wait a minute?

DAUBER QUICKLY DUCKS BACK OUT. AS HAYDEN AND KELLY
CONTINUE TO HOLD EACH OTHER, WE . . .

> FADE OUT.

THE END

APPENDIX B

Pilot Script:
Law and Order

EXEC. PRODUCER: Dick Wolf   PROD. #86250
                                   Rev. 1/13/88

LAW AND ORDER

PILOT

"EVERYBODY'S FAVORITE BAGMAN"

Written by

Dick Wolf

PRODUCTION NOTE

"Law and Order" represents a conscious shift away
from many of the conventions of one hour dramatic
series. Aside from the format change of following
one case through the criminal justice system by
telling two discrete stories with two separate sets
of stars (Police and D.A.'s), there will be a
visual difference which will help set the tone of
the series. It is anticipated that the show will be
shot on 16mm Panaflex and finished on tape, the aim
being to achieve a <u>cinema verite</u>, semi-documentary
look, replete with hand held camera and
naturalistic lighting. In line with this look,
almost all locations, with the exception of the
requisite standing sets, will be practical. In
addition, there will be an editorial style of "hard
cutting". The series will avoid the use of
transition shots of cars driving up, exterior
establishing shots of buildings, people walking
into rooms, etc. This style will also influence
pace, which will, of necessity, be quick, as we
will move from story point to story point. In
addition, there will be a locked P.O.V. -- the
audience will see or hear only what the cops or
D.A.'s do. The fact that each half hour will
essentially be telling the same type of story that
might be seen in an entire hour of a typical cop
show, necessitates a certain economy of style which
will, in turn, become the series' stylistic
signature.

TEASER

FADE IN

EXT. WAREHOUSE DISTRICT - NIGHT

Deserted streets. The intermittent high pitched
whine of garbage trucks compacting the day's
industrial waste. The background jabbering of a
police radio is a continuous, unemotional
chronicler of the night.

CONTINUED

CONTINUED

                    POLICE RADIO (V.O.)
          . . . 340 West 26th . . . see the
          manager . . . man with a knife
          . . . all available units sector
          eight . . . Code 3 . . . shots
          fired . . . hit and run, Park and
          Astor, pedestrian down . . .

                                        CUT TO

INT. PATROL CAR - NIGHT

Their P.O.V. is through the windshield, we can
hear, but not see, the two patrol cops, as the car
cruises the industrial area.

                    POLICE RADIO
          Sector Four, nearest unit, domestic
          disturbance . . . 540 West three
          one . . . 3rd floor rear . . .

                    DRIVER
          I want the Coupe De Ville . . . I'm
          happy with the velour, not even
          leather . . . what do I end up
          with? A goddam Nipponese bug
          box . . .

The unit turns a corner into an alley bordering a
series of loading docks. Nosed into one of them is
a Mercedes 560 SEL. As the headlights wash over the
car, two black seventeen year-olds, "Simonize"
Jackson and Tremaine Lewis, bolt from the Benz and
head down the alley.

                    SHOTGUN COP (V.O.)
          Must've forgotten their keys . . .

His hand moves into frame and hits the lights and
siren as the V8 opens up and the patrol car leaps
forward. Tremaine turns, sees the black and white
hurtling down the alley and starts climbing the
chain link fence that runs along one side. Simonize
joins him as the cops fly past the Mercedes.

                                        CONTINUED

CONTINUED

SHOTGUN COP'S POV:

Charles Halsey, an overweight fifty year-old, is sprawled half in and half out of the car, the entire front of his Vicuna coat blood stained.

> SHOTGUN COP
> Hold it . . . we got a vic . . .

CUT TO

EXT. ALLEY - NIGHT

The patrol car comes to a screeching halt. Tremaine and Simonize roll over the top of the chain link fence and drop into the courtyard of a deserted tenement. They pick themselves up and run into the gutted building. As the shotgun cop runs to Halsey the camera follows the driver as he takes off after the two perps, scaling the chain link fence, dropping into the courtyard and running to the door of the tenement. He stops, sticks his head into the hallway, comes back out and unholsters his gun. He wipes a thin film of sweat off his upper lip, and swallows off a sudden case of dry mouth. This is a cop's nightmare and the camera is right with him, showing us why -- the building is dark and ominous.

CUT TO

INT. TENEMENT - NIGHT - CONTINUOUS

The driver takes a deep breath, listens to the thundering silence, races through the first floor and continues out to the street, the camera with him, step for step, as leather squeaks and handcuffs jingle.

EXT. TENEMENT - NIGHT- CONTINUOUS

The driver comes out of the tenement and checks out the bombed-out looking street. It's totally deserted. Breathing hard, he holsters his weapon and puts his fists on his hips, a portrait of total frustration, as he tries to get his breathing back under control.

CUT TO

CONTINUED

CONTINUED

INT. BOGEDA - NIGHT

Detective Sergeant Max Greevey, 40's, is counting
out four dollars and twenty-eight cents from a
clumped up mass of small bills and change cupped in
a ham sized paw. Three inches of cheap cigar are
burning in the corner of his mouth. He's wearing a
two hundred dollar suit and a tie a blind man
wouldn't be seen in. What can't be seen is the
mind, which on one level is a cornucopia of
seemingly useless information, and on another is a
veritable data base of Police information. He's
been married to his high school sweetheart for
twenty years and has three daughters, nineteen,
fifteen and six, all of whom can wrap him around
their little fingers. He's also an NBA fanatic, and
a Knicks fan, an unfortunate combination that has
cost him thousands in lost bets since the team's
glory days of the early seventies. Greevey's been a
cop for eighteen years and has seen everything
twice, but he can't stand seeing the bad guys win.
He squints at Jesus, the clerk, through a swirl of
cigar smoke and shakes his head in disbelief.

                    GREEVEY
          Since when's a ham sandwich two
          seventy-five, Jesus?

                    JESUS
          Since last Friday.

                    GREEVEY
          Didn't know ptomaine had gone
          up . . .

The line goes right over Jesus' head.

                    JESUS
          We don't use none of that . . .
          it's all home made.

There's an impatient honk from outside. We follow
him out the door.

                                        CONTINUOUS

                                        CONTINUED

CONTINUED

EXT. STREET - NIGHT

A green Plymouth Fury with no chrome's parked at the curb. Detective Mike Logan, early 30's, is a good looking Irishman with a temper to match. He's been Greevey's partner for the past two years. There's a mutual trust and respect, but it's a professional relationship - these guys don't spend any more time with each other than the job demands. They don't confide their secret fears to each other, they don't socialize, but they both know that the other would put his life on the line if the situation required it.

Logan has a B.S. in Police Science, reads books, likes Woody Allen's early comedies, has a Marine Corps screaming eagle tattooed on his forearm, drinks Bushmills, and has a mostly monogamous relationship with a uniformed policewoman. He's never been married, but he has a five year-old daughter that he supports and sees. He's putting a bubble gum light on the roof of the unmarked car as Greevey comes out of the bodega, pulls open the passenger door and climbs in.

> GREEVEY
> What?

> LOGAN
> We got a 211 . . . could turn into a homicide.

> GREEVEY
> Vic conscious?

> LOGAN
> (shaking his head)
> Ambulance is on the way.

Greevey takes the lid off his coffee, sips and nods for Logan to drive.

> GREEVEY
> <u>Around</u> the potholes . . . suit's just back from the cleaner.

> CUT TO

> CONTINUED

CONTINUED

EXT. LOADING DOCK - NIGHT

Halsey, unconscious, is being lifted into the back
of an ambulance. Logan looks at the paramedic.

> LOGAN
> Odds?

> PARAMEDIC
> Fifty-fifty . . . but I'm an
> optimist.

Greevey looks down at the bloodless face.

> GREEVEY
> I've seen this guy . . .
> (calling uniform over)
> Hey, Hochmeyer.

One of the uniforms leaves the Mercedes and crosses
to the ambulance.

> GREEVEY
> Any I.D.?

> HOCHMEYER
> (shaking his head)
> Took his wallet, but we ran the
> car.
> (yells to other uniform)
> Who owns the Benz, Eddie?

The other uniform comes over, pulling out his
notebook.

> EDDIE
> Registered to Charles Halsey, Kew
> Gardens.

Greevey's face twists into a pissed off frown.

> GREEVEY
> Oh, great . . . that's just
> terrific.

> LOGAN
> You know him?

CONTINUED

CONTINUED

> GREEVEY
> Councilman Halsey? Ring a bell?

> LOGAN
> The tubesteak who's always mouthing
> off about the streets being unsafe?

Greevey tosses away his cigar stub in annoyance and
shakes his head in frustration.

> GREEVEY
> I hate media cases.

> FADE OUT

END OF TEASER

ACT ONE

FADE IN

INT. HOSPITAL CORRIDOR - NIGHT

Greevey and Logan stride down the corridor.
Greevey's got another cigar jammed between his
teeth. He shoots Logan a look.

GREEVEY

> You ever had one?

Logan shakes his head.

GREEVEY

> Reporters try to get close to you,
> looking for anything they can get
> five hundred words out of . . . if
> you talk to them they start calling
> you at home at three in the morning
> . . . if you don't talk to them
> they start writing about how the
> Police are stymied . . . then the
> phone calls start from the brass
> downtown . . .

They pass a nurses station. An irate battle axe
spots Greevey's cigar.

NURSE

> You can't smoke that in here.

GREEVEY
(not slowing down)

> It's not lit.

They turn a corner and enter another corridor.

LOGAN

> Not bad, Max. A prophet in your own
> time . . .

There's a full scale media invasion at the far end.
Borough President Richard Conti, washed in the hot
lights of a half dozen mini-cams, faces a phalanx
of TV and print reporters. He's clearly pissed off
and emotional. A distraught looking, overly made-
up, forty year-old woman in a plain cloth coat,
Alice Halsey, is by his side.

CONTINUED

CONTINUED

                    CONTI
          . . . you all were at his press
          conferences, but he was just
          pissing into the wind. Now do you
          understand what Chuck Halsey was
          screaming about?
          Our streets aren't safe for anyone.
                    (beat; controlling himself)
          You can check with my office about
          Chuck's condition . . . we'll have
          regular updates . . . thank you,
          ladies and gentlemen.

The lights go off. A reporter, Fred Lasco, shouts a
question.

                    LASCO
          Mrs. Halsey - what do you think
          your husband was doing in that
          neighborhood late at night?

Before she can answer, Conti puts an arm around her
shoulder and pushes through a pair of swinging
doors into a doctor's lounge. The camera follows
into --

                                        CONTINUOUS

INT. DOCTOR'S LOUNGE - NIGHT

Conti and Mrs. Halsey approach a surgeon in a sweat
stained set of O.R. greens as Greevey and Logan
enter the lounge behind them. Conti turns and
shoots them an annoyed look as the surgeon pats
Mrs. Halsey's arm.

                    SURGEON
          Go home and get some sleep. He came
          through the surgery, which is half
          the battle . . . we'll call you
          immediately if there's any change.

As the doctor leaves, Conti moves toward Greevey
and Logan.

                    CONTI
          Who are you?

                                        CONTINUED

CONTINUED

                    LOGAN
              (flashing shield)
     I'm Detective Logan, this is
     Sergeant Greevey . . .

                    CONTI
     You're the investigating officers?

                    LOGAN
     Yes, sir.

                    CONTI
     We heard it was two black kids.

                    GREEVEY
     Two suspects were seen fleeing the
     scene.

                    CONTI
     You have anything else?

                    GREEVEY
     Not yet.

                    LOGAN
              (to Mrs. Halsey)
     Could you give us a description of
     his personal items, ma'am?

                    MRS. HALSEY
              (swallowing)
     He always carried a brown alligator
     wallet, a star sapphire ring, and a
     gold and diamond Rolex . . . he
     usually had about five hundred
     dollars in cash.

                    LOGAN
              (writing notes)
     Diamonds around the outside or on
     the face?

                    MRS. HALSEY
     Around the outside.

                    GREEVEY
     Your husband have any enemies?

                                        CONTINUED

CONTINUED

                    CONTI
        Chuck Halsey is one of the most
        respected and liked men in this
        district.

                    GREEVEY
        I'm sure he is . . .
                (looking at Mrs. Halsey)
        Ma'am?

                    MRS. HALSEY
        What are you asking? I thought you
        knew who did it.

                    LOGAN
        We know two black kids were there,
        but they didn't drive your husband
        to that location. You have any idea
        what he was doing way out there?

                    MRS. HALSEY
                (shaking her head)
        Chuck had a political dinner.

                    CONTI
        I was there. It ended around ten-
        thirty.

                    LOGAN
        Did he leave alone?

                    CONTI
        I have no idea . . . are you going
        to be able to catch those nig . . .
        kids?

                    GREEVEY
        I'm not going to lie to you – it'll
        take a break or a miracle.

                    MRS. HALSEY
        What kind of miracle?

                    LOGAN
        One of them walking in and
        confessing would help.

        Conti shoots him a look.

                                    CONTINUED

CONTINUED

> GREEVEY
> We're on our way over to the
> impound garage . . . we'll get
> your car back to you as soon as
> possible, ma'am.

> MRS. HALSEY
> Thank you, Sergeant.

CUT TO

EXT. HOSPITAL - NIGHT

Greevey and Logan come out of the building and head
for the parking lot.

> GREEVEY
> That was smart.

> LOGAN
> No sense in her having any false
> illusions . . .

> GREEVEY
> Right. Conti got a real charge out
> of your sense of humor.

Logan stops and looks at Greevey, who stops and
lifts an expectant eyebrow.

> GREEVEY
> Yeah?

> LOGAN
> You going to try and tell me that
> this plays right?

> GREEVEY
> Let's check the car.

> LOGAN
> What was he doing out there after a
> political dinner?

> GREEVEY
> (slowly; deliberately)
> Let's check the car.

Logan's eyes narrow. He knows his partner.

CONTINUED

CONTINUED

                    LOGAN
         Wait a minute, wait a minute . . .
         what have you got?

                    GREEVEY
         Old rumors.

                    LOGAN
                (getting pissed)
         That's great. When were you
         planning on telling me? What kind?

                    GREEVEY
         <u>Rumor</u> was that he ran the pad in
         the Criminal Courts.

                    LOGAN
                (can't believe it)
         He's a bagman!

                    GREEVEY
         Was . . . <u>if</u> you believe the
         rumors.

                    LOGAN
         This really frosts my cookies, Max.
         You mind telling me why you <u>didn't</u>
         tell me?

                    GREEVEY
                (unrepentant)
         Because you're <u>already</u> leaping to
         conclusions, for God's sake . . .
         about the only <u>probable</u> conclusion
         we can draw is that the black kids
         took whatever they found.

Logan's as pissed at himself as he is at Greevey.
His partner's absolutely right.

                    LOGAN
         Let's check the car.

                                        CUT TO

INT. IMPOUND GARAGE - NIGHT

A grease stained impound lot manager watches as
Greevey puts a key in the Mercedes' trunk.

                                        CONTINUED

CONTINUED

> MANAGER
> . . . sixty bucks for a damn key,
> Sergeant. I coulda popped it for
> nothing.

> GREEVEY
> Car belongs to a city councilman.

The manager's eyes widen.

> MANAGER
> That real?

Greevey reaches into the trunk and comes out
holding a lynx coat.

> GREEVEY
> (to Logan)
> How much?

> LOGAN
> Twenty-five and up.
> (beat; deadpan)
> He must be crazy about his old
> lady.

CUT TO

INT. CAPTAIN CRAGEN'S OFFICE - DAY

Cragen's in his early fifties and is looking at the
Lynx coat on his desk like it's a large turd.

> GREEVEY
> I don't want to tell her.

> CRAGEN
> Odds?

> LOGAN
> (flip)
> Eight to five.

Cragen shoots him an unamused look.

> GREEVEY
> Surgeon says it's in God's hands.

> CRAGEN
> That must be comforting.

CONTINUED

CONTINUED

                    GREEVEY
  Well?

                    CRAGEN
    (shaking his head)
  The guy wakes up and it wasn't for
  the wife and we've told her . . .

Greevey nods, shoves the coat back in the bag.

                    GREEVEY
  Thanks for your help, Captain.

                              CUT TO

INT. SQUADROOM - DAY

Logan and Greevey move to their opposite facing
desks in the corner of the run down, chaotic room.
Greevey nods at the coat.

                    GREEVEY
  No labels.

                    LOGAN
  Maggie's best friend works for a
  furrier.

Greevey pushes the bag toward Logan. They both turn
as a voice yells out Greevey's name. Profaci,
another detective, is at the far end of the
squadroom.

                    PROFACI
  You catch the Halsey mugging?

Greevey nods.

                    PROFACI
  Give Chang a call in Narco.

                              CUT TO

INT. NARCOTICS SQUADROOM - DAY

Jimmy Chang, an undercover narcotics detective in
his late twenties, brings Greevey and Logan up to
speed.

                            CONTINUED

CONTINUED

                  CHANG
. . . so we take down the crack
house and roll up this scumball
dealer Rodriguez along with half a
dozen customers. Rodriguez is on
probation and knows he's going back
for a deuce so he gives us this kid
who he says came in with a wad that
he had taken off some white dude in
a Mercedes. I got in here, read the
APB and called upstairs.

                  GREEVEY
Where's the kid?

Chang jerks his finger back toward the holding
cell. Simonize Jackson, one of the crack-fried kids
from the Teaser, is pacing the cage like a neurotic
zoo animal.

                  LOGAN
Monster case of the yips . . .

                  GREEVEY
             (shaking his head)
He's good for nothin'.

                  LOGAN
             (cocky)
I'll have him singing the name game
in two minutes . . .

                  GREEVEY
             (a snort)
Twenty?

Logan sticks his hand out. They shake.

                            CUT TO

INT. INTERROGATION ROOM - DAY

Greevey sits facing Simonize while Logan paces
behind the kid. The table's scarred, the walls
grimy.

                       CONTINUED

```
CONTINUED

                    SIMONIZE
          Rodriguez'd rat out his momma . . .
          junkie gimp don't know nothing, and
          you ain't got squat on me except
          what he said, and that's just
          heresy.

                    GREEVEY
          Word's hearsay, Simonize.

                    SIMONIZE
          Yeah. That's it.
                (cocky)
          And I be good for nosay.

Logan gives the back of Simonize's head a good
smack with his open hand. He's getting frustrated.

                    LOGAN
          We don't dig being dissed by
          lightweights.

Greevey looks at his watch and smiles at Logan.

                    GREEVEY
          Mike, Mike, he's not being
          disrespectful, he's just being
          . . . reflective.

Simonize's head comes up and he looks at Greevey
suspiciously as Logan scans his rap sheet.

                    LOGAN
          Eight arrests and he still hasn't
          caught on that Judges help those
          who help themselves.

There's a knock at the door.

                    LOGAN
          Going, going . . . last chance
          . . .
                (nervous; pissed)
          Don't be stupid . . .

Simonize looks at the door, swallows hard and
remains silent. Greevey check his watch again.


                                          CONTINUED
```

```
CONTINUED
                    GREEVEY
         Gone . . . come in.

The door opens and Rosen, Gang Detail, comes into
the room. He shakes his head with a disgusted half
chuckle. Simonize looks totally confused as Greevey
rubs his fingers together with a smile, Logan
reaches into his pocket and reluctantly hands
Greevey a twenty.

                    ROSEN
         Si-mo-nize! What a sur-prise.
              (looking around room)
         Getting some career counselling
         from Greevey and Logan?

                    SIMONIZE
         I ain't done nothin'.

                    ROSEN
              (to Greevey)
         Such a polite boy . . .
              (to Simonize)
         Of course you didn't. We always go
         out and arrest innocent people in
         shooting galleries.

                    GREEVEY
         Who's this jerk hang with?

                    ROSEN
         How's Tremaine these days?

                    SIMONIZE
         Ain't seen him.

                    ROSEN
         Amazing how you homeboys are always
         apart.
              (to Greevey)
         Tremaine Lewis. I got the address
         upstairs. Simonize lives with his
         grandmother.
                                        CUT TO
```

INT. TENEMENT – DAY

Greevey and Logan enter a decaying tenement. Gang graffiti's on the walls. A stale urine stench makes Logan grimace. They pass a serious looking eight year-old girl. She follows them with her eyes, finally talking to their backs.

                    GIRL
          You the man?

Neither of them look back.

                    GREEVEY
          We sure are, honey.

The two cops stop in front of a door on the third floor and knock.

                    WOMAN'S VOICE
          Who is it?

                    GREEVEY
          Police, Mrs. Jackson.

                                        CUT TO

INT. MRS. JACKSON'S APARTMENT – DAY

Greevey and Logan are in a tiny back bedroom going through a collection of pants, jackets and basketball shoes. Mrs. Jackson is a sixty year-old dipso. She's looking at a warrant dubiously.

                    MRS. JACKSON
          You sure this paper says you can do
          that? When he ain't even here?

                    GREEVEY
          Yes, ma'am. That's a search
          warrant. It's signed by a judge.

                    MRS. JACKSON
          Police ain't never come with no
          search warrant before . . . Simon
          done something real bad, this time,
          huh?

Logan's picked up an Air Jordan basketball shoe. Something clinks. He turns the shoe upside down and Halsey's Rolex drops out.

                                        CONTINUED

CONTINUED

>>>   LOGAN
>>>   Yes, Ma'am. Looks that way.

>>>   CUT TO

EXT. TENEMENT #2 - DAY

Greevey and Logan are outside the building.

>>>   LOGAN
>>>   Lot of noise?

>>>   GREEVEY
>>>   Plenty of warning.

Logan nods and heads toward the alley in back of
the building as Greevey enters.

>>>   CUT TO

EXT. ALLEY - DAY

Logan hugs a wall as he hears the sound of running
feet on a firescape. Tremaine is boogeying down the
metal steps, a .38 in his hand. Above him, Greevey
carefully crawls out a window. Logan reaches for
his gun, thinks better of it, and picks up a metal
garbage can lid. Tremaine comes running down the
alley, looking over his shoulder. Logan steps
around the corner of the wall and slams the lid
into Tremaine's face as if it was a metal cream
pie. Tremaine goes down like he's been poleaxed.

>>>   FADE OUT

>>>   END OF ACT ONE

<pre>
                    ACT TWO

FADE IN

INT. INTERROGATION ROOM - NIGHT

Greevey's in the interrogation room with Simonize
and Tremaine, explaining the facts of life, a game
show host lilt to his voice. Tremaine's wearing a
bandage over a broken nose.

                    GREEVEY
          . . . and if the vic croaks, you
          guys move up to the bigs . . .
          murder two . . .

                    TREMAINE
          We're tellin' the truth, man. We
          didn't do nothin'.

                    GREEVEY
          You're willing to swear you two
          were together the whole night . . .

                    SIMONIZE
          You got that right.

Greevey reaches into his jacket pocket.

                    GREEVEY
          Know what we found at Simonize's
          apartment?

Simonize squeezes his eyes shut with an "oh shit"
expression as Greevey drops the Rolex on the table.

                    TREMAINE
          I ain't never seen that.

                    GREEVEY
          You holding out on your main man,
          Simonize?
                    (to Tremaine)
          That's the vic's watch.

Tremaine's face hardens and he stares straight
ahead.

                    GREEVEY
          Anybody want to make a deal?

                                        CONTINUED
</pre>

CONTINUED

Silence. The door opens. Logan looks at the two
perps, his expression dead serious.

> LOGAN
> You didn't plea these jerks, did
> you?

> GREEVEY
> We're still talking.

> LOGAN
> Stop.

Tremaine and Simonize look at each other as Greevey
and Logan exchange looks.

> GREEVEY
> The vic?

Logan shakes his head. Tremaine's eyes widen.

> TREMAINE
> Wait a damn minute . . .

> SIMONIZE
> You sayin' the dude croaked?

> LOGAN
> (letting them believe it)
> You blew it, my man . . .

Tremaine won't take 'no' for an answer. He comes
out of his chair.

> TREMAINE
> He was already cut . . . we took
> the guy off, but we didn't do
> nothin' to him . . .

> SIMONIZE
> It's the truth, man . . . he was
> just lying there bleeding . . .

> TREMAINE
> It was the white cat . . . he got
> out of the Mercedes as soon as the
> truck left . . .

Greevey and Logan look at each other. It has the
unfortunate ring of truth.

CONTINUED

```
CONTINUED
                        LOGAN
              What truck?

                                        CUT TO


EXT. LOADING DOCK - DAY

Greevey and Logan walk up to a semi that's just
pulling in.

                        GREEVEY
                      (to Logan)
              That wasn't bad - I thought Halsey
              had croaked . . . you join the
              actor's studio or something?

Before Logan can say anything, Greevey goes up to
the thirty year-old driver as he hops down from the
cab.

                        GREEVEY
              Tony Halliwell?

                        HALLIWELL
              Yeah?

                        GREEVEY
                    (flashing badge)
              I'm Sergeant Greevey, this is
              Detective Logan.

                        HALLIWELL
              There a problem?

                        LOGAN
              Dispatcher said you made a real
              late delivery Tuesday night?

Halliwell nods.

                        GREEVEY
              Anybody else here when you arrived?

                        HALLIWELL
              Just the night man. He was inside.

                        LOGAN
              Outside.

                                     CONTINUED
```

CONTINUED

> HALLIWELL
>
> Outside?
> (remembering)
> Yeah . . . yeah. There were a
> couple of cars parked next to each
> other down the end of the dock
> . . . a silver Mercedes and a red
> Jag XJ-S.

> LOGAN
> (pleased)
> Very observant, Tony.

Halliwell really doesn't know what to make of
Logan's attitude.

> HALLIWELL
>
> I like cars.

> LOGAN
>
> See anything else?

> HALLIWELL
>
> Yeah . . . when I drove in, there
> were two guys at the rear of the
> Jag. Trunk pops, guy reaches in,
> out comes a fur coat and he hands
> it to the other guy.

> GREEVEY
>
> Could you identify them again?

> HALLIWELL
>
> Yeah. Sure.

> LOGAN
>
> Then what happened?

> HALLIWELL
>
> The other guy opens the trunk of
> the Mercedes and puts it in there.
> Then they both climb into the
> Mercedes, and I go inside. When I
> come out, the Jag's gone.
> (beat)
> Heard you caught the black kids who
> did it.

CONTINUED

CONTINUED

                    GREEVEY
            (patting Halliwell's
            shoulder)
        Thanks. You've been very helpful.

Halliwell takes the hint and moves off. Logan looks
at Greevey and shakes his head.

                    LOGAN
        I don't like this. I really don't.

                                        CUT TO

EXT. HIGH RENT SHOPPING AREA - DAY

Greevey and Logan pull in to the curb behind a
black and white. A good looking thirty year-old
policewoman, Maggie Pierson, climbs out from behind
the wheel and crosses to Logan and Greevey. Logan
looks at the expensive shops.

                    LOGAN
        Didn't know you hung with the
        carriage trade.

                    MAGGIE
        Hello to you, too . . .
            (to Greevey)
        Hi, Max.

                    GREEVEY
        Maggie . . .

                    MAGGIE
            (to Logan)
        Third floor. You can talk to her
        boss - he thinks he knows who made
        it.
            (sotto; to Logan)
        This good for a dinner?

                    LOGAN
            (deadpan)
        Depends what the dinner'll be good
        for.

                    MAGGIE
        Let's put it this way . . . you
        don't have a prayer without it.

                                        CONTINUED

CONTINUED

                 , LOGAN
       Really cold, Mags.

                MAGGIE
       So light my fire.

                               CUT TO

INT. FUR SALON - DAY

Soft lighting, gray flannel furniture, no stock
visible except for a pair of mannequins swathed in
sable and ermine, and an address that justifies a
two hundred per cent mark-up. Greevey and Logan
walk through the showroom and into a small office
behind Louis Farber, a fifty year-old furrier in an
Italian suit cut so tight it doesn't leave room for
lunch. The lynx coat is thrown across a desk.

                FARBER
       . . . and then among lynx . . .
       there are as many variations as
       there are among . . . people.

               GREEVEY
       So is this coat Meryl Streep or
       Whoopi Goldberg?

                FARBER
       More the latter than the former,
       I'm afraid . . . Canadian farm
       grown, male pelts . . . basic coat,
       not a designer's . . . flash but
       basically trash.

                LOGAN
       You mind if we cut to the chase,
       Mr. Farber?

                FARBER
       I called around . . . there are
       three furriers who do this kind of
       garbage goods, but your best bet's
       Kornbluth on twenty-second.

                                 CUT TO

INT. KORNBLUTH FURS - DAY

The opposite end of the spectrum from Farber's. The
place is a claustrophic sweat shop. Laborers clean
pelts. The skins hang from the overhead pipes and
cover every other flat surface. Greevey and Logan
move through the labyrinth and into the office
area, where Nate Swersky is screaming into a phone.

                    SWERSKY
          They're <u>Russians</u>, you cretin. Don't
          give 'em a dime 'till you have the
          pelts.

He slams the phone down and turns to Greevey and
Logan.

                    SWERSKY
          What?

                    LOGAN
          You Kornbluth?

                    SWERSKY
          There hasn't been a Kornbluth since
          1957. I'm Swersky. What do you
          want?

                    GREEVEY
          Where's the owner?

                    SWERSKY
          What is this, Twenty Questions?

                    LOGAN
               (flashing shield)
          I'm Detective Logan, this is
          Sergeant Greevey . . .
               (tossing him coat)
          This yours?

Swersky looks at it without much enthusiasm, then
shrugs.

                    SWERSKY
          It's possible.

Greevey's and Logan's faces go cold. The
transformation is instantaneous. This guy's
bullshitting them. Swersky picks up on it.

                                   CONTINUED

CONTINUED

                SWERSKY
I mean it looks like one of mine,
but I don't know every coat.

                GREEVEY
Now you're starting to piss me off,
Mr. Swersky.

                LOGAN
     (to Greevey)
Why do I think Mr. Swersky
recognized that coat as it was
walking in?

                SWERSKY
     (visibly nervous)
You want to tell me what this is
about?

                GREEVEY
Nope.

                LOGAN
Who bought the coat?

                SWERSKY
It was a gift.

                GREEVEY
What kind of car do you drive?

                SWERSKY
Cadillac . . . a Coupe de Ville.
Why?

                LOGAN
Who was the gift for?

Swersky looks distinctly uncomfortable again.

                SWERSKY
I really think maybe I should give
my attorney a call.

                GREEVEY
Absolutely. Feel free.

Logan walks to the office door and looks out at the
obviously under code work area.

                          CONTINUED

CONTINUED

> LOGAN
> (to Greevey)
> Maybe I should give Gaffney a call
> over at the Fire Department . .
> (pointing)
> Aren't some of those pelts covering
> sprinkler heads?

> GREEVEY
> And call Ulasewicz over in the
> Buildings Department . . . I saw a
> lot of violations.

Swersky rubs his face in pain. The name's a squeak.

> Swersky
> Tony Scalisi.

> LOGAN
> (to Greevey)
> Don't we know that name?

> GREEVEY
> (to Swersky)
> Masucci family?

> SWERSKY
> God . . . he finds out I told
> you . . .

> GREEVEY
> Why'd he want the coat?

> SWERSKY
> What am I, Karnak?

>   CUT TO

INT. CAPTAIN CRAGEN'S OFFICE - NIGHT

Cragen's reading a yellow sheet. There's a picture
of Scalisi on the desk.

> CRAGEN
> Trucker give you a positive I.D?

> LOGAN
> (nodding at photo)
> Right from the picture. So did
> Lewis and Jackson.

>   CONTINUED

CONTINUED

               GREEVEY
Read the rap sheet -- Mr. Scalisi
likes to cut.

               LOGAN
And guess who leases a red Jaguar
XJ-S?

               CRAGEN
Halsey regained consciousness?

               GREEVEY
       (shaking his head)
Doctors aren't very optimistic
. . . I wouldn't mind waiting to
see if Halsey buys the farm . . .
murder's a better collar.

Cragen looks up at them.

               CRAGEN
I'm getting my butt barbequed.
Borough President called for a task
force . . . he wants to take it
away from us . . . Deputy
Commissioner Jefferson calls twice
a day . . .

               LOGAN
What's <u>he</u> want?

               CRAGEN
Doesn't want me to forget that this
is a politically sensitive case.
       (shaking his head)
I don't want to wait. Get a
warrant.

INT. D.A.'S OFFICE - DAY

Greevey and Logan walk into a cavernous high
ceilinged room. Logan looks around at the various
prosecutors with ill concealed disdain.

               LOGAN
Which night school Clarence
Darrow's handling this?

                             CONTINUED

CONTINUED

               GREEVEY
Name's Robinette.

               LOGAN
Twenty says he won't file.

               GREEVEY
        (nods, then sighs)
These defensive bets are going to
kill you.

Greevey walks over to the guard.

               GREEVEY
ADA Robinette?

The guard points to the back corner of the room.
Lower level prosecutors have desks in an enormous
open bullpen. Supervisors and senior ADAs are in
cubic sized offices around the perimeter. Cacophony
-- ringing telephones, shouted questions, snatches
of Spanish, Yiddish, Russian, Farsi. Robinette
passes a rumpled junior prosecutor with sympathetic
eyes who's taking notes as a girl in her late teens
looks past him with a thousand mile stare.

               GIRL
. . . then he picked up the baby
and started shaking her and her
head was flopping . . .

Robinette keeps moving, approaches a desk where a
Cuban defense attorney is arguing with a nerdy
prosecutor while an uncomprehending Marielito drug
dealer watches.

            DEFENSE ATTORNEY
It's a simple possession case!

             PROSECUTOR
No, no, my friend. Eight grams of
cocaine in the possession of an
habitual criminal is possession of
narcotics for sale which means
mandatory twenty to life . . .

The lawyer looks like he's going to faint. Greevey
and Logan come up to a desk. Paul Robinette, a

                              CONTINUED

CONTINUED

black, 26 year-old assistant district attorney
looks up. He's a product of Stuyvesant High, NYU
and Columbia Law. Bright, bordering on brilliant,
he could move to a high priced litigation firm and
quintuple his salary, but he gets off on being in
court on a daily basis. He also likes seeing the
good guys occasionally win. Right now he doesn't
look happy.

>   ROBINETTE
>   Stone's willing to file, but it's a
>   reach . . .

Logan mutters on expletive under his breath.
Greevey gives him an I-told-you-so smile.

>   GREEVEY
>   I've sent a lot of guys away on
>   circumstantial evidence . . .
>   anyway, I think this is more than
>   that.

>   ROBINETTE
>   What kind of more?

>   LOGAN
>   You know Halsey was a bagman?

>   ROBINETTE
>   Stone mentioned that.

>   GREEVEY
>   Then mention to Stone that Deputy
>   Commissioner Jefferson's been
>   nosing around . . . tell him I
>   thought he'd like to know . . .
>   You're new . . . how long have you
>   been with Stone?

>   ROBINETTE
>   Eight months.

>   GREEVEY
>   (standing)
>   Must be a record . . . see you in
>   court.

>   CUT TO

EXT. APARTMENT BUILDING - NIGHT

A doorman attended high rise. Greevey and Logan
watch while the doorman uses the house phone.

> DOORMAN
> He must be out . . . no answer.
> (looking over their
> shoulders)
> You guys just got lucky . . . here
> he comes . . .

Greevey and Logan turn. Scalisi, a balding guy in
his late thirties, is coming up the sidewalk with a
bag of groceries in each arm.

> LOGAN
> Oh, no . . .

Scalisi is also walking a pit bull on a leash.

> LOGAN
> I hate pit bulls.

> GREEVEY
> (sotto)
> He lets go of that leash, shoot the
> dog first . . .

They split up on the sidewalk. When Scalisi gets
twenty feet away, Logan yells out to him.

> LOGAN
> Anthony Scalisi, I have a warrant
> for your arrest . . .

The dog starts to growl.

> SCALISI
> What's the charge?

> LOGAN
> Assault with a deadly weapon and
> the attempted murder of Charles
> Halsey.

Scalisi considers whether to make a play. Greevey
steps out of the shadows, his .38 out.

> GREEVEY
> Spuds MacKenzie moves he's history.

CONTINUED

CONTINUED

Scalisi's eyes go from cop to cop, measuring, deciding, while the dog's growls get louder. He comes to a decision and raises his hand over his head.

                    LOGAN
          You have the right to remain
          silent . . .

The dog growls even louder as we

                                        FADE OUT

                    END OF ACT TWO

<pre>
                         ACT THREE

FADE IN

INT. COURTROOM - DAY

An arraignment in progress. Scalisi's standing next
to Edward Cosmatos, a $400 an hour mob mouthpiece.
                         BAILIFF
              . . . possession of an unregistered
              weapon, possession of a concealed
              weapon, assault, assault with
              a deadly weapon, attempted
              murder . . .

At the prosecution table Paul Robinette looks up as
the bailiff finishes his recitation.
                         JUDGE
              Does the defendant wish to enter a
              plea at this time?

                         SCALISI
                   (strong clear voice)
              Not guilty.

                         COSMATOS
              Request for bail, your Honor.

                         JUDGE
              Mr. Robinette?

                         ROBINETTE
                   (standing)
              Your honor, the defendant has been
              convicted of murder once before. He
              is an habitual criminal, is a
              soldier in the Masucci family, and
              is considered a flight risk. This
              office requests that he be held
              without bail.

                         JUDGE
              I'm afraid that I'm loathe to
              withhold bail except in homicide
              cases, counsellor.
                        (to Cosmatos)
                            (MORE)

                                          CONTINUED
</pre>

CONTINUED

             JUDGE (Cont'd)
     Five hundred thousand, cash or
     bond.
          (to bailiff)
     Short date.

                              CUT TO

INT. COURTHOUSE HALLWAY — DAY

Cosmatos catches up to Robinette at the elevator.

             COSMATOS
     Thought Stone would be here.

             ROBINETTE
     Have no fear, Eddie . . . he's
     looking forward to seeing you in
     court.   .

             COSMATOS
     What's his schedule like?

             ROBINETTE
     Depends on who's coming to call.

             COSMATOS
          (wave of derision)
     C'mon, Paul, this whole thing's one
     step above a roust.
          (beat)
     It's a two minute negotiation.

             ROBINETTE
          (shrugs)
     I wouldn't count on it. Halsey's
     still touch and go.

             COSMATOS
     Give me a break . . . nobody dies
     of a knife wound a week later.

The elevator door opens. Robinette shrugs, dubious.

             ROBINETTE
     <u>Multiple</u> felonies . . . Stone hates
     pleading out multiples.

Robinette smiles politely as the doors close.

                              CUT TO

INT. D.A.'S OFFICE - DAY

Robinette moves past the single guard, goes through the open bullpen, knocks on Stone's door, and enters.

                                                  CUT TO

INT. STONE'S OFFICE - DAY

Ben Stone, late thirties, sits behind a mound of paperwork at a chaotic desk. He covers the mouthpiece as Robinette enters and mouths "Cosmatos."

                          STONE
               Eddie, call me irresponsible, but I
               like you. You're a helluva lawyer.
               That's why I'm always amazed at how
               incredibly guilty your clients are.
               Scalisi's lower than cat crap, but
               if you want to waste some more of
               his money, come on down Thursday.

Stone hangs up and looks at Robinette. The older lawyer exudes intelligence, confidence and the don't-screw-with-me attitude of a street fighter. Hunter College, NYU Law on a full scholarship, then three years as a PD before joining the DA's office. He's twice divorced and has a twelve year-old girl that he sees on major holidays. The rest of the time he's married to his job, though he's had a five year relationship with Sarah Nicksey, a pediatrician. While he's more than willing to use every prosecutorial trick available to get a conviction, he's always felt that the real work happens long before he walks into court -- trials are won on preparation.

                          STONE
                      (ruminating)
               I'm Eddie Cosmatos, I can't wait to
               take this in front of a jury. Two
               black kids are found with the
               victim's possessions, the other
               eyewitness puts Scalisi there, but
                      (MORE)

                                            CONTINUED

CONTINUED

                    STONE (Cont'd)
          the only time he saw him was when
          he was with Halsey, who was
          perfectly fine. So why does he want
          to plea his client?

                    ROBINETTE
          Judicial calendar doesn't publish
          until next week . . . Scalisi draws
          Robards or Kapstein . . .

                    STONE
          He gets fifteen to life . . . and
          he draws Rosen or Gonzales he gets
          an apology.
                    (beat)
          So what do ninety-nine defense
          lawyers out of a hundred do?

                    ROBINETTE
                    (seeing his point)
          Wait for the calendar to come out.

                    STONE
          And you only make five per cent of
          what Eddie makes.

                    ROBINETTE
          What did Greevey mean about Deputy
          Commissioner Jefferson?

                    STONE
          Jefferson and I don't dance.

                    ROBINETTE
          The guy's a hero.

                    STONE
                    (controlled)
          He's a lying, two-faced bastard.

Robinette looks like he's been slapped.

                    ROBINETTE
          Now wait a minute. I grew up around
          the corner from him. He coached my
                    (MORE)

                                        CONTINUED

```
CONTINUED
                    ROBINETTE (Cont'd)
          little league team . . . I wouldn't
          even be a lawyer if it wasn't for
          him . . .

                    STONE
          I'm sure his dog loves him too.

                    ROBINETTE
          You know how many black kids look
          up to him? He's the highest ranking
          black cop ever.

Stone cuts him off with a frown, a raised index
finger and a lowered, steely, voice.

                    STONE
          Don't ever bring race into a case
          in this office. If the guy's wrong,
          he's wrong.

                    ROBINETTE
                 (not giving ground)
          If he's so wrong, how come nobody
          knows it?

                    STONE
          I know it . . .

Stone pushes himself back from his desk and stands
up.

                    STONE
          Traffic's going to be a bitch . . .
          we'd better get out of here.

                                        CUT TO

INT. HALSEY HOUSE - NIGHT

Stone, Robinette, Mrs. Halsey and Warren Wentzel, a
lawyer, sit in a living room done in expensive bad
taste.

                    MRS. HALSEY
          . . . and since he never discussed
          business with me, I had no
          idea . . .
                 (MORE)

                                        CONTINUED
```

CONTINUED

> MRS. HALSEY (Cont'd)
> (starting to cry)
> that he was involved in illegal
> activities . . . we just had dinner
> with Deputy Police Commissioner
> Jefferson and his wife, for God's
> sake.

Stone shoots Robinette a look, which he ignores.
As Mrs. Halsey dabs at her eyes, Eric Halsey, 17,
enters the room. He's good looking, with a football
player's tight body and a look of sheer panic
lurking just behind his eyes. He walks over to his
mother, bends down and kisses her forehead.

> ERIC
> (sotto)
> I'm going over to Gran's. She's a
> little shaky. I'll be back in an
> hour . . .

She watches her son's back as he disappears,
breathes deeply, and turns to Stone, her flat voice
an accusation.

> MRS. HALSEY
> Eric was going to Annapolis, but
> with what's going to come out,
> he'll never be able to get a
> Congressional appointment.

> WENTZEL
> Mr. Halsey never wanted Mrs. Halsey
> to be burdened with unnecessary
> business details. Is there anything
> else you'd like to know?

> STONE
> Her coat size.

Wentzel is taken completely by surprise, but
manages to keep his face under control. Mrs. Halsey
looks at him and he nods slightly.

> MRS. HALSEY
> Twelve . . . I wear a twelve.

CONTINUED

```
CONTINUED

                    STONE
          Thank you, Mrs. Halsey . . . oh,
          just one other thing : . . . did you
          ever hear of somebody called
          Anthony Scalisi?

                    MRS. HALSEY
               (thinks; shakes her head)
          No . . . no, I don't recall that
          name. Why?

                    STONE
          He was the man who we suspect
          attacked your husband.

                    MRS. HALSEY
          A black boy named Scalisi?

                    STONE
          The two blacks are in custody.
          They've confessed to robbing your
          husband, but Scalisi was the one
          who slashed him.

                    ROBINETTE
          Do you have any idea why somebody
          might want to attack Mr. Halsey?

                    WENTZEL
               (frosty)
          Mrs. Halsey has already told you
          that she didn't know Tony Scalisi.

                    STONE
               (pleasant)
          We don't want to take up any more
          of Mrs. Halsey's time . . .


Stone looks at Wentzel, his face hardening but his
voice staying soft, issuing a command, not a
request.

                    STONE (cont'd)
          . . . but why don't you let us buy
          you a cup a coffee? We'll meet you
          at Lindy's.

                                   CUT TO
```

INT. N.D. SEDAN - NIGHT

Stone drives through the dark streets, clearly
preoccupied. Robinette looks at him curiously.

                    ROBINETTE
          Thinking about Wentzel?

                    STONE
              (shaking his head)
          The kid . . . Halsey's
          reputation'll only get what it
          deserves, but the kid's getting
          screwed for it . . . it's a bitch.

                    ROBINETTE
          Funny thing about reputations.

                    STONE
          Don't start on this, Paul . . .

                    ROBINETTE
          I just think . . .

                    STONE
          No, you're <u>not</u> thinking. If
          Jefferson <u>was</u> white, you wouldn't
          doubt what I'm saying.
              (annoyed)
          The only reason he's still got a
          badge is <u>because</u> he's black.

                    ROBINETTE
          Really. Then why don't you just
          tell me what the hell he did?

                    STONE
          He perjured himself when he was a
          Captain. Changed his testimony on
          me . . . somebody bought him. That
          was one. Another time he doctored
          evidence in a numbers case . . .
              (stopping himself)
          I'm not going to do this, Paul.
          You're either on my team or
          Jefferson's.

Off Robinette's discomfort --

                                        CUT TO

```
INT. COFFEE SHOP - NIGHT

Stone and Robinette face an uncomfortable looking
Wentzel in a booth. The lawyer stares down at the
table as Robinette finishes taking him through the
evidence.

                   ROBINETTE
          . . . and the coat's an eight.

Wentzel's head pops up.

                    STONE
          Who is she, Mr. Wentzel?

He looks at Stone in disbelief.

                   WENTZEL
          You can't be serious . . . I
          can't . . .

                    STONE
               (ice)
          You're going to make me very angry
          if you finish that sentence.

Wentzel flushes. He doesn't like being pushed.

                   WENTZEL
          Hey! What is this? We're talking
          privilege here.

                    STONE
          My ass. We're talking obstruction
          here, that's what we're talking.

Wentzel looks like he's just been jolted by a
cattle prod.

                   WENTZEL
          Now wait a damn minute.

                    STONE
          You wait . . . this case stinks.
          Your client was a bagman long
          before he was a Councilman . . .
          old habits die hard.
               (beat)
          I'm going to start deposing some
          people. I find out that you had any
                   (MORE)
                                        CONTINUED
```

CONTINUED

                    STONE (Cont'd)
        knowledge of person or persons who
        were involved with your client in
        illegal activity, and therefore
        have a motive, I'll have your
        license . . . now, what's her name?

Robinette flips open a notebook and looks at
Wentzel expectantly.

                                    CUT TO

INT. CARTIER - DAY

Robinette walks into the jewelry store and goes up
to the armed guard.

                    ROBINETTE
        Alicia Heslin?

                    GUARD
                (pointing)
        Right over there.

Robinette crosses to a good looking woman in her
late twenties. She looks more like a customer than
most of the customers.

                    ROBINETTE
        Miss Heslin?

                    Heslin
        Yes.

                    ROBINETTE
        My name's Paul Robinette. I'm from
        the District Attorney's office.

                    HESLIN
        Yes?

                    ROBINETTE
        I'd like to ask you a few
        questions.

                    HESLIN
        About what?

                                    CONTINUED

CONTINUED

> ROBINETTE
>   (evenly)
>   Charles Halsey.

The color completely drains from Heslin's face.

> HESLIN
>   (barely a whisper)
>   I've been expecting you . . .

>   CUT TO

INT. RESTAURANT - NIGHT

A decidedly masculine steakhouse. Stone sits across
from Fred Lasco, the reporter who had asked Mrs.
Halsey a question at the hospital the night Halsey
was slashed. The waiter takes away their dishes as
Lasco leans back and pats his stomach.

> LASCO
>   Tasty thirty pieces of silver.

Stone refills Lasco's wineglass.

> LASCO
>   (continuing)
>   So . . . what do you want?

> STONE
>   Everything you've got on Charles
>   Halsey.

Lasco swirls his wine while he considers the
request, then finally shrugs.

> LASCO
>   How much do you know about parking
>   meters?

> STONE
>   They all run fast.

> LASCO
>   And a lot of the people who get
>   tickets don't pay them . . .
>   getting the money for those unpaid
>   tickets is a big headache for the
>   head of the Parking Violations
>   Bureau. He has to get outside help.

>   CONTINUED

CONTINUED

>   STONE
> And that means a big contract.

>   LASCO
> A <u>very</u> big, <u>very</u> lucrative
> contract.

>   STONE
> Who has it?

>   LASCO
> An interesting little company
> called Carnegie Collections . . .

>   CUT TO

INT. STONE'S OFFICE — DAY

Robinette's bringing him up to date on the Heslin
meeting.

>   ROBINETTE
> . . . she's got champagne tastes
> . . . Cartier watch, alligator
> shoes . . . when she first heard
> about it, she thought that he might
> have been trying to commit suicide.

>   STONE
> Why? Was he depressed?

>   ROBINETTE
> He had been subpoenaed . . . the
> Federal Grand Jury on municipal
> corruption. Oh . . . how's this
> grab you . . . her apartment
> lease is made out to Carnegie
> Collections.

>   STONE
> She wear a size eight coat?

>   ROBINETTE
> Right off the rack.

>   STONE
> He tell her names?

>   CONTINUED

CONTINUED

> ROBINETTE
> The last month, it was all he
> talked about. Told her who had done
> what to whom and how they had done
> it.

> STONE
> Will she testify?

> ROBINETTE
>   (shaking his head)
> Most of it's unusable anyway . . .
> "Chuck told me that Scalisi had
> told him that Brademas had told
> him" . . . that kind of thing . . .
>   (beat; not pleased)
> She did say that he couldn't figure
> out how this was happening since he
> had a Deputy Police Commissioner in
> his pocket.

Stone leans back in his chair and rubs his temples.

> STONE
> I can't use her at trial, but I can
> bring her in front of the Grand
> Jury . . .
>   (coming to decision)
> I've got to see the boss . . .

>   CUT TO

INT. D.A.'S OFFICE - DAY

Stone brings District Attorney Alfred Wentworth up
to speed. The venerable, silver-haired D.A. hasn't
tried a case in twelve years but looks great behind
a forest of mics.

> WENTWORTH
> How deep does it go?

> STONE
> It's not confined to the Parking
> Violations Bureau, that's for sure.

> WENTWORTH
> Why not?

>   CONTINUED

CONTINUED

>   STONE
> Because Halsey's been a bagman for
> twenty years. Scalisi's mobbed up
> . . . plus, a reporter I know told
> me that several other councilmen
> and politicians are stockholders in
> Carnegie Collections . . . as well
> as a Deputy Police Commissioner
> . . . one William Jefferson . . .

>   WENTWORTH
> Is that why you want to bring the
> Feds in? This personal?

>   STONE
> Look . . . I'd love to nail the
> bastard, but the fact is, with him
> involved we get one surveillance
> leak, we're dead. At least I'll
> know we're secure with the Bureau
> doing it . . . let the Feds have
> the ink on Municipal corruption –
> they may help me get a conspiracy
> to murder on these bozos.

>   WENTWORTH
>   (not happy, a raised finger
>   of warning)
> You never know whose pants are
> going to get dropped in a
> corruption scandal.

>   STONE
> Hey – this started out as a
> mugging.

>   WENTWORTH
> I'll back you, but don't give me
> any names that aren't dead bang
> guilty . . . I want a smoking gun
> and I want it in somebody's hand.

>   STONE
> Are you telling me tape?

                                    CONTINUED

CONTINUED

> WENTWORTH
> Tape would be a start.

> STONE
> Can I offer Scalisi immunity?

> WENTWORTH
> Nope . . . it'll look like he's
> naming people to save himself.

> STONE
> (sarcastic)
> I wouldn't want you to go out on a
> limb here, Alfred.

> WENTWORTH
> That's not what I get the big bucks
> for.

The intercom buzzes.

> WENTWORTH
> Yes.

> SECRETARY (V.O.)
> Mr. Stone has an urgent call . . .
> a lawyer named Cosmatos.

> STONE
> (pleased)
> Somebody wants to make a deal . . .

> CUT TO

INT. D.A.'S OFFICE - DAY

Stone and Robinette stride through the madhouse of
the bullpen.

> ROBINETTE
> Cosmatos and Scalisi are in your
> office . . .

> STONE
> Call Judge Ichaso . . . get
> warrants for Halsey, Scalisi and
> Jefferson's phone records, and talk
> to Halsey's doctor - see when we'll
> be able to interrogate him.

> CUT TO

INT. STONE'S OFFICE - DAY

Stone is behind his desk, facing Scalisi and
Cosmatos.

                    COSMATOS
          . . . so, while we steadfastly
          maintain that the slashing was done
          by the black youths seen fleeing
          the scene, we all know that you
          never know what will happen with
          a jury, so we would be willing
          to negotiate some sort of
          agreement . . .

                    STONE
          Don't do me any favors . . . I'm
          more than willing to let the people
          decide.

Scalisi shoots his lawyer a disgusted look.

                    SCALISI
               (to Stone)
          Bottom line . . . what do you want?

                    STONE
          Who paid you to do Halsey?

                    SCALISI
          Look, you want to talk city
          corruption . . .

                    STONE
          No deal without the name.

Scalisi shakes his head.

                    SCALISI
          Pass.

As he starts to stand the door opens and Robinette
walks in.

                    STONE
          What's up?

Robinette's eyes go from Stone to Cosmatos to
Scalisi.

                                        CONTINUED

```
CONTINUED
                    ROBINETTE
          Hospital just called . . . Charles
          Halsey died half an hour ago.

Off Scalisi's shocked expression --

                                      FADE OUT

                    END OF ACT THREE
```

ACT FOUR

FADE IN

INT. STONE'S OFFICE - DAY

He waves his hand in dismissal.

>   STONE
>   We'll get back to you . . .

>   COSMATOS
>   I haven't even made an offer.

>   STONE
>   Trust me . . . you wouldn't like
>   the counter.

Scalisi glares at his lawyer, then turns to Stone.

>   SCALISI
>   I can tell you things . . .

Stone turns his poker face to Scalisi.

>   STONE
>   What? You going to tell me all
>   about Parking Tickets?
>   (shaking his head)
>   Yours is already punched, pal . . .
>   we know all about Carnegie
>   Collections.

Scalisi is rocked by Stone's announcement.

>   SCALISI
>   I've got a lot of names.

Stone shakes his head and points to the door.

>   STONE
>   See you in court.

>   SCALISI
>   (getting upset)
>   Hey! I'm not talking G-4s here
>   . . . these are your basic elected
>   officials and a deputy Police
>   Commissioner.

>   CONTINUED

```
CONTINUED
                    STONE
               (to Cosmatos)
          Don't have him make me call
          security.

Cosmatos takes his client's elbow.

                    COSMATOS
          Come on, Tony.

                    SCALISI
               (facade cracking)
          I ain't going down alone behind
          this . . .
               (to Stone)
          What do you want?

Stone manages a tiny smile.

                    STONE
          Want? I want it all. You testify.
          You give names, dates and amounts.
          You flush all those true blue
          public officials.

                    SCALISI
          That gets me a walk?

                    STONE
               (shaking his head)
          Only way you walk is you tell me
          who gave the order.

Silence. Scalisi looks at Stone.

                    SCALISI
          You know I can't.

                    STONE
               (shrugging)
          No Masucci, no free ride.

Cosmatos takes off his glasses and cleans them with
his tie.

                    COSMATOS
          But the public officials could lead
          to a plea of let's say . . .
          assault?

                                        CONTINUED
```

CONTINUED

                    STONE
        Let's say voluntary manslaughter.

                    COSMATOS
        Let's say involuntary.

                    STONE
        Then he wears a wire.

                    SCALISI
        Are you crazy? They know I've been
        busted . . . they'll smell it.

                    STONE
        You let me worry about that.

                    COSMATOS
        What kind of sentencing
        recommendation?

                    STONE
        Depends what's on the tape.

He looks from Scalisi to Cosmatos, then looks at
his watch.

                    STONE (cont'd)
        Tick tock, gentlemen . . .

Scalisi nods miserably.

                    STONE
                (nodding back; satisfied)
        I'll have it typed up.

                    ROBINETTE
                (to Stone)
        We'd better get to the
        hospital . . .

                                        CUT TO

INT. SURGEON'S SCRUB ROOM - DAY

Stone and Robinette talk to Dr. Goldberg, a
cardiologist in a sweat stained operating gown.

                    GOLDBERG
        They guy had arteries the diameter
        of capillaries.

                                        CONTINUED

```
CONTINUED
                     ROBINETTE
          So with the traumatic loss of six
          units of blood, there was a
          causative connection between the
          assault and the coronary?

                     GOLDBERG
          C'mon, guys . . . you don't want
          to ask me that . . . "causative
          connection?"

                     STONE
          Whoa, whoa . . . excuse me . . .
                (adopting a courtroom
                demeanor)
          Mr. Halsey had a regular doctor,
          right, Dr. Goldberg?

                     GOLDBERG
          Yes, he did.

                     STONE
          And he described Halsey as being in
          good health?

                     GOLDBERG
          Uh-huh.

                     STONE
          And he was alive a week ago,
          correct?

                     GOLDBERG
                (almost smiling)
          Far as I could tell.

                     STONE
          And then somebody cut his throat
          with a straight razor, severing an
          artery and his vocal chords?

                     GOLDBERG
                (nodding)
          As well as other connective tissue.

                     STONE
          And now Mr. Halsey is dead?

                                      CONTINUED
```

CONTINUED

                    GOLDBERG
          Yes. That's correct.

                    STONE
          Thank you, doctor . . .

                                        CUT TO

INT. U.S. ATTORNEY'S OFFICE - DAY

Stone and Robinette sit facing McCormack, a guy
about 30, with a desktop nameplate that says, "John
McCormack, Assistant U.S. Attorney."

                    ROBINETTE
          . . . it's neat, it's clean, it's
          inter-agency cooperation and we may
          get a murder-for-hire conspiracy
          while you get another nail for your
          RICO . . .

                    MC CORMACK
          How did I get so lucky?

                    STONE
          A high level cop's involved. I
          can't run it through the P.D.

                    MC CORMACK
          The D.A. know about this?

                    STONE
          It has his full approval.

                    MC CORMACK
          We go to trial first . . .

                    STONE
          You want to win your RICO?

McCormack gives him a frosty stare. He's not about
to answer a rhetorical question.

                    STONE (cont'd)
          Go in with one of the five counts
          already having been proven in State
          Court . . .

McCormack considers the response. He doesn't like
it, but he knows Stone's right.

                                        CONTINUED

CONTINUED

               MC CORMACK
What do you need?

               STONE
An FBI surveillance team.

McCormack hits his intercom.

               MC CORMACK
Get me Jackson at the Bureau . . .

                         CUT TO

EXT. PARK — NIGHT

Overlooking the water. The lights of downtown towering in back of Stone and Lasco.

               LASCO
Let me see if I've got this . . .
Halsey had been called in front of
the Grand Jury, big names figure
he's going to name them, give the
contract to Scalisi . . .

               STONE
. . . but Scalisi screwed up. . . .

               LASCO
The black kids come along . . .

               STONE
    (nodding)
And we got lucky . . . they came up
with the I.D.

               LASCO
So why are you kicking him?

               STONE
I told you, it's a weak case . . .
all circumstantial and no choirboys
as witnesses for the
prosecution . . .

               LASCO
Spare me the waltz, alright?

                    CONTINUED

CONTINUED

>   STONE
>   (cautionary finger)
>   Off the record until after an
>   indictment?

>   LASCO
>   But I get an exclusive on the
>   arrest . . .

>   STONE
>   I can't promise that.

>   LASCO
>   Sure you can.

>   STONE
>   You get the exclusive on highest
>   ranking defendant's arrest site
>   . . . will you run it?

Lasco considers, then nods.

>   CUT TO

INT. STONE'S OFFICE - DAY

Stone and Robinette read copies of the Post.

>   ROBINETTE
>   "Assistant District Attorney
>   Benjamin Stone stated that his
>   office did not feel that Scalisi's
>   causative role in Halsey's death
>   could be proven beyond a reasonable
>   doubt. . . "A tad doctrinaire, but
>   not too bad . . .

>   STONE
>   Scalisi comes out smelling like a
>   rose . . .

>   ROBINETTE
>   Long as they buy he held his
>   mud . . .
>   (beat)
>   Jefferson called me for a status
>   report . . .

>   CONTINUED

CONTINUED

                    STONE
               (shocked; pissed)
      You talked to him about <u>this</u> case?

Robinette's in pain. His voice drops to a near
whisper.

                  ROBINETTE
      I had to. He would have been
      suspicious if I didn't talk to
      him . . . I gave him the "we had to
      let Scalisi walk" rap.

Stone and Robinette lock eyes. Robinette's made his
clearly painful decision to stay with Stone, who
eases up.

                    STONE
      How did he take it?

                  ROBINETTE
      He was absolutely furious . . .

                    STONE
      I'm sure it was an Oscar
      performance.

                  ROBINETTE
           (can't help himself)
      You're certain he's guilty, right?

                    STONE
      Not certain, positive.
           (checking watch)
      Let's go . . . you take her through
      her testimony?

                  ROBINETTE
           (nodding)
      She's still upset about not having
      a lawyer.

                    STONE
      You explain how the Grand Jury
      works? That we need her testimony
      to get a wiretap?

                                  CONTINUED

CONTINUED

> ROBINETTE
> She understands . . . she's not
> happy about it, but she gets it.

> CUT TO

INT. GRAND JURY ROOM – DAY

The members of the Jury sit in two semi-circular
tiers of overstuffed chairs. Alicia Heslin sits
in the well facing them while Stone asks her
questions.

> STONE
> And did Charles Halsey tell you of
> other officials who were involved
> in the conspiracy to award the
> Parking Violation Bureau collection
> contract to Carnegie Collections?

> HESLIN
> He mentioned people that I knew, as
> well as other people that I had
> never heard of.

> STONE
> Which people that you knew
> personally?

> HESLIN
> Anthony Scalisi and William
> Jefferson.

> STONE
> And did he tell you the amount of
> money involved?

> HESLIN
> He said that there was over a
> million dollars available to pay
> off city officials per year.

> CUT TO

INT. COURTHOUSE HALLWAY – DAY

Stone and Robinette come out of the Grand Jury Room
and are intercepted by Cosmatos. Stone chuckles.

CONTINUED

CONTINUED

                   STONE
Pleased with who your client drew?

                 COSMATOS
Haven't seen the calendar.

                   STONE
"Let 'em walk" Falk.

                 COSMATOS
Hey, I didn't want him to plead
. . . it was his decision . . .
anyway, he got the call.

                   STONE
From whom?

                 COSMATOS
       (shaking his head)
Scalisi wants it to be a surprise.

                   STONE
This isn't a parlor game, Eddie.

                 COSMATOS
       (leveling)
He's worried that somebody might
not show and you'll think he's
lying.

                   STONE
Where's the meet?

                 COSMATOS
Alberto's Clam House.

                   STONE
       (pissed)
Terrific. They'll never notice a
surveillance van in Little Italy.
       (sighs)
When?

                 COSMATOS
Tomorrow night . . . eight.

                                   CONTINUED

CONTINUED

              STONE
Bring him to the Bureau at six.
      (beat; searching Cosmatos'
      face)
You know?

              COSMATOS
      (not pleased)
Umh-hmm.

              STONE
Bad?

              COSMATOS
You're not going to be winning any
political popularity contests.

              STONE
      (spotting Greevey and Logan)
Just make sure he's on time.

Stone and Robinette move to Greevey and Logan and
shake hands.

              STONE
      (to Logan)
I'll start with you, take you
through the arrest of Jackson and
Lewis . . .
      (nods at Greevey)
Then let Max do Scalisi.

              LOGAN
How'd you let those two do-wops
plead?

              ROBINETTE
Possession of stolen property. Six
months.

Logan squeezes his eyes shut in frustration.
Greevey shakes his head with an "I-told-you-so"
smirk and holds out his hand. Logan slaps a twenty
into it. Greevey pockets it and turns to Stone.

              GREEVEY
You going to be able to nail
Jefferson for anything worse?

                     CONTINUED

```
CONTINUED
                    STONE
          Looks like it.

                    GREEVEY
               (satisfied)
          What goes around comes around.

                                        CUT TO


INT. FBI HEADQUARTERS - DAY

Scalisi is in the middle of a conference room, his
pants around his ankles as an FBI agent works on
taping a wire inside his boxer shorts. Stone,
Robinette, McCormack and a group of agents watch.

                    SCALISI
          These guys smell anything hinky,
          they're gonna clam up.

                    ROBINETTE
          So just be cool . . . you beat the
          system . . . you told the cops to
          shine it on . . .

                    MC CORMACK
          You want to tell us who's coming to
          the party now?

                    SCALISI
               (nervous; pissed; to Stone)
          Didn't you tell him the deal?
          Whoever comes, comes. I want these
          guys to hang themselves . . . I
          ain't rattin' on them . . . I'll
          tell you who ain't coming . . .
          Masucci . . . no way I give up my
          boss . . .

                    STONE
          Hold your water, Tony . . . we
          wouldn't want you to short yourself
          out.

                    ROBINETTE
          Just make sure one of the
          principals implicates himself . . .

                                        CUT TO
```

INT. SURVEILLANCE VAN - NIGHT

Stone, Robinette, McCormack and a couple of F.B.I. agents look through a smoked van window at Alberto's Clam House. The diners are clearly visible through the front plate glass which runs the length of the restaurant. Scalisi's visible at the back corner table. Above the stack of sophisticated electronics, on one wall of the van, a digital clock reads 8:10.

                  MC CORMACK
        Scalisi and Halsey I understand,
        but why Jefferson?

                  STONE
        He's a Deputy Commissioner and
        he's in charge of traffic, which
        includes parking.

                  ROBINETTE
        Look at this . . . you believe the
        stones on these guys?

A stretch limousine with a City shield pulls up to the curb. The back door opens and Borough President Conti, Deputy Police Commissioner Jefferson and a guy in a double breasted blazer climb out.

                  STONE
        Bingo.

                  MC CORMACK
        Who are they?

                  STONE
        Borough President Conti's in front,
        the black guy's Jefferson and the
        one in the Admiral's outfit is
        Deputy Mayor Kostmeyer.

McCormack lets out a low whistle.

                  STONE (cont'd)
        Ain't politics great?

                            CUT TO

INT. VAN — LATER

The clock reads 9:55. Through the van window, Stone
sees Conti wait until the waiter finishes refilling
wineglasses and leaves. He picks up a fork and taps
it on his wine glass. The table falls silent.

                     CONTI
          This has been a rough couple of
          weeks for all of us. The D.A.'s
          decision is extremely gratifying.
               (raising glass)
          I'd like to propose a toast to Tony
          Scalisi, who knows how to be a
          stand up guy . . .

They raise their glasses.

                                    CUT TO

INT. SURVEILLANCE VAN — NIGHT

Stone, Robinette and McCormack listen glumly to
the bug, which is picking up the sounds of people
enjoying themselves.

                   MC CORMACK
          That was about as damning as a
          Rotary Club meeting.
                     STONE
          Ssssh!

Stone's listening to the bug. Conti's voice takes
over. It's a barely audible whisper.

                   CONTI (V.O.)
          Tony . . .

                                      CUT TO

EXT. ALBERTO'S CLAM HOUSE — NIGHT
A red Cadillac Eldorado pulls in to a parking spot
diagonally across from the van.

                                    CUT TO

INT. VAN — NIGHT
The driver sits bolt upright as a guy in his early
thirties climbs out of the Eldorado.

                               CONTINUED

CONTINUED

> AGENT #1
> God Almighty . . .

> ROBINETTE
> What's the problem?

> AGENT #1
> That's Vinny Capelleti . . .

Capelleti is moving down the sidewalk towards Alberto's.

> STONE
> Who is he?

> MC CORMACK
> One of Masucci's mechanics . . .
> eats at Alberto's regularly . . .
> what do you want to do?

Stone listens. Scalisi is drawing Conti out in a whisper.

> SCALISI (V.O.)
> So? Everybody happy with me?

> CONTI (V.O.)
> We're all real thankful.

> SCALISI (V.O.)
> I thought the jerk was never gonna
> croak. . .

> STONE
> (begging)
> Come on, come on . . .

The other F.B.I. agent leans in.

> AGENT #2
> He's getting close . . .

STONE'S POINT OF VIEW:

Capelleti's almost at the door. McCormack, Stone and Robinette look at each other, the tension palpable, then look out the smoked window.

CONTINUED

```
CONTINUED
                    MC CORMACK
          He's probably just going in for
          dinner . . .
                  (beat)
          Your call . . .

                    ROBINETTE
                  (pleading; looking at
                  speaker)
          He's going to incriminate
          himself . . .

Conti's voice is soothing.
                    CONTI (V.O.)
          I . . . we . . . want you to have
          this.

STONE'S POINT OF VIEW:

Conti is slipping an envelope that's bulging with
hundreds to Scalisi.
                    SCALISI (V.O.)
                  (smiling)
          Who contributed?

                    CONTI (V.O.)
          You really want to know?

                    SCALISI (V.O.)
          Absolutely.

                    CONTI (V.O.)
          Me, Jefferson . . .

The door opens and Cappeletti walks in.

                                        CUT TO

INT. SURVEILLANCE VAN - NIGHT
                    CONTI (V.O.)
          . . . and Kostmeyer.

                    STONE
          Go! Take them! Tell the agents
          inside the restaurant.

They start out of the van.

                                     CONTINUED
```

CONTINUED

MC CORMACK
They're not wearing radios . . .
can't hide the wires . . .

STONE
Oh, God . . .

He's looking through the front window. Capelleti
spots Scalisi and starts moving toward the back
table, his hand going in to his jacket. Stone,
Robinette and McCormack break into a run as
Capelleti pulls out a gun. They're still on the
street as Capelleti walks up behind Scalisi and
puts four into the back of his head, propelling him
face down into his spaghetti marinara, the gunshots
and screams muffled by the glass.

CONTINUOUS

INT. ALBERTO'S CLAM HOUSE - NIGHT

Stone, Robinette and McCormack burst in just as two
F.B.I. agents stand up from a table with guns
drawn.

AGENT #4
Freeze, Capelleti!

Capelleti turns towards the agents bringing his gun
up. The two F.B.I. men fire simultaneously, sending
him crashing into the table. His and Scalisi's
bodies roll to the floor, grotesquely intertwined,
as Stone, Robinette, McCormack and the outside
agents race toward the table. Total pandemonium.
Women are screaming. Stone looks at Robinette,
tight lipped, then looks down at the bodies. It's
less than a minute since Capelleti was spotted on
the street. At the table, Jefferson is getting the
rest of the conspirator's attention.

JEFFERSON
(loud)
Do not say anything! Not a word!
Wait for your lawyer . . .

Robinette looks at him, his disappointment and
revulsion obvious, then glances at Stone, who's
also watching, and shakes his head.

CUT TO

INT. COURTROOM — DAY

Twelve jurors listen intently as Stone delivers an
opening statement. At the defense table sit Borough
President Conti, Deputy Mayor Kostmeyer, and Deputy
Police Commissioner Jefferson.

                    STONE
          Ladies and Gentlemen of the Jury,
          over the coming weeks you will hear
          how an investigation of what seemed
          to be a common mugging uncovered a
          conspiracy at the highest levels of
          city government . . . a conspiracy
          that led to the violent deaths of
          three men . . .
                (pointing to defendants)
          You will learn how these men,
          driven by the basest kind of greed,
          violated their public trust and
          contracted with a member of
          organized crime to murder another
          public official who they were
          afraid was about to turn State's
          evidence.

Stone stops pacing and looks at the jury.

                    STONE
          I ask you to weigh all the evidence
          that's presented. It is my
          responsibility to show you their
          crimes. It is your responsibility
          to decide whether they will be
          punished for them . . .

SUPER OVER BLACK:

After a ten week trial, all three defendants were
found guilty of being accessories before the fact
and solicitation of murder. They are free on their
own recognizance while their convictions are being
appealed.

                                        FADE OUT

                    END OF ACT FOUR

Index